Word, Words and World

Religions and Discourse

Edited by James M. M. Francis

Volume 50

PETER LANG
Oxford • Bern • Berlin • Bruxelles • Frankfurt am Main • New York • Wien

Sue Patterson

Word, Words and World

How a Wittgensteinian Perspective on Metaphor-Making Reveals the Theo-logic of Reality

PETER LANG
Oxford • Bern • Berlin • Bruxelles • Frankfurt am Main • New York • Wien

Bibliographic information published by Die Deutsche Nationalbibliothek.
Die Deutsche Nationalbibliothek lists this publication in the Deutsche Nationalbibliografie; detailed bibliographic data is available on the Internet at http://dnb.d-nb.de.

A catalogue record for this book is available from the British Library.

Library of Congress Control Number: 2013944393

ISSN 1422-8998
ISBN 978-3-0343-0230-2

Hochfeldstrasse 32, CH-3012 Bern, Switzerland
info@peterlang.com, www.peterlang.com, www.peterlang.net

Printed in Germany

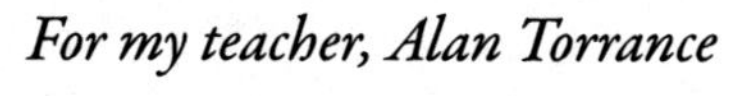

For my teacher, Alan Torrance

Contents

Preface

This book began as a thesis submitted for the degree of Doctor of Philosophy at the University of Otago, Dunedin, New Zealand, in October 1991. The thesis itself was a direct response to questions which stubbornly persisted beyond the end of a Bachelor of Divinity course in philosophical theology. The questions themselves were not entirely laid to rest by the thesis and were subsequently taken up in my book, *Realist Christian Theology in a Postmodern Age*,[1] which was the product of postdoctoral research at the Center of Theological Inquiry in Princeton, New Jersey. Meanwhile the thesis itself remained unpublished for the next twenty years while I taught and ministered in Bristol, England, the Midlands and West of Ireland, and most recently, Nelson, New Zealand. For various reasons, it now seems the right time for this work to be made public.

As a Bachelor of Divinity student in mid-life, I struggled to master first theological, then philosophical paradigms. My fascination with Wittgenstein came out of a course in philosophical hermeneutics in my final year and was encouraged by my then teacher, Alan Torrance. Reading Wittgenstein did not give me a store of knowledge; it brought about a change of perspective that altered permanently the way I saw the world. Out of this change of perspective came the conviction that there were aspects of Wittgenstein's thinking which were very important for theology that had been largely missed to date.

The passage of time and the intervening book have meant that the work has required some editing and updating of references, but these have been kept to a minimum. The title, '*Word*, Words and World', is that of my first published paper[2] which covers some of the ground of this book.

1 Sue Patterson, *Realist Christian Theology in a Postmodern Age* (Cambridge UK: Cambridge University Press, 1999).

2 Sue Patterson, '*Word*, Words and World', *Colloquium* 23/2 (1991), 71–84.

I remain grateful to my teacher, Alan Torrance, to whom this book is dedicated, not only for inspiring my research questions, but also for his preparedness to take the risk of letting me pursue them in my own way with his inimitably enthusiastic encouragement. Others to whom I am grateful for their helpful comments and willingness to make unpublished papers available include Grant Gillett, the late Daniel Hardy, Alvin Plantinga, Janet Martin Soskice and the late Thomas F. Torrance. I would like to thank series editor James M. M. Francis for his reading of the revised manuscript and advice regarding publication. Thanks are due also to the editors and staff at Peter Lang Publishers for their support and patience during the publication process. Last but hardly least, I have a debt of gratitude to my husband John for his support and forbearance during both the original period of doctoral research and this subsequent editing for publication two decades on.

Sue Patterson
Nelson, New Zealand
August 2013

Introduction

On revisiting this work after two decades, I have been convinced once more that the questions it grapples with are not only still at the forefront of theological research but are also of vital importance for the Church. As Barth rightly insists, theology is always done by and for the Church. Theological thinking is for the service of the Church and this thinking must filter down to the daily lives and beliefs of its members in local Christian communities.

Accordingly, this work on the fundamental theology of revelation which explores the God-language-world relationship is not prolegomenal in the sense that Barth decries – that is, as an academic exercise in (in effect) the philosophy of religion, to pre-determine the shape and limits of Christian doctrine. Rather, it aims to carry out the role of philosophy as handmaid to theology – a role established by Aquinas[1] and maintained by many others since, including Barth and T. F. Torrance. This role is, first, to articulate and establish coherence. This includes correcting mistakes in theological thinking (such as Platonic and Cartesian dualisms) which may have hidden under the carpet of doctrine until revealed by late-modern and postmodern scholarship to have the capacity to undermine what is central to Christian thought and belief.[2] The second role of philosophy in the service of theology is to enable the assimilation of insights from what Bruce Marshall has called 'the universe of truths',[3] to achieve a more comprehensive explanation of doctrine without departing materially from

1 Thomas Aquinas, *Super Boethium De Trinitate*, Rose E. Brennan S.H.N. (tr.), (New York: Herder and Herder, 1946), I.2.3.

2 See, for instance, Fergus Kerr, *Theology After Wittgenstein* (Oxford: Blackwell, 1986) and Colin E. Gunton, *The One, The Three and the Many: Creation and the Culture of Modernity* (Cambridge UK: Cambridge University Press, 1993).

3 Bruce D. Marshall, 'Absorbing the World: Christianity and the Universe of Truths', in B. D. Marshall (ed.), *Theology and Dialogue: Essays in Conversation with George Lindbeck* (Indiana: University of Notre Dame Press, 1990), 69ff.

that doctrine. This may be done by establishing approximate equivalences between paradigms. Without such connections to promote a gain to meaning, theological discussion tends to go round in jargon circles within its own paradigm. Yet the exercise of explaining theological truths by way of another paradigm (as Daniel Hardy exemplifies in employing the terminology of science)[4] must also extend understanding to a far wider audience of readers and thinkers, while at the same time facilitating the connection between theology and contemporary culture. One of the purposes of seeking more comprehensive explanation is to bridge the epistemological gap within the Church between the academy or seminary and the educated Christian layperson.

To reiterate the questions that provoked this research in the first place: how do we take on board postmodern insights regarding the relationship between language and world without losing our grip on theological truth? Then, how do we refute the arguments of those scholars who hold that human beings construct their own (including divine) reality with our language without throwing out the baby with the constructivist bathwater? – that is, without settling for a rigid realism which poses problems for orthodox Christian theology, biblical interpretation, and ecclesiality.

Why are these questions still at the forefront of theological research, as I maintain? While a number of scholars have identified the linguistic philosopher, Ludwig Wittgenstein, as a valuable dialogue partner for theology and philosophy of religion, the theological implications of the ontology (understanding of the nature of reality) inferable from Wittgenstein's philosophy have been largely ignored. I argue in this work and its sequel that these implications are fundamental to an understanding of the place of language in a reality that embraces both divine and human spheres. However, a further reason why the ontological fruit of engaging with Wittgenstein has been ignored is that discussion on the language-world relation has tended to be pre-empted by theological constructivists and deconstructionists who embrace a species of linguistic idealism which takes

4 See Daniel Hardy, 'The Spirit of God in Creation and Reconciliation', in H. Regan and A. J. Torrance (eds), *Christ and Context* (Edinburgh: T. & T. Clark, 1993), 237–58.

language alone as basic to reality. Undertaking this research has involved tackling these scholars on their own ground to challenge their interpretation of the ontological and theological entailments of the postmodern 'linguistic turn'.

At the other end of the theological spectrum, traditional Evangelical theologians have tended to display a 'ghetto mentality' in holding fast to a direct-realist correspondence theory of truth which not only opens them to a charge of incoherence (as the logical deficiencies of this are easily demonstrated), but also introduces some self-defeating hermeneutical implications as the language-world dualism inherent in direct realism places a truly contextual biblical theology out of reach, and thus abandons the field of contextual theology to the theological relativists.

In this work I argue that both the linguistic idealists and the direct realists are mistaken. The unavoidable socio-cultural relativities of human reality do not entail a constructivist metaphysic or other species of theological relativism. This argument involves engaging with Wittgenstein on different terms, asking the question, how, is his philosophy able to be the handmaid of theology rather than its jailor or executioner? I demonstrate not only that theology is possible from the perspective of a Wittgensteinian 'language-game' ontology, and as such, consistent with a Trinitarian theology, but also show that certain intractable and frequently glossed over problems may be solved through the ousting of some deeply entrenched ways of understanding reality that have stymied theological attempts to grapple with the God-language-world relation. Notable among these problems is the traditional separation of language and world. This may be a less obvious dualism than the more familiar Platonic and Cartesian mind-body varieties (although related to them), and one that is harder to eradicate, but the coherence of the Christian doctrine of God depends upon our doing so. Indeed, the Trinitarian theological conclusions I reach are an inescapable consequence of working through this eradication process. To run with a language-game ontology is to beg certain questions, which exploration of the nature and role of metaphor-making at the creative edge of language merely compounds, unless and until a theological, indeed Trinitarian, conclusion becomes the inevitable end-point.

The repercussions of all this for Christian discipleship, worship, prayer and proclamation are only hinted at here. Due to the unwieldiness of straddling several disciples, this work can do no more than provide a scaffold on which to build such applications. If it does indeed provide that scaffold, it will have achieved its purpose.

The Structure of the Argument

In Part One I argue for the basicality of Wittgensteinian language-games as the language-world link upon which all human experience and comprehension depends.

In Part Two I explore the relationship between language-games and metaphor-making as the creator of new language-world links, coining the term 'metaphorising' (hereafter without inverted commas) as a short-hand way of talking about metaphor-making as I develop a theory of metaphorising in relation to language-games.

In Part Three I relate metaphorising and language-games to aspects of the metaphysics of possibility and actuality.

In Part Four I relate all of the foregoing to theology in respect to revelation and make a case for a 'language-game theology'.

The argument develops through a series of paradigm shifts or syntheses. With the change in paradigm comes a change in or a superimposition of perspectives as each absorbs and assimilates the other. Finally, however, all is assimilated to theology, not because this *must* happen because, after all, this is a theological exercise, but rather because, as I have already indicated, there is no other solution to the argument.

PART ONE

A Wittgensteinian Foundation

CHAPTER ONE

The Case for Language-Games as Basic

1.1.1. Introduction

In this chapter I make particular use of Merrill and Jaakko Hintikkas' exposition of Wittgenstein's philosophy.[1] Central to the Hintikkas' exposition is, first, the need to take account of some neglected aspects in the development of Wittgenstein's thinking during his career; second, the unparalleled (and similarly neglected) importance of language-games in the philosophy of the later Wittgenstein. The primacy of language-games for Wittgenstein, the Hintikkas contend, is necessitated by (and is only understandable in the light of) certain earlier developments in his thinking which became the basis for his later philosophy, namely his conviction regarding language as universal medium (hereafter referred to as LUM), his concern with verification, his rejection of a phenomenological paradigm and his realisation that the linguistic and the nonlinguistic alike are part of the physical world. My case for the basicality of language-games rests on the strength of Wittgenstein's own reasoning as presented by the Hintikkas.

Here I set out to demonstrate the importance to theology of an ontology which takes language-games as basic. I could, of course, simply have assumed this basicality of language-games and treated the steps Wittgenstein trod along the way as entailments of this basicality in an

1 Merrill B. and Jaakko Hintikka, *Investigating Wittgenstein* (Oxford: Basil Blackwell, 1986); Jaakko Hintikka, 'Semantics: a Revolt against Frege', *Contemporary Philosophy: A New Survey*. Vol. 1, G. Floistad, Martinus (ed.), (The Hague: Nijhoff Publishers, 1981), 57–82.

if-then argument. However, the potential significance of this concept for theology requires a more thorough logical basis than a simple axiomatic assertion. In this first chapter of Part One I will seek to establish this basis.

1.1.2. The Web of Language-World

Merrill and Jaakko Hintikka suggest that Wittgenstein employs two arguments which combine to furnish his conclusion regarding the primacy of language-games. Both arguments rest on a basic premise:

[1] Language is universal medium.[2]

Without this premise the basicality of language-games cannot be inferred. How reasonable is this premise? It seems self-evident that when we think or talk about language we must do so using language. If the nature of language, its structures and content, is primitive, that is, presupposed in all examinations or explanations of language, then such examinations or explanations are precluded. This seems to be irrefutable logic. The use of language to explain language entails that the conclusion will always be at least in part begged by the premise:

The way language is → the way language is.

2 Jaakko and Merrill Hintikka see Wittgenstein's view of language as universal medium as fundamental to his philosophy. This view may be outlined as follows: 'One cannot as it were look at one's language from outside and describe it, as one can do to other objects that can be specified, referred to, described, discussed, and theorized about in language. The reason for this alleged impossibility is that one can use language to talk about something only if one can rely on a given definite interpretation, a given network of meaning relations obtaining between language and the world. Hence one cannot meaningfully and significantly say in language what these meaning relations are, for in any attempt to do so one must already presuppose them'. (Hintikka and Hintikka, *Investigating Wittgenstein*, 1–2.)

The Hintikkas note that the idea of language as universal medium may be seen to have an affinity with certain Kantian doctrines. Wittgenstein himself notes this. 'The limit of language shows itself in the impossibility of describing the fact that corresponds to a sentence without repeating that very sentence. What we are dealing with here is the Kantian solution to the problem of philosophy.'[3] As the uniqueness of language lies in its indescribability from outside of itself, it is accordingly uniquely universal medium. This unique universality has an important and inconvenient consequence: LUM entails the ineffability of semantics.[4] The Hintikkas contend that both LUM and the ineffability of semantics are ideas found in Wittgenstein from the beginning.

> [The] thesis of language as the universal medium implies primarily the inexpressibility of semantics rather than the impossibility of semantics ... Unlike Frege, the young Wittgenstein ... believed that he could convey his vision [of semantics] by an oblique [ostensive] use of language ... showing as distinguished from saying.[5]

Hence Wittgenstein in the *Tractatus* argues that '[t]he world as a whole is inexpressible because its boundaries are inexpressible. For these boundaries are determined by the totality of objects, or equivalently, the total of elementary propositions.'[6]

It follows from the thesis of language as universal medium that it is impossible to vary the interpretation of our language other than heuristically or hypothetically. Such a thesis rules out logical semantics and model theory in semantics, requiring as they do the systematic variation of the relations between language and world. That is, semantics as a 'systematic enterprise whose results are codifiable in language' is ruled out by LUM.[7] If the ineffability of semantics means that the language-world link cannot

3 Ludwig Wittgenstein, *Vermischte Bemerkungen* (Frankfurt Am Main: Suhrkamp Verlag, 1977), translation in this instance by Jaakko Hintikka (ibid. 4), 27.

4 Ibid. 6.

5 Ibid. 2.

6 Ludwig Wittgenstein, *Tractatus Logico-Philosophicus* (London: Routledge, 1922), #5.61.

7 Hintikka and Hintikka, *Investigating Wittgenstein*, 3.

be contained in language, it follows that it cannot be expressed in language, for 'one cannot transcend language in language or transcend one's thoughts in thinking'.[8]

As has been noted, on this point Wittgenstein identified himself with Kant. However, this argument appears to do away with the whole field of semantics, which after all is the 'study of the representative relations (meaning relations) between language and reality'.[9] Semantics seems to presuppose the sort of separation of language and nonlinguistic reality denied by the notions of language as universal medium and language as a component of physical reality. Conversely, as 'we can practise systematical semantics only if we can meaningfully discuss these relationships', the denial of a suitable (outside language) vantage point to view the language-world relationships appears to preclude the possibility of a systematic semantics.[10] For this reason, LUM and its semantically inconvenient consequences were abandoned by many semanticists.[11]

Yet it will be seen that Wittgenstein does not dispense with semantics so much as 'contain' the semantic relation within the language-game. For Wittgenstein the meanings we find in the world are not totally reducible to a set of propositions but, in order for such propositions to be meaningful, there must also be a context of use and skills, practices or techniques; that is, a context of using the propositions according to a set of lived 'rules'.

Wittgenstein never approved of Russell's 'solution' of a meta-language. Yet, in spite of the obvious circularity in so doing, it seems that we do habitually use language in this way. Wittgenstein himself on at least one occasion distinguished between primary and secondary language-games. There are

8 Ibid. 185.

9 Hintikka, 'Semantics', 58.

10 One is condemned to circularity if one attempts to explain the thing one's argument takes as primitive, upon which the foundation of one's logic rests. However, Paul Ricoeur talks about language's unique ability to be self-regarding (see Part Two) and in practice there is a constant need to suspend this circularity objection for heuristic purposes. Wittgenstein himself did this on occasion, but much less so in his later work.

11 In what Jaakko Hintikka calls the 'anti-Fregean revolt'. (See Hintikka, 'Semantics'.)

games such as verifying and believing and doubting which evaluate other games. Somehow language permits (or, more sceptically, gives the illusion that it permits) the stepping back from parts of itself and assumption of a partial and temporary objectivity without actually stepping outside of language. It is arguable that these two deductions are not as incompatible as they seem and that it can both be acknowledged that we inhabit language as a universal medium and are able to make meaningful non-tautological observations about language. Perhaps language can be both universal and incomplete or open-ended.[12]

However, Wittgenstein's main concern was not with the tautological consequences of talking about language in language, rather with the impossibility of explaining how language connects with the nonlinguistic aspects of reality. To take language as primitive, which seems on this account quite an inescapable position, means that it is impossible to explain that which accounts for language: the language-world link. Words or nonverbal communications are simply that link; how they are so is unknowable. Thus, the language-world link is not impossible but ineffable and the primitiveness of language per se entails the primitiveness of language as irreducible unit of language-world connection. This unit is what Wittgenstein calls the language-game.

12 Theories of semantics tend to make the assumption that it is essential to come up with a general theory of meaning which fits all contingencies. Jaakko Hintikka disputes this need: 'There is … too much of an attempt to give a uniform one-level explanation of the workings of a natural language. This is as futile as it would be to essay a uniform explanation of all the main observable macroscopic physical phenomena, from the fall of a feather to the workings of a steam engine. No wonder the result is a situation in which exceptions can be found to most regularities that linguists have actually proposed'. (Jaakko Hintikka, 'The Semantics of Questions and the Questions of Semantics', *Acta Philosophica Fennica* (28) No. 4: Chapter One: 'Questions of Semantics', 16.

1.1.2. Language-Games[13]

If, because language is universal medium, we cannot escape the basic semantical relationships that connect our language with reality, all examinations of language take place within language and mix up our linguistic conceptions of world with the nonlinguistic world. It is therefore necessary to deal with language-world 'chunks' rather than language and world as separate entities. On this view, then, neither language nor world can be basic or primitive in isolation. The basic unit is one of language-world. Wittgenstein calls these units 'forms of life' or 'language-games'.

Language-games do more than connect language and world: they integrate them in their interwoven patterns of activity and words. Wittgenstein illustrates this thus: 'It is like looking into the cabin of a locomotive. We see handles all looking more or less alike ... But one is the handle of a crank which can be moved continuously ... [A]nother is the handle of a switch, which has only two effective positions ... a third is the handle of a brake-lever, the harder one pulls on it, the harder it brakes; a fourth, the handle of a pump: it has an effect only so long as it is moved to and fro'.[14] Later Wittgenstein talks of the multiplicity of kinds of language-game and goes on to list some of this multiplicity:

> Giving orders and obeying them – Describing the appearance of an object, or giving its measurements – Constructing an object from a description (a drawing) – Reporting an event – Speculating about an event – Forming and testing a hypothesis – Presenting the results of an experiment in tables and diagrams – Making up a story; and reading it – Play-acting – Singing catches – Guessing riddles – Making a joke; telling it – Solving a problem in practical arithmetic – Translating from one language into another – Asking, thanking, cursing, greeting, praying.[15]

13 Some of the material in this chapter has appeared previously in my paper, Patterson, '*Word*, Words and World'.

14 Ludwig Wittgenstein, *Philosophical Investigations* (Oxford: Blackwell, 2nd edn, 1958): #12.

15 Ibid. #23.

As it is of the nature of the language-game (being practice) to defy definition, our understanding of what language-games are must come in part from such lists or descriptions of actual instances (although the Hintikkas warn that such lists over-emphasise intra-linguistic games – see below). For Wittgenstein 'the use is the life of the sign'.[16] Meaning is demonstrated by practice; signs are related to their context by use: 'Look at the sentence as an instrument and at its sense as its employment'.[17] 'If language-games are prior to their rules ... then the only criterion for the use of a word is in the last analysis the entire language-game in which it plays a role ... [T]he only criterion is the application of the word.'[18] Therefore, the only way of learning the use of words is by observing or engaging in the practice of a language-game.[19] The use of language, which for Wittgenstein is in most cases identical to its meaning, is learned by training, not by the learning of propositional rules; a language-game cannot be learnt simply from such articulation of rules. To learn a language-game, then, is to be trained in the practice of a skill.[20]

Wittgenstein makes it clear that 'the term "language-game" is meant to bring into prominence the fact that the speaking of language is part of an activity, or of a form of life'.[21] However, he does not simply use the terms language-games and forms of life interchangeably. Language-games are activities involving language (language broadly defined therefore not necessarily verbal language), whereas forms of life are the institutions or ways of being in the world constituted by complexes of language-games. A form of life is a community of consensual acted-out beliefs. As Wittgenstein says, 'It is what human beings say that is true and false; and they agree in the language they use. This is not agreement in opinions but in forms of life'.[22]

16 Ludwig Wittgenstein, *Blue and Brown Books* (Oxford: Blackwell, 1958), 4.
17 Wittgenstein, *Philosophical Investigations*, #421.
18 Ibid. #146.
19 Ibid. #31.
20 Ibid. #6.
21 Ibid. #23.
22 Ibid. #24.

A language-game is a language-involving activity or micro-practice which is part of, and together with other language-games, occurs within and constitutes a form of life. Whereas a given language-game is not (broadly speaking) confined to a particular form of life – the same sorts of language-games are played in various forms of life – a new situation means that a language-game will be used differently. If, with a change in use, the meanings of words and actions change, there must come a point where the difference in use is such that it is questionable if the game is still the same game.

For Wittgenstein, '[w]hat has to be accepted, the given, is – so one could say – forms of life.'[23] Yet the human activities which give rise to a state of affairs or an institution are logically and historically prior: it is the language-game which is properly basic. Language-games are connectors both of words and sentences and objects and facts. They are the '"missing links" between the expressions of our language and reality with which the language helps us to deal [and] are recognised by observing certain rule-governed human activities …'[24]

This understanding of language-games goes against what the Hintikkas call the 'received' view which is 'based on ascribing to Wittgenstein the idea that to understand language amounts to understanding the role in our lives played by different kinds of utterance in different circumstances'.[25] This view asserts that, according to Wittgenstein 'not even the ordinary descriptive meaning is based on truth-conditions'. Instead they posit a counterpart in assertibility or justifiability conditions – that is, justification by local, relative experience.[26] The Hintikkas' view is almost diametrically opposed to this view. Far from trying to get rid of language-world links, Wittgenstein emphasises them (while still maintaining their ineffability). The 'received' view in fact confuses Wittgenstein's lack of explanation of the language-world link with its implicit denial or nonexistence. Wittgenstein does not talk about the link between language and world because he believes

23 Ibid. 226e.

24 Hintikka and Hintikka, 212–13.

25 Ibid. 213.

26 Ibid. 214.

it is unsayable on an understanding of language as universal medium. This is why, according to the Hintikkas, he deals almost exclusively with intralinguistic phenomena.[27] It is only the external 'grammar' (or 'rules') of language-games that can be expressed in language. This is because, as LUM requires, '[a]ll use of language presupposes certain language-games and is a move in some language-game. These games are presupposed when any use is made of language. Hence we cannot in our language theoretically discuss the language-games which this language presupposes, or say what would happen if e.g. their rules were varied.'[28]

Thus it may be seen that Wittgenstein's apparent emphasis on the 'horizontal' intralinguistic relations 'is an optical illusion.' These horizontal connections are important in displaying and instantiating the language-games which give our sentences their meanings, that is, their various connections with reality. They are the game counterparts to the 'elucidations' mentioned in the *Tractatus*.[29] Moreover, such horizontal moves in language-games are all we can, strictly speaking, convey to the next person about those familiar but theoretically elusive language-games by means of the literal meaning of our words, for we cannot say what these games are like; we cannot describe them, nor can we formulate a systematic theory about them in language. But the main function of language-games themselves is to establish such vertical connections. 'Ironically, the impossibility (for Wittgenstein) of saying anything about language-games in language stems from this very semantical function they perform.'[30]

Use of a term in a language-game is what links it to the (nonlinguistic) world. 'Use' here means utilisation in contrast to the 'received' view of use as usage (see last footnote). Far from being simply speech-acts, language-game 'moves' 'consist of transitions in which utterances can play a role but

27 Ibid. 215.

28 Ibid. 216.

29 Wittgenstein, *Tractatus*, #3.263.

30 Hintikka and Hintikka, *Investigating Wittgenstein*, 216. The Hintikkas consider that we do not ourselves have to take such a strict line, that it is more helpful than misleading or redundant to attempt some explanation of the operation of the 'vertical' function of language-games.

normally not the only role; on the contrary, many moves need not involve any verbal utterance'.[31] In other words, it is the *use* of language (verbal and/or nonverbal) by speakers which gives it its meaning.[32] However, the Hintikkas make the point that it cannot be every language-game in which a word or expression is used which gives a word its meaning. Some language-games create new uses of terms; others utilise existing ones, preserving their identities more or less.[33] The Hintikkas observe that, realistically speaking, we can only preserve the concept of meaning as use in a language-game if we do indeed make this distinction, otherwise meaning becomes hopelessly unstable, changing with every slight variation in use. As has been noted, Wittgenstein himself makes the distinction between the two types of language-game at least once, but it is not clear 'to what extent Wittgenstein explicitly acknowledges the distinction in its full generality'.[34]

It is misleading that Wittgenstein appears to have used the term 'language-game' 'to highlight two entirely different (although compatible) ideas': first, 'the role of rule-governed human activities in instituting the basic representative relationships between language and [nonlinguistic] reality'; second, 'to highlight the fact that language can be used in many different ways, not just descriptively ... [T]here are many different language-games besides the descriptive (fact-stating) ones'.[35] However, Wittgenstein

31 Ibid. 217. The Hintikkas call the confusion of language-games with speech-acts 'the fallacy of verbal language-games' and regard it as 'one of the most widespread misunderstandings of Wittgenstein's later philosophy'. (Ibid. 218.) Wittgenstein himself appears to warn against this fallacy: 'The word "language-game" is here meant to emphasize that the speaking of language is part of an activity or a form of life.' (*Philosophical Investigations*, #23); and, 'I shall also call the whole, consisting of language and the actions with which it is interwoven, the "language-game".' (Ibid. #7.) And, 'Our talk gets its meaning from the rest of our proceedings'. (Ludwig Wittgenstein, *On Certainty* (Oxford: Blackwell, 1969), #229.)

32 Ibid. 219.

33 Although, as previously noted, it is a moot point whether a change of language-game can leave a use completely unscathed when use is the key to meaning.

34 Hintikka and Hintikka, *Investigating Wittgenstein*, 220.

35 For example, in *Philosophical Investigations*, ##23, 24, 27. Ibid. 220–1.

is not merely saying that there are a variety of language-games; he is saying that language-games constitute descriptive meaning.[36]

That language is universal medium is, it is contended, Wittgenstein's first argument. His second argument does not follow directly but first provides a further two premises regarding language to accompany LUM:

> [2] Language is a part of the physical world.
>
> [3] Language is not confined to verbal expressions but includes non-verbal forms of communication such as noises and gestures.

The first premise entails that language is primarily both object-language and (as the physical world exists in time and space) an activity which forms part of other activities in the physical world. This premise then ultimately requires not only the abandonment of a phenomenological language but also, as will be seen later, an abandonment of the distinction between semantics and pragmatics.

1.1.3. The Interweavings of Language-World

If language and nonlinguistic reality are both parts of the physical world, they cannot be dichotomised into separate spheres or realms. Instead, they exist as part of an interwoven whole. It is Wittgenstein's recognition that language itself is part of the physical world which finally destroys for him the plausibility of a phenomenological foundation: 'The language itself belongs to the second [i.e. physicalist] system. If I describe a language, I am essentially describing something that belongs to physics. But how can

36 Therefore 'there is no obstacle to saying, for instance, that descriptive meaning is truth-conditional as long as we realise how it is that those truth-conditions are determined [that is, through the language-game].' (Ibid.)

a physicalist language describe the phenomenal?'[37] As the language-world comparison takes place in the physical world itself, it can only be achieved via 'physicalist' (or physical object) language. If physical object language is that which is closest to our experience, it is so because it is directly linked to the world of objects. The recognition that language itself is a part of physical reality may be seen to stem directly from this point.[38]

Thus Wittgenstein comes to see the connection of language with physical objects as basic. For Wittgenstein the bottom line of accessibility through language to the world has ceased to be the human ability to receive and articulate sense-data and has become instead human ability to access the physical world through our use of (activities involving) it. Because language belongs to the physical world and the world exists in time, language-world relations must also take place in time. They have ceased to be the atemporal entities of the *Tractatus*.[39]

Once Wittgenstein has come to this realisation, his next concern is the nature of this integration, the way in which the language-world links operate: in a physicalist language the intricate web of language-world relations becomes a problem. Many physical objects are too large, too small, too distant, or otherwise too inaccessible to our sense to allow us to confront them directly in our experience ... Thus Wittgenstein's change of his language paradigm meant that language-world relations become a problem for him, whether they are considered from the vantage point of name-object

37 Ludwig Wittgenstein, *Philosophical Remarks*, Rush Rhees (ed.), Raymond Hargreaves and Roger White (trs.) (Oxford: Blackwell, 1975), VII, #68. In fact, the nonbasicality of phenomenology is entailed by the basicality of language-games. See Chapter 2 of Part One.

38 As the Hintikkas put it: 'It was only when Wittgenstein was hit by the full force of the idea that language itself belongs to the physical world and that the process of the verification of a proposition, which amounts to a comparison between language and the world, must therefore take place in the same world, that he came to be ready to draw the right conclusion from premisses to which he had subscribed for weeks and months. That is what happened in October 1929.' (Hintikka and Hintikka, *Investigating Wittgenstein*, 165.)

39 Ibid. 168–9.

relations, language teaching and language learning, or from the vantage point of comparisons between a proposition and reality.[40]

It is the second premise:

> [3] Language is not confined to verbal expressions but includes nonverbal forms of communication such as noises and gestures.

which forces Wittgenstein to abandon ostension (or showing) as a way of explaining the language-world link without recourse to language. If ostension is a form of nonverbal language, it stands to reason that it cannot carry out the language-world-linking task.[41] A simple two-place naming relation model is now seen to be hopelessly inadequate unless the more complicated and inaccessible objects can be reached from the simpler accessible one via a system of rules (for example, definitions) for the use of words.[42] But ostensive relations prove unable to bear this burden. Because ostension as a means of communication is also part of language, the problem of 'How does the sign link up with the world?' has merely been pushed back a step. Ostension cannot 'step outside of language and connect signs with reality'. Wittgenstein's view of language simply does not allow the drawing of a line between the verbal and the nonverbal. An ostensive gesture is instead a link between verbal and nonverbal language. Therefore for Wittgenstein after 1932, language is not only verbal but encompasses all communication of a meaningful kind.[43]

While Wittgenstein's idea of (propositional) rules may be seen as a halfway house which still relied on ostension to establish the language-world link, Wittgenstein came to see that rules were as nonbasic in their own way as the phenomenological paradigm was in its way. More basic than the rule itself was the following of it. Rules are not simply statements or orders, but things which are acted upon. Ultimately, it is the activity of rule-following which expresses the rule; therefore the following of the rule is

40 Ibid. 177.

41 'How do you point to the State of California?' Ibid. 178.

42 Ibid. 180.

43 Ibid. 183–4.

the rule. In this way, Wittgenstein came to see as basic the structured activities which he called language-games. It is the playing of the language-game which expresses the rule.[44] Once the basicality of language-games is fully established, the idea of rule as a separate entity is redundant. Rules are no longer a product of language-games; the entire language-game is the rule.

By the time of the *Brown Book*, Wittgenstein has arrived at the insight that the use of a sign constitutes the link between sign and world and is the 'mode of existence' of 'the basic semantical relations'.[45] This implies that it is the language-game and not the simple naming relation that is primitive, but Wittgenstein does not appear to conceive of the language-game as prior to the propositional rules which may be inferred from it until *Philosophical Investigations*. Then he tells us to 'look on the language-game as the primary thing'.[46] It may be seen from the present discussion that (as the Hintikkas observe) this conclusion is a product of logical inference.[47]

1.1.4. The Foundations of Language-World

Two premises have been suggested as the basis of Wittgenstein's second argument:

[2] Language is a part of the physical world.

[3] Language is not confined to verbal expressions but includes non-verbal forms of communication such as noises and gestures.

44 Ibid. 189–90. 'One has already to know (or to be able to do) something in order to be capable of asking a thing's name. But what does one have to know?' (Wittgenstein, *Philosophical Investigations*, #30; see also #37.)

45 Hintikka and Hintikka, *Investigating Wittgenstein*, 193.

46 Wittgenstein, *Philosophical Investigations*, #654. 'Our mistake is to look for an explanation where we ought to look at what happens as a "proto-phenomenon". That is, where we ought to have said: this language-game is played' (ibid. #656).

47 Hintikka and Hintikka, *Investigating Wittgenstein*, 199.

A complementary reading of these premises and their entailments assuming Wittgenstein's first premise:

[1] Language is universal medium

necessitates the conclusion that language-games are basic. First, the primitiveness of language per se entails the primitiveness of language as the basic unit of language-world connection. That is, the language-world link is basic. Second, the premise that language is a part of the physical world entails that language is primarily both physical object language and (as the physical world exists in time and space) an activity which forms part of other activities in the physical world. That is, the nature of this basic language-world link is not simply linguistic but is concrete and active. The language-world link is an activity involving the use of concrete physical object language. Third, this concrete language is not confined to verbal expressions but includes nonverbal forms of communication such as noises and gestures. The language-world linking activity need not involve the use of verbal language at all but may instead employ ostension or gestures or bodily orientations. This is the Hintikkas' definition of Wittgenstein's primary language-game.

Can we describe these primary language-games as epistemically foundational? According to Michael Williams,[48] 'knowledge to which nothing is epistemologically prior may be called "epistemologically basic" or "foundational"'. As not everything that we know can be justified by appeal to further knowledge of some kind (so foundationalists argue), there must be some things we know which do not need justification, either because they are self-justifying or because they are intrinsically credible in some other way. Williams is concerned to expose foundationalism as both redundant and incoherent. Alvin Plantinga, on the other hand, has no objection to the structure of foundationalism as such, although he regards both classical and modern foundationalism as falling into the trap of self-referential

48 Michael Williams, *Groundless Belief* (Oxford: Blackwell, 1977), 13–22.

incoherence by being too narrow in their stipulations.[49] Plantinga proposes the more flexible requirement of apparent self-evidence or incorrigibility as grounds for accepting a proposition as properly basic; this solves the incoherence problem as well as avoiding the notorious difficulty of trying to find criteria for self-evidence. On this understanding of foundationalism, the criteria are subjective, relative to the believer: what is self-evident is what is self-evident to me or to us. In other words, this is a relativistic view of foundationalism. It is a view which has not gone without criticism from those who hold that what is foundational is necessarily absolute because what is foundational has to be *logically* or rationally foundational. According to Plantinga, what we have instead of objective self-evidence is *commitment* to the reliability of what we have learned: our knowledge.[50]

It seems reasonable, on the face of it, to ascribe a Plantingan kind of foundationalism[51] to Wittgenstein in that he treats language-games and forms of life as primitive and these entities arguably comprise a form of knowing.[52] The incorrigibility and self-evidence of primary language-games

49 Alvin Plantinga, 'Is Belief in God Properly Basic?' *Nous 15*. 41–51. The material in this section also draws on unpublished lectures and seminars given by Alvin Plantinga at the University of Otago, Dunedin, New Zealand, July/August 1991.

50 William P. Alston, 'Plantinga's Epistemology of Religious Belief', *Profiles 5: Alvin Plantinga*, James E. Tomberlin and Peter van Inwagen (eds), (Dortrecht: D. Reidel, 1985), 289–312: 385.

51 Some shortcomings of Plantingan foundationalism will be discussed in Part Four Chapter 2.

52 Wittgenstein, *Philosophical Investigations*, 226e. A 'bedrock' consisting of forms of life is incompatible with classical foundationalism because it is only within a context of usage and use that we refer to something as true or false. Wittgenstein himself notes that 'What stands fast does so, not because it is intrinsically obvious or convincing; it is rather held fast by what lies around it.' (Wittgenstein, *On Certainty*, #144.) John Downey, in noting this Wittgensteinian refutation of classical foundationalism, comments that 'When one pronounces some object as the clear giver of life to mere words, a weave of life and language is read into the situation and not noted ... A whole form of life is projected into the object or experience and its unnoticed presence makes it look as if the object or experience were doing all the work'. (John Downey, *Beginning at the Beginning: Wittgenstein and Theological Conversation* (Lanham: University Press of America, 1986), 136–8.) Such an understanding may

(in that each constitutes a self-contained, self-verifying world of beliefs whose justifications come to an end in the 'bedrock' of 'This is what I do'[53]) amounts to a commitment to what is communally normative as foundational. 'What has to be accepted, the given, is – so one could say – forms of life'.[54]

For Wittgenstein also, then, an epistemic foundation is a local, relative thing (if one accepts that this is not in fact a contradiction in terms). It also may vary temporally. To be foundational, Williams writes, systems of belief do not have to be unrevisable; their intrinsic credibility can be temporary.[55] Forms of life are created and maintained by the playing of various language-games. The identity of these language-games both depends on and informs the content of the form of life. If a form of life changes, it is because of a change in the information its language-games provide about the world. Language-games and forms of life are always changing and new ones coming into being. As a language-game in relation to a form of life is a lived axiom upon which the whole logic of our understanding rests, it is not just that we do not see the need to question this axiom just now; it is to say that 'there is a logical presumption in favour of the belief's being true, although not a guarantee'.[56]

That is, what is axiomatic for us need not be strictly incorrigible, nor need it be unchangeable; if something is built upon or lived by, that is enough to make it foundational. However, it makes no sense to doubt what is foundational for us. As Wittgenstein observes, 'I must not saw off the branch on which I am sitting'.[57] For this reason Williams shows a fundamental misunderstanding of how foundational beliefs operate when he disparages people for wanting to have incorrigible foundations even

---

not be compatible with classical foundationalism, but might be thought to be so with an epistemic foundation which includes practices as well as concepts. See also Part Four Chapter 2.

53 Wittgenstein, *Philosophical Investigations*,#217.

54 Ibid. 226e.

55 Williams, *Groundless Belief*, 62.

56 Ibid.

57 Wittgenstein, *Philosophical Investigations*, #55.

though they are not (sic) necessary.[58] It is a part of being human and living forms of life for it to be mandatory to commit oneself to certain beliefs. This is not a matter of choice. A form of foundationalism may, therefore, be inevitable. It is rather a matter of endeavouring to ensure that our theories regarding the form of knowledge which is foundational have the best explanatory power.

1.1.5. Summary

The argument so far may be summarised as follows:

1. If all human experience requires language (verbal and nonverbal) for its comprehension and hence its accessibility, then language is universal medium.
2. If the linguistic and nonlinguistic are both subsumed by physical reality and their relation therefore takes place in space-time, then language and world are integrated, not separate.
3. Therefore the language-game is basic or primitive, and arguably epistemically foundational.

The aim of the foregoing discussion has been to demonstrate the coherence of Wittgenstein's premises and deductions regarding the relation of language to world as here presented and as they have been interpreted by the Hintikkas. In the following chapter I examine some of the consequences of such an ontology.

58 Williams, *Groundless Belief*, 74.

CHAPTER TWO

The Consequences of Language-Games as Basic

1.2.1. Pragmatics Subsumes Semantics

If language-games constitute the language-world link, then language-games provide the meanings of words and sentences and the descriptive language-game provides the verification of a proposition. If the language-game is basic, language utilisation is prior to language as such. As language-games determine the meanings of words, pragmatics takes over the work of semantics. It is the living of life in the context of world and language (as opposed to showing or explaining) which is the semantical link. What this entails is revolutionary for the relationship between semantics and pragmatics. It means that the pragmatic must subsume the semantic. Wittgenstein is not alone in arguing for the primacy of language use over language *per se*. Robert Stalnaker, observes that:

> accounting for the relation between language and propositions still falls partly within the domain of semantics. One of the jobs of natural language is to express propositions, and it is a semantical problem to specify the rules for matching up sentences of a natural language with the propositions that they express. In most cases, however, the rules will not match sentences directly with propositions, but will match sentences with propositions relative to features of the context in which the sentence is used. These contextual features are part of the subject matter of pragmatics.[1]

Accordingly, a mix of the semantical and pragmatical aspects of language is required for an adequate explanation of reference. Stalnaker goes on to

1 Robert C. Stalnaker, 'Pragmatics', in *Semantics of Natural Language*, Gilbert Harman and Donald Davidson (eds), (Dortrecht: D. Reidel, 1972), 383.

say: '[i]n most cases ... the context of utterance affects not only the force with which the proposition is expressed, but also the proposition itself. It may be that the semantical rules determine the proposition expressed by a sentence or clause only relative to some feature of the situation in which the sentence is used'.[2]

Kambartel and Schneider[3] reach similar conclusions, seeing Wittgenstein as part of the broad pragmatic tradition and regarding a pragmatic foundation for semantics as essential because understanding of language comes from social activity, not from internal, private meanings. This means that actions, or situations involving use of language are the source of linguistic meanings. Pragmatics is prior to semantics which is in fact subsumed by pragmatics. That is (as has already been argued), language use is prior to language as such and it is necessary to study word meanings in the context of use. On this view pragmatics is no longer seen as an accessory to semantics but as central and basic. In a pragmatical theory of semantics '[l]anguage structures are reconstructed throughout as parts of a rational practice rather than as objects'. Activity, rather than substance, is basic.[4] This leads to Wittgenstein's point that '[s]uch a reconstruction cannot draw on those conceptions of language and logic that at present are dominant in formal logic and linguistics'.[5]

2 Furthermore, '[a]ccording to the pragmatical conception, presupposition is a propositional attitude, not a semantic relation. People, rather than sentences or propositions, are said to have, or make, presuppositions in this sense'. In general, any semantic presuppositions of a proposition expressed in a given context will be a pragmatic presupposition of the people in that context, but the converse clearly does not hold.' (Ibid. 384–5, 387.)

3 F. Kambartel and H. J. Schneider, 'Constructing a Pragmatic Foundation for Semantics', in Floistad, *Contemporary Philosophy*, 155–78.

4 See Part Four for a discussion of the theological ramifications of this.

5 Ibid. 155–8. Incompleteness of description is the price paid for the abandonment of meta-language. Therefore, I take Wittgenstein's objection to semantic models to be to this sort of 'complete functional analysis'. Kambartel and Schneider go on to say: '... even if we had a *Tractatus*-world and an appropriate "ideal" metalanguage ... we would find it impossible to formulate for any natural language a comprehensive system of features and rules in the sense considered above. It is an important feature

These writers demonstrate that pragmatics cannot be used merely as a sort of reference-enricher because it is 'too inexhaustible and vague' to fit into the semantical category of reference. Rather the reverse is the case; the semantical category 'reference' is to be fitted into the pragmatic mix of communicating activities which Wittgenstein calls language-games. To call this mix 'reference' is, therefore, to stretch the term somewhat.[6] Wittgenstein prefers to talk in terms of language-games having (in appropriate cases) a verification function.

While pragmatics subsumes semantics, semantics itself does not disappear. Through regular use of a particular kind, words acquire some stability of meaning(s) that is carried with them to new or less familiar language-games. This could not, however, be described as a 'fixed semantics', although it is temporarily and partially fixed.

As a Wittgensteinian semantics is seen to be subsumed within pragmatics, depending upon prior social consensus and as such demonstrable rather than articulable, Grant Gillett considers that to play a language-game is to be engaged in 'tacit semantics'.[7]

> [T]he thinker masters an ability (structurally located within his conceptual system) to recognise items of a given kind through his own encounters with them and knowledge gained from other thinkers about such items. He learns what counts as 'going on in the same way' by drawing on his experience to organise his responses to items of the type in question as structured by the many intersecting practices in which he participates. His attitudes are therefore shaped by the practices in which he has grasped the use of a term.[8]

As practice-based, a pragmatical theory of knowledge requires a broadening of traditional theories of knowledge to include tacit knowing that is,

---

of language that its use will always be ahead of any set of pragmatic rules ... Natural languages ... characteristically are not closed ...' (Ibid. 161.)

6 Such a stretching of the term 'reference' to apply to the function of language-games, can, however, be of heuristic value (see Part Two).

7 Grant Gillett, 'Tacit Semantics' *Philosophical Investigations*, 2/1 (1988), 1–12.

8 Grant Gillett, *Representation, Meaning and Thought* (London: Oxford University Press, 1992), 25.

'knowing how' as well as 'knowing that'. 'For a large class of cases – though not for all – in which we employ the word "meaning" it can be defined thus: the meaning of a word is its use in the language.'[9] Such know-how is demonstrable but not necessarily articulable. 'Tacit knowledge is seen as a state which explains a skill similar to the ability to tie knots (where, although one cannot describe what one is doing, nevertheless, at a certain stage and in virtue of one's competence, one can be said to know how to tie the knot in question). The skill we are concerned with is the analysis and composition of complex or novel linguistic expressions by use of the components they share with familiar forms.'[10]

Tacit semantics as a category is not exhausted by simply knowing how to use words. Nor is it about merely knowing how to use words to some purpose. The question still remains of how we knew the meanings of the words and word-combinations in the first place. What constrains the acquisition of tacit knowledge is the goal of communicating or understanding certain things in a certain time and place. What counts as 'knowing how' in a particular instance depends on a consensus or norm which constitutes part of a form of life. 'The mapping of expressions on to the world and thus the meaning of these expressions or the content of the thoughts which they can be taken to express, is part of an interwoven network of activities which share human (and usually interpersonal) features'.[11] These enacted 'rules' are what shape our practices (acted-upon know-how) and our conception of these practices. 'It is the forms that such activities take and the rules that govern them – themselves internally related to our capacities for selective attention to aspects, abilities to act, and the need for regularity in our inferences – which impose categorical and lexical structure on our thought and this is precisely where the explanation of that structure must be sought.'[12]

9 Wittgenstein, *Philosophical Investigations*, #43; Gillett, 'Tacit Semantics', 6.

10 Gareth Evans, 'Reply: Semantic Theory and Tacit Knowledge', in S. Holzman and C. Leich, *Wittgenstein: To Follow a Rule* (London: Routledge, 1981), 133. Gillett, 'Tacit Semantics', 6.

11 Ibid. 6–7.

12 Ibid. 12.

In a parallel way, working within a phenomenological paradigm, Michael Polanyi uses the term 'subception' to mean 'having the structure of a skill'.[13] Polanyi distinguishes two kinds of knowing – specifiable and non-specifiable. Subception, once organised into specifiable knowledge, becomes conception. As this process of organisation must, in requiring thinking, involve language of some sort,[14] what Polanyi is in effect describing, in relating tacit to explicit knowledge, are language-games. Polanyi's perspective highlights a feature of language-games: that they are a mixture of specifiable and non-specifiable knowing. The non-specifiable part of knowing is the unreflective use of words and other forms of language as a part of activities, the intertwining of language with the rest of the world. What Polanyi terms 'non-specifiable' is equivalent to what Wittgenstein terms 'ineffable'. The role of words in practice constitutes a first-order use of words. To specify this use (that is, to articulate what we mean by our practices which involve the first-order use of words) is to translate actions or experiences into concepts: 'when we use a tool we are attending to the meaning of its impact on our hands in terms of its effect on the things to which we are applying it. We may call this the semantic aspect of tacit knowing. All meaning tends to be displaced away from ourselves.[15]

1.2.2. The Bedrock of Doing

The idea that individuals or objects have inherent properties and that we understand them solely in terms of these properties entails that meaning is seen as a function of these 'inherent' properties rather than as a function of

13 Michael Polanyi, *The Tacit Dimension* (London: Routledge, 1966), 8. (This material concerning Polanyi previously appeared in my article, Patterson, '*Word*, Words and World'.)

14 Not necessarily verbal language – images, ostensive gestures, postures etc. are adequate communication in some practices.

15 Polanyi, *Tacit Dimension*, 13. Wittgenstein also refers to language as a tool.

use. According to this understanding, our concept of a given individual is a sort of compendium of its properties.[16] However, a language-game ontology entails that both properties and individuals are defined by the various language-games in which they play a part. Viewed in this light, semantic *relata* (language and objects) cannot be distinct items or entities, but by nature are interwoven in activities, in roles and language-games.

Moreover, as the language-game is both our access to the world and the source of our comprehension (concepts) of the physical world, it is doubtful, as Jaakko Hintikka observes, whether individuals can even exist for us as such independently of our (changing) conceptualisation. That is, to question the idea of an individual as a distinct entity is also (again) to call into question the classical notion of 'substance' as basic,[17] for the very idea of an individual has, on this account, become the product of language-games and will vary between language-games: 'The notion of individual *simpliciter* makes no sense. The reality can be conceptualised – structured into individuals – in more than one way, none of which reduces to the others.'[18]

Nelson Goodman (here not necessarily nominalist in his view) concurs. If there are many different ways an object is, then none of these ways can be *the* way. Goodman also utilises Kant: 'The innocent eye is blind and the virgin mind empty' and adds that '[c]ontent cannot be separated from

16 George Lakoff and Mark Johnson, *Metaphors We Live By* (Chicago: University of Chicago Press, 1980), 119.

17 This point is important theologically, as will be seen below. It again shows Wittgenstein's (and Hintikka's) debt to Kant. It is not necessary to accept Kant's Cartesianism to appreciate some of his other insights. Gillett notes that while '[f]or Kant experience was the primary datum for the rational subject and comprised intuitions – sensory matter structured according to the forms of space and time' – he does not see that experience as simply impinging on the subject as 'a "given" or a set of stimulations; rather it involves conceptual judgments which should appear in an adequate account of thought and its content'. (Gillett, *Representation, Meaning and Thought*, 9n, 10.) See also Jaakko Hintikka, 'Self-Profile' in *Profiles 8: Jaakko Hintikka*, Radu J. Bogdan (ed.), (Dortrecht: D. Reidel, 1987), 3–38: 25.

18 Esa Saarinen, 'Continuity and Similarity in Cross-Identification', in *Essays in Honour of Jaakko Hintikka*, E. Saarinen, R. Hilpinen, I. Niiniluoto and M. Provence Hintikka (eds) (Dortrecht: D. Reidel, 1979), 89–215; 97.

comment'. Goodman observes that the inherent relativity of what we regard as real or true 'is obscured by our tendency to omit specifying a frame of reference when it is our own'. The custom is the standard.[19]

1.2.3. How does the Sign Link up with the World?

To the extent that realism and the correspondence theory of truth have depended on an isomorphism between language and world, Wittgenstein's adherence to these perspectives did not survive the transition from the *Tractatus* to the *Philosophical Investigations*. The Hintikkas, however, suggest that Wittgenstein's picture and mirroring theories did not so much disappear as picturing and mirroring ceased to be primary language-world connectors. This does not mean, contrary to the 'received view', that Wittgenstein abandoned the idea of correspondence. He merely abandoned a general theory of simple isomorphic naming or picturing relations. Post *Tractatus*, Wittgenstein continued to be concerned with verification and truth-conditions. However, the method of verification became more complex. As the Hintikkas observe, in later Wittgenstein there are no longer one-to-one language-world relations. One language-game links several different words with the world. Linguistic 'pictures', insofar as they can still be said to be pictures, are pictures of reality as represented by language-games. At the same time, these language-games as the 'projective links with reality' also have to be incorporated in the 'picture' if the picture is to serve its purpose of depiction. The verbal picture or proposition has become sentence plus use of sentence. Accordingly, language-games must be seen as components of propositions and conversely, the terms which express propositions receive their meaning from the language-games.[20]

19 Nelson Goodman, *Languages of Art: an Approach to a Theory of Symbols*, 2nd edn (Indianapolis: Hackett Publishing Co., 1976), 6–8, 38.

20 Hintikka and Hintikka, *Investigating Wittgenstein*, 226–7, 230–1, 235.

The construal of a separation between language and world (which, as Wittgenstein has observed, has caused philosophers to pose and answer the wrong questions[21]) has led to the continual tendency for the ostensibly opposed positions of realism and modern idealism or nominalism to revert to the one (idealist) position of their common basis because 'for all their passionate insistence on having knowledge of things outside our minds, [they] never look outside the world as representable. They too, that is to say, take it for granted that the debate is about matching ideas in our heads with items in the world ... Realists, just as much as idealists, fail to acknowledge that *das leben* is "the given"'.[22] However, 'Words have meaning only in the stream of life'.[23] The basicality of the language-game offers an epistemology which combines realist and non-realist insights in regarding language as an inextricable component of the practices of our living in the world.[24] Language-games as language-world links (activities or practices which interweave language and world) 'slice reality up vertically' as it were into a multitude of language-world 'pieces'. Here questions of truth are not seen as a simple one-to-one correspondence between propositions and states of affairs. It is language-games which effect that correspondence and at the same time determine the meanings of the propositions and states of affairs. Language and world are inextricably interwoven in the practices of living. Human confidence about 'knowing the way things are' is not a matter of explicit statement or belief so much as a matter of living according to patterns or axioms generated by communal experience,

21 As Wittgenstein points out, realists and nominalists alike are trying to answer the same question in opposite ways, but the question is the wrong question (see *On Certainty* #37). For a discussion on this point see Thomas Morawetz, *Wittgenstein and Knowledge* (Amherst: University of Massachusetts Press, 1978), 141–4.

22 Wittgenstein, *Philosophical Remarks*, #47), paraphrased in Kerr, *Theology After Wittgenstein*, 133.

23 Ludwig Wittgenstein, *Remarks on the Philosophy of Psychology Vol. II*, G. H. von Wright and Heikki Nyman (eds), E. G. Luckhardt and M. A. E. Aue (trs.), (Oxford: Blackwell, 1980), #687. See also Wittgenstein, *Philosophical Investigations*, ##96, 428, 435.

24 For an extended discussion on this, see my subsequent book, *Realist Christian Theology*.

the doubting of which would destroy that pattern because it would be to doubt the very structure of existence.

The semiotic theory of Charles Sanders Peirce provides a comparable way of going beyond realist and anti-realist perspectives. According to John Deely, Peirce's category of the semiotic subsumes the concerns of realism and idealism in their common dependency on experience, thus exposing their dichotomy as false.[25] To begin with 'There is no atomic structure to the world such that words can be made to correspond to it point-by-point'.[26] Thus,

> [I]t is not enough to recognise that language itself is a system of relationships and contrasts between elements ... Language itself as an objective network is part of a larger whole of objective relations ... the *Umwelt* or 'objective world' of experience integrally taken in relation to which the linguistic network exists symbiotically – that is, as itself feeding upon and being transformed by the structure of experience as a whole in its irreducibility to the physical environment.[27]

25 John Deely, *Basics of Semiotics* (Indiana: Indiana University Press, 1990): 109, 116. Of course, the affinity between Peirce and Wittgenstein has been previously noted (see Kambartel and Schneider, 'Constructing a Pragmatic Foundation for Semantics', 56).

26 Deely's sentence here demonstrates the difficulty of finding expressions that do not connote a separation of language and world, so built-in to our language-world is this assumption! I have struggled with this problem throughout the present work and apologise for its remaining inadequacies in this respect.

27 Ibid. 18–19. This is to be contrasted with Saussure's 'fatally flawed' view of semiotics as a subordinate rather than all-embracing discipline in which the 'arbitrariness of signs' is a general principle of analysis. Saussure's 'duality of significant and *signifie* lacked the thirdness whereby the sign in its foundation (and whether or not this foundation be essentially arbitrary or "stipulated") undergoes transformation into first an object and then into other signs'. (Ibid. 115, 118.) 'Peirce's idea of interpretive processes does not commit him to construing referents as purely linguistic or symbolic, arbitrary conventions. They are not arbitrary for two reasons. First, at each stage of reinterpretation, or new interpretation, what is interpreted is an Immediate Object that is constituted within the interpretive structure of a sign relation. In each sign relation, the sign represents an object to an interpretant. This relation gives semiotic structure to each stage of interpretation. Consequently, no instance of interpretation is wholly self-contained and decisive for establishing a set of meanings

It is possible to recognise here Wittgenstein's insight that language is a part of physical reality, which, as such, interweaves with other aspects of the physical world in our lives or experiences. Experience as a complex of activities (language-games and forms of life) subsumes the nonlinguistic physical environment and is not therefore reducible to it. However, Peirce (as represented by Deely at least) appears to see things in far more general terms than Wittgenstein. He does not appear to have any 'equivalent notion' to language-games as 'micro' practices and forms of life as local ways of being in the world which vary with culture and subculture. Yet for Peirce, like Wittgenstein, language-world connections are dynamic, a process, not a static atemporal network.[28] Peirce is also committed to the primacy of pragmatics: 'The sign not only stands for something other than itself, it does so for some third'[29] – that is, a sign (whether verbal or nonverbal) represents something *for someone*. Thus the meaning of the sign is dependent not only on its referent but also on its utilisation by a user in terms of the referent. For Peirce, therefore, as for Wittgenstein, meaning is a product of use.[30]

When dependence on cognition for comprehension of the sign-object is taken into account, Peirce's ontology also seems implicitly Kantian,[31] for basic here is the notion of experience as equivalent to the 'semiotic web'

arbitrarily. There is, then, an objectivity of growing interpretations converging on a larger, coherent community of interpretations.' [Carl E. Hausman, *Metaphor and Art: Interactionism and Reference in the Verbal and Nonverbal Arts* (Cambridge UK: Cambridge University Press, 1989), 214.]

28 Deely, *Basics of Semiotics*, 51.

29 Ibid. 33.

30 According to Deely, Peirce considers experience to be epistemically basic. However his is a wider view of experience because he does not confine signifying activities to the human sphere but extends it to the whole of the living world. To exist is to be signifier and signified (ibid. 58–9). 'There is no object that does not depend in its objectivity on the simultaneous action of the sign as making present in experience something other than itself, something that it itself is not.' (Ibid. 61.)

31 'If there is an 'independent, extralinguistic, extra-conceptual condition ... but the condition is not knowable in itself, then the position is Kantian'. (Hausman, *Metaphor and Art*, 84.)

(universal process of signifying as access to comprehension of the world). However, 'while the being proper to signs exists actually only within the context of experience (in precisely the sense that experience presupposes cognition), the action that underlies this possible being by no means presupposes cognition.'[32]

It is not hard to see the affinity with a language-game ontology. Likewise Peirce's *Umwelt*, as 'the environment selectively reconstituted and organised according to the specific needs and interests of the individual organism,'[33] can be seen to correspond to Wittgenstein's form of life. The scale is different, but the idea is basically the same. Likewise, Peirce's concept of the code as the 'correlation and proportioning of a sensibly accessible element to an objectivity that is understood as correlated thereto' resembles the concept of language-game as language-world link. 'The idea must be correlated with some physical element within experience that is taken to serve as ground for the relation in which the idea expressly consists.' This correlation or effecting of correspondence is the code (language-game equivalent). 'A code thus channels and directs relations among objects in a publicly accessible way.'[34]

1.2.4. The Problem with 'Being Appeared To'

If language-games are basic, language-world linking activity is epistemically prior to individual perceptions of world, therefore sense-data are epistemically nonbasic.

An essential feature of foundationalism, according to Williams, is that 'the intrinsically credible beliefs must be directly knowable.' This, he contends, requires a 'permanent body of observational knowledge independent

32 Deely, *Basics of Semiotics*, 83.

33 Ibid. 59–60.

34 Ibid. 66.

of all theory, against which any theory is to be tested'.[35] Phenomenalism is the archetypical and, according to Williams, the most plausible form of foundationalism. It has certainly been the most prevalent. This school of thought, traceable to Brentano, could be called the 'theory of the absolute self-evidence of inner perception'. Its legacy from Descartes is obvious; the indubitability of consciousness as 'self-transparent' provides a 'presupposition-less' basis for phenomenalism. Phenomenology accordingly is the 'science of the manifestations of consciousness'.[36] It recognises two components in knowledge: the given (sense-data) and the interpretation (activity of thought). 'The content of awareness of the given is non-propositional.'[37]

Knowledge of the physical world may be caused by the having of sensations, but one does not have to be a phenomenological foundationalist and claim that this sensory mediation is epistemic. Williams warns that it is easy to confuse the mediated with the mediation. 'If having a sensation is not an episode of "knowing that", the having of sensations cannot constitute the foundations of empirical knowledge'. If one subscribes to this theory of knowledge, a removal of the foundation back a step to 'beliefs about how one is appeared to' (as Roderick Chisholm does[38]) does not solve the problem as this tends to reduce to talk about the sensations themselves.[39]

While I acknowledge Williams's warning, I suggest there are two problems with his argument. The first problem is that it relies upon a certain assumption of what sort of knowledge can count as foundational.[40] Why

35 Williams, *Groundless Belief*, 61, 70.

36 Gilbert Ryle, 'Heidegger's "Sein und Zeit"', *Critical Essays: Collected Papers Vol. 1* (London: Hutchison, 1971), 200ff: 167. 'Meanings are the gift of consciousness; so that consciousness is constitutive of all objects that are (or pretend to be) transcendent ...' (Ibid. 212.)

37 Williams, *Groundless Belief*, 26, 32.

38 See Roderick Chisholm, *Theory of Knowledge* (New Jersey: Prentice Hall), 1966.

39 Williams, *Groundless Belief*, 73–5. Rather than being a primary mediator of reality, phenomenological language proves to be nonbasic because it is parasitic on ordinary everyday 'object-language'. (See Hintikka and Hintikka, *Investigating Wittgenstein*, 148–9.)

40 This is due to Williams's restriction of what counts as knowledge in the first place: 'a person becomes a fully-fledged knower only when his linguistic and other practices

is 'knowing that' to be preferred over 'knowing how'? Wittgenstein maintains that acting accordance with a rule is prior to the explicit articulation of or comprehension of the rule. We can play the game in accordance with the rules without ever knowing that it has particular rules. The game *is* its rules; the rules are enacted, lived ('Now I know how to go on'[41]). Why then cannot the 'knowing how' of knowing the moves of certain language-games which are played subject to local modifications in relation to the lived belief-structure of a form of life, be a foundation of empirical knowledge? If a language-game ontology is maintained, there is in fact no option. Given that the system of language-games is a complex entity which includes secondary, interpretative games, 'language-game' as foundational is an irreducible composite of 'knowing how' and 'knowing that'.[42]

Gillett applies a Wittgensteinian perspective in a critique of phenomenology.[43] 'Attempts to connect our concepts with the world via a sort of causal chain' – that is, to construe perception as such a chain – is firstly ruled out by the fact that concepts structure our perceptual experience and secondly by the fact that an epistemic gap will still remain between

---

have reached a degree of complexity sufficient for it to be apparent that he accepts sentences of many different kinds, that he has various general as well as particular beliefs.' (Ibid. 91.)

41 Wittgenstein, *Philosophical Investigations*, ##151, 179.

42 Jaakko Hintikka identifies sense-perception games as a subset of the language-games of seeking and finding. These games also comprise a subset of Wittgenstein's primary (often nonverbalised) physiological, physiognomic and sensory language-games. They are language-games, then, both in the broader sense of language which includes nonverbal communications, and in the sense that perception must involve language to be comprehensible. Hintikka sees that what is needed to explain perception is a stronger (rather than a non-existent) phenomenological thesis 'which goes further than conceptual realism itself'. According to such a thesis 'the most primitive and spontaneous sense-impressions which can surface in one's consciousness are already articulated into perceptions of physical objects, of persons, and of the rest of the regular inhabitants of the real world'. (Jaakko Hintikka, 'Reply to Romane Clark's "What is a 'Perceptually Well-Defined Individual"? Hintikka's views on Perception', *Profiles 8: Jaakko Hintikka*, 215–32: 324–5.)

43 See Gillett, *Representation, Meaning and Thought*, 179ff. (See also his 'Learning to Perceive', *Philosophical and Phenomenological Research* 48 (1987–1988), 601ff.)

mind and world. This is so because of the need in such a chain to posit an intermediate 'range of proximal states' which are neither world nor concept.[44] Our perception, dependent as it is on our learning to perceive (our being trained in the comprehension or the ordering of our sense-data by the community of which we are a part), is secondary to our practices.[45] The object of our perception comes clothed in the dress of the training we have received in the use of it.[46]

Training in the language-games which constitute forms of life provides both the perception and the articulation of the perception which is empirical knowledge. 'One might say that understanding the meaning of a term involves a familiarity with its application with a range of activities and interpersonal context or a form of life.'[47] We are trained by our social

44 Gillett, *Representation, Meaning and Thought*, 190–1. Gillett suspects that 'similar problems attach to any theory which bases thought on "informational states" of the subject because these tend to lock the thinker within the veil of the senses rather than to allow his mind to directly engage with the real world'.

45 On a Wittgensteinian view, the primacy of the language-game takes care of the special case of private experiences: 'the job of phenomenological languages can be done [in the case of private languages] by language based on public language-games'. One learns how to comprehend our private experiences through public language-games. Accordingly, Wittgenstein sees that relations of (private) sensations to their (public) behavioural counterparts as a necessary, not a contingent one. 'These "external manifestations" are needed in the language-games which give our talk of our private experiences their meaning. They are therefore logically (semantically) connected with the experiences themselves; they enter essentially in the relevant language-games.' (Hintikka and Hintikka, *Investigating Wittgenstein*, 245, 258.)

46 It is important to remember here the point made in Chapter 1 that in language-games 'language' is not confined to purely verbal expressions but includes nonverbal forms of communication such as noises and gestures. Wittgenstein's view of language simply does not allow a discrete step from the verbal and the nonverbal because for him language is a part of the physical world. An implication of this is that we may not, when it comes to language-games, draw a line between human and animal communications. Communicating activities come in all shapes and degrees of sophistication.

47 Gillett sees that it is through activity (into which fragments of words are interwoven) that our perceptual world acquires its shape. 'The rules which informally constitute meaning and allow the construction of linguistic complexes from their component

milieu in the moves of matching sense-impressions to physical object language (we have 'stabbing' or 'dull' pains). Without the meaning conferred by use in a language-game, the objects of sensations can have no meaning. Therefore the sensations in themselves are devoid of content and communicate no information.[48]

Williams agrees that 'The credibility of sensation reports can be attributed to training'.[49] Under this interpretation, any reduction from Chisholm's appearance-beliefs cannot be a reduction of beliefs about sensations to the sensations themselves. Williams is right to regard these as incapable, being epistemically inaccessible, of constituting a foundation of empirical knowledge. Instead the reduction is from one type of language to another, more basic type.[50] Wittgenstein takes this path in

---

terms, depend for their content and form on the activities in which those terms have been learnt.' (Gillett, 'Learning to Perceive', 609–10.)

48 'Mental content, one might say, constitutively embraces things we perceive in the world and it is within its structure that we live and move and do our seeing.' (Gillett, *Representation, Meaning and Thought*, 198.) Also, '[i]n a sense ... items or features [of the world] do not exist as objects of attention to be thought about until the child learns to perceive them: they are given through the skills or abilities refined in practices which pick them out' ('Learning to Perceive', 13). Downey notes that 'Phenomenology sets the problematic as a radical attention to the structures of experience and this selective focus blurs the linguistic environment ... [w]hile attention is directed to experience, a definition of "secular man" is quietly at work.' (Downey, *Beginning at the Beginning*, 123.)

49 'Phenomenological perceptual reports involve implicit comparisons and appeals to norms so that such statements cannot be epistemologically basic.' (Williams, *Groundless Belief*, 163, 165.)

50 This turns on its head the meaning of Chisholm's observation reported by Williams that 'that which is only indirectly evident can be "known through" that which is directly evident, although the relation between the directly and indirectly evident is neither inductive nor deductive.' (Williams, *Groundless Belief*, 166.) As I have suggested, this relation is metaphorical or analogous. This can be seen when Chisholm's 'directly evident', namely sense-data, is equated with Wittgenstein's 'indirectly evident' (Wittgenstein's 'directly evident' being our conceptions of everyday objects). Of course, when this way of solving the problem is followed, phenomenology loses its foundationality. In having become one set of language-games among others, it is

recognising that talk of sensations relies in turn upon physical object language.[51]

The second problem with Williams's argument is to do with his dismissal of phenomenalism, and hence foundationalism, on the grounds of its requirement that the 'permanent body of knowledge' which qualifies to be foundational must be independent of all theory. As 'knowing-that' is impossible without theory, this stricture, coupled with Williams's seeming limitation of knowledge to 'knowing-that', appears effectively to rule out the viability of foundationalism. However, all this does is rule out the phenomenalistic version of foundationalism. The empirical evidence that there is an inextricable mix of empirical data with theory involved in comprehension of the world suggests an irreducible combination of 'knowing-how' and 'knowing-that' as a foundation of knowledge. If 'knowing how' is treated as an admissible component of this 'permanent body of knowledge', then this body may be said to be at best partially theory-independent. Of course, as Williams rightly points out, complete freedom from theory is impossible where considerations of knowledge are involved. To suggest that it is possible is to attempt to make knowledge independent of concept formation. It is to be expected that this would be the phenomenalists' intention.

I suggest that Williams has confused the requirements of foundationality with the requirements of phenomenalism; foundationalism does not require freedom from theory of that which is foundational. However, the presence (necessarily, it is contended) of theory in an epistemic foundation which is not completely theoretical, such as language-games, means that there will be a circularity operating within that foundation between its

---

superseded by a language-game foundationality. In other words, a kind of foundationalism survives (arguably), but not phenomenalism.

51 There is nothing in Wittgenstein's middle period that 'prima facie rules out a language of the immediately given' – in fact ostension encourages it; likewise, the idea of rules is compatible with a phenomenological language'. However, 'with the primacy of language-games as language-world links, the idea of a private language has to go, for to understand a word is to witness the entire language-game which is its "logical home" – and this cannot be private'. (Hintikka and Hintikka, *Investigating Wittgenstein*, 242–3.)

theoretical and non-theoretical components. Perhaps this does not matter. If the components of the compound foundational entity are inseparable, and the language-game thus irreducibly basic, why should they not form a self-justifying system? For that is what the language-game is.

It is unfortunate that when Williams turns his attention to the idea of linguistic rules as basic, he does not see that the fault lies with the notion of *linguistic* rules as basic.[52] Certainly, 'a class of basic predicates applicable without criteria' can easily be shown to be nonbasic. How can predicates be meaningful without criteria? However, the idea of rule as basic does work when rule is understood as language-game. It is surprising that Williams does not consider this option, as he allows that justifications must come to an end somewhere (a direct although unacknowledged quote from Wittgenstein).[53] However, Williams is committed to the defence of a kind of direct realism against foundationalism and therefore cannot entertain the possibility of any coherent form of foundationalism, let alone any such notion as language-games.[54] His narrow definition of knowledge as 'knowing that' is a safeguard against the need to consider such partially conceptual foundations.

It may be objected that the notion of language-game is too vague to be epistemically foundational. It may be argued that there is little use in having a foundation which is so general as to include all actions involving a mix of objects and language of all kinds. The language-game may be general as a concept but it is most specific and small-scale as an empirical entity. The difficulty is that thinking has been traditionally done 'horizontally' in language or activity or object 'layers' whereas language-games are carvings-up up these layers into quite circumscribed 'vertical blocks' of reality. It is a matter of re-educating one's thinking. A language-game foundation is

52 Williams, *Groundless Belief*, 79–80.

53 Ibid. 83 (see also Wittgenstein, *Philosophical Investigations*, #217).

54 Williams seems to accept as valid a foundational view of knowledge, which ascribes intrinsic credibility to knowledge of physical objects as this is compatible with direct realism (ibid. 70), however he does not see the necessity for this unless one maintains a correspondence theory of truth (which he does not).

not a solid floor one's beliefs rest on, but rather resembles a high-rise tower which harbours a whole community of thinking and doing.

That this section has warranted the time spent on it will, it is suggested, become apparent later. A phenomenalistic foundationalism has implications for the theory of knowledge which are unhelpful in theology. As this sort of foundation is usually the 'default' (and often tacit) position adopted in the absence of the choice of any other, and as it seems to be difficult if not impossible for human beings to operate conceptually without some sort of foundation (see Williams's disparagement of this above), it is important to make a case for the proper foundationality of language-games. It is more constructive (although perhaps less conventional) to offer a positive alternative than merely to refute an inadequate one. It is not denied that there are problems with any human ideas of basicality. This more fundamental issue will be addressed in Part Four.

1.2.5. Language-Games and Local Truths

A language-game foundation is plausibly a local or relative foundation in the Plantingan sense in that the content of language-games varies in time and space. To say that the language-game is foundational is to say that a certain structured activity is basic, not a particular content of that activity. To be committed to the reality of language-games is not to be committed to the absolute truth of any propositions related to any language-game. This means that a further important consequence of the basicality of language-games is linguistic relativism. The Hintikkas note that the ineffability of the semantical language-world link 'entails, among other things, the linguistic inaccessibility of the relation of a true sentence to the fact which makes it true'.[55] This means that human access to truth is to local truths only, no one of which appears to have any claim to be absolute. Linguistic relativ-

55 Hintikka and Hintikka, *Investigating Wittgenstein*, 8.

ism may be seen thus to preclude an 'eye of God' stance.[56] This is not as troublesome (or indeed fatal) for theology as might be thought. If truth is believed, in any case, to repose ultimately in God, it may be argued that what linguistic relativism does is merely to restore the 'eye' to its rightful owner. Human access to truth is necessarily given and partial. This subject will be taken further in Part Four.

1.2.6. An Ontology of Practice

There is an intimate connection between correspondence as the measure of truth and a foundational view of knowledge. It is the epistemic foundation which verifies other, nonbasic, knowledge. From a Wittgensteinian perspective, it is the language-game which provides the verification of propositions because it is there that justification comes to an end; forms of life provide the warrant for our beliefs.[57] Likewise, the Peircean understanding of experience is the dynamic world of the use of signs – of relation of sign to signified; it is necessarily temporal as well as public (occurring in observable space). 'Semiosis' (the action of signs) applies wherever there is 'a question of future outcomes and law-governed interactions'.[58]

While both of these positions occupy territory beyond the usual direct-realist and idealist categories, as has been seen, both are consistent with a kind of realism. Reality has merely been redefined. It has become a compound of mind and world. While Wittgenstein, Peirce, Gillett and Hausman would not deny that our thoughts and actions are subject to

56 Ibid. 21. While this may be worrying for traditional realists, I will argue later that this need not be a problem for theology as it merely sweeps away some inadequately founded claims to absolute truth.

57 'If I have exhausted the justifications I have reached bedrock and my spade is turned. Then I am inclined to say: "This is simply what I do".' (Wittgenstein, *Philosophical Investigations* #217.)

58 Deely, *Basics of Semiotics*, 67.

extra-conceptual constraint – that is, are to some extent limited by the 'shape' of the reality which lies beyond our conceptions of it – they are also concerned to recognise the social and cultural constraints which modify our understanding of reality.

The basicality of language-games again suggests a Kantian relation between ontology and epistemology.[59] According to such a position, one cannot approach ontology except through epistemology – thought about both is constrained by the limits of language in general and local forms of life in particular. Speaking about what is the case takes place with an assumption of knowledge. That is, ontology assumes knowledge (or belief about) what is. The limits of what can be expressed and comprehended are set by forms of life. The strength of the Kantian position is its very failure ultimately to be relativist or positivist. Whatever understanding of the world is allowed by the limitations of comprehension placed on us by our forms of life, for the Kantian this is not to be equated with the nature of reality itself. This always lies beyond the reach of our knowledge.

Thus this sort of 'conceptual realism' accepts a local and partial verification – a correspondence between our ideas about reality and what is foundational for us: the language-games which comprise our forms of life. However, the correspondence between this foundation and the transcending reality it mediates is unverifiable because it is inaccessible: the ineffable language-world link is subsumed by the inaccessible language-game.[60] As Gillett observes:

> if the mind dictates the form of knowledge and the objects of experience must conform to it then how can we have an idea of what reality is really like? ... On such a conception, thoughts of the world are 'mind-dependent – not really describing a mind-independent reality at all, but in some sense creating the reality they describe' ...

59 Hausman suggests that the ontology which results from an experiential foundation may be construed as either community generated (cultural relativism) or general to human experience. If the latter, the position is Kantian. Without the extra-conceptual constraints, the position would be idealism. (Hausman, *Metaphor and Art*, 186.)

60 Ibid. 183–7.

> The difficulty is to acknowledge that human judgments make sense of experience and yet retain some objectivity for that experience.[61]
>
> How can we say that we do not merely 'construct an hypothesis of perception' which, as it turns out, is remarkably useful to us? If a perception at time *t1* is merely a part of a mind-dependent construct with an unspecified relation to that which is 'outer', then a sequence of such perceptions, however they are related to each other, merely multiply our evidence at the same level and cannot validate it.[62]

In other words, what validates the language-games themselves? What is the reality against which they may be measured? One finds that this validation may not even be attempted via analogy because how then is the analogy validated? 'There are no terms which make a formed thought available.'[63] Gillett, following Wittgenstein, considers such questions to be confused and ultimately meaningless.

> Beyond their applications, actual and hypothetical, within this milieu, the terms, and their meanings, will not go. The attempt to make them go further is just confused. Kant argued this but Wittgenstein supplied the aphorism: 'That whereof we cannot speak, thereof we must be silent'. To attempt to discuss a conception of reality which outstrips the meaning in which conceptions have their life is to attempt nothing … The grander question of whether we could have any conception of objective reality against which the totality of our thought might be gauged is meaningless.[64]

Thus on a Kantian (and, it is suggested, Wittgensteinian) view, what is basic epistemologically must also be basic ontologically. It makes no sense to talk about a basic ontology in the sense of the way things are in themselves. To assume the incorrigibility of one's beliefs about the nature of reality is to equate what is known or believed to be so with what is the case. The world that is the case is either concept-conditioned or nonsense. Wittgenstein talks about the ungroundedness of concept and belief as

61 Gillett, *Representation, Meaning and Thought*, 180, quoting S. Blackburn, *Spreading the Word* (London: Oxford University Press, 1984), 146.

62 Ibid. 182.

63 Ibid. 200.

64 Ibid. See also Grant Gillett, 'An Antisceptical Fugue', *Philosophical Investigations* 13/4 (1990), 304ff.

if to underscore their local circularity with experience. However much such a circle (or spiral) engages with other circles, the system of circles is free-wheeling. It is also subject to change. Self-evidence is only local and temporary. Knowledge and belief may seem to coalesce but neither can be known to coalesce or not with a hypothetical reality beyond language. The interweavings of first-order use of language, primary language-games, with the activities and objects they relate provide the verification of our concepts. Yet in the language-game one seems to act purely in accordance with what is axiomatic for that game: forms of life. As we have no way of knowing (through our ordinary human experience) what lies beyond the foundation of our knowledge, ultimately the verificational requirements of realism can only be met, if met at all, theistically.[65]

This issue will be revisited in Part Four. For the time being, the way forward is hinted at by Gillett who suggests that, to solve this problem, we may posit a '"given" element in perception which impinges on the mind'.[66] Such an element is not mind-independent or extralinguistic, resembling a Peircean 'intentional object' that 'is given by a word or phrase which gives a description under which'.[67] The givenness of forms of life (a givenness of both form and content), while only accessible via conceptual structuring, 'assures us of something beyond the mind', however inconceivable. Here philosophy ends and theology takes over.

65 This is Michael Dummett's point. (See 'Introduction', *Truth and Other Enigmas*, London: Duckworth, 1978.)

66 Gillett, *Representation, Meaning and Thought*, 183.

67 G. E. M. Anscombe, *Metaphysics and the Philosophy of Mind* (Oxford: Blackwell, 1981), 9, quoted in ibid. 'Dummett suggests that this pervasive feature of experience be named Kant's principle: 'Every object is given to us in some particular way'. (Lectures on Gareth Evans's Varieties of Experience, Oxford, Trinity Term, 1986; ibid. 183n.)

1.2.7. Summary and Conclusions to Part One

The primacy of language-games may be seen to be a logical inference. If all human experience requires language (verbal and nonverbal) for its comprehension and hence its accessibility, then language is universal medium. This means that nonlinguistic reality is accessible only through our contact with it via language. But language is a part of the physical world, therefore physical-object language is basic and constitutes our access to the nonlinguistic world.

If the linguistic and nonlinguistic are both subsumed by physical reality and their relation therefore takes place in space-time, then language and world are integrated, not separate. Moreover, the language-world relation as subsumed by physical reality takes place in time. In-time-ness means that we must understand the language-world relation in spatio-temporal terms as activity. Therefore the language-world connecting activity (language-game) is prior to the connections it makes (rules), so cannot be justified in terms of rules inferable from it. Therefore the language-game is basic or primitive.

This conclusion entails that:

1. Pragmatics subsumes semantics and language-world-linking activity is prior to language per se. Thus, knowledge is inclusive of 'knowing how' (tacit knowledge) and not restricted to 'knowing that' and the basicality of language-games constitutes an epistemic foundation;

2. Language-world linking activity is prior to individual perceptions of world, therefore phenomenology is nonbasic. It is also prior to any distinction between or correspondence of language and world, therefore the traditional categories of direct realism and idealism are superseded;

3. The epistemic foundation is a relativistic one (and thus hints at its own ultimate nonbasicality). However, a purely extralinguistic reality (and the accompanying notion of absolute truth) is either a meaningless concept or inaccessible by definition unless 'given'

> within the epistemic foundation (in which case it is not extralinguistic at all). Hence any conception of ontology is contingent on the epistemic foundation.

In Part Two, I deal with the question of how, if the reality of language-world is 'given', an epistemic foundation comprising language-games is able to explain and incorporate new information.

PART TWO

Moving the Foundation

CHAPTER ONE

A Wittgensteinian Explanation of Metaphor

2.1.1. Why Metaphor?

In Part One I left two issues open: first, the possibility of epistemic access to a reality beyond the limits of human knowing: to (in effect) a more basic foundation than that of language-games. The second (related) issue is the ability of a language-game ontology to incorporate and explain gains to knowledge. It may be seen that, for the purposes of this study, the first issue depends upon the second.

A gain to conceptual knowledge ('knowing-that') takes the form of new propositions, concepts or categories whereas a gain to tacit or pre-conceptual knowledge ('knowing how') occurs through activities or practices. On a Wittgensteinian view, these two types of knowledge are intertwined in language-games. Therefore, any gain to knowledge involves a gain to language-games. My aim is to incorporate within a Wittgensteinian perspective another area of linguistic theory which identifies metaphor as an incremental agent of knowledge. I demonstrate in Part Four that metaphor-making (hereafter metaphorising[1]) is integral to a theology of revelation. The task at this point is to establish a specifically Wittgensteinian perspec-

1 See Introduction. While specifically metaphor is referred to here and elsewhere, I will argue that the process of metaphorising (metaphor-making) is not restricted to the making of figures of speech alone but may be said to include all ways in which new knowledge is arrived at by means of a recombination and reassignment of the old. While it is obvious that metaphor as such requires the involvement of words, metaphorising is rather broader in its scope, including actions and other forms of communication as well as words. Models may also be produced through the metaphorising process (see below).

tive on metaphor, drawing parallels and making comparisons with various theories of metaphor where appropriate without undertaking full scale critiques of these theories.[2]

Following on from the conclusions drawn in Part One, I argue that a Wittgensteinian explanation of metaphor must first, take the language-game as basic or primitive; second, subsume its semantics within its pragmatics (seeing metaphorical language-world linking activity as prior to metaphorical language per se); third, accordingly understand knowledge as inclusive of 'knowing-how' and not restricted to 'knowing that'; fourth, in its integration of language and world, bypass or supersede the traditional categories of realism and idealism; and fifth, show how metaphorical activity is part of the totality of language-games and yet effects an increment to knowledge as understood in terms of that totality.

I suggest that this inclusion of metaphor within the Wittgensteinian language-game concept will produce a synthesis with greater explanatory power. In the second chapter of Part Two I set out to demonstrate this.

2.1.2. The Metaphorising Language-Game

> [1] *A Wittgensteinian explanation of metaphor takes the language-game as basic or primitive.*

If language is universal medium and all human activities involve language of some sort and are therefore language-games (and incorporated in LUM), then the activity of metaphorising (making of metaphors) is a language-game. What is the significance of understanding metaphor in this way?

2 As the reviewing of various theories of metaphor has been done very extensively by others, I do not propose to do this here. Nor is it the aim of this study to produce yet another theory of metaphor, although this is to a degree unavoidable if, for the purposes of the later theological argument, a Wittgensteinian understanding of metaphor is to be employed.

A metaphor is commonly taken to be a verbal utterance or statement expressing an unconventional use of terms. This new use somehow both depends on the antecedent conventional use of the terms in question and, at the same time, suggests (and may come to establish) a new use resulting from the new combination of terms. Because of metaphor's dependence on use, semanticists have tended to regard metaphor as an aberration or special case belonging in the domain of pragmatics. Of course, this view reflects the semanticist's prejudice that pragmatics is simply an add-on category of peripheral relevance to language meaning. However, this relegation of metaphor to the domain of pragmatics exposes as unsustainable the judgment that pragmatical concerns are merely peripheral with respect to meaning and at the same time reveals the true nature of metaphor. If metaphor is simply or largely a matter of language use, and yet metaphor conveys new meaning, then for metaphor meaning is intimately connected with use. Therefore the pragmatic cannot be merely peripheral with respect to meaning, at least not for metaphor. Wittgenstein's thesis of meaning as a creation of use is, of course, not restricted to metaphor. For Wittgenstein, in a great many if not all instances of linguistic expression, the way a term is used establishes its meaning. Thus, as has been seen, pragmatics is a foundation for semantics and not the reverse, because understanding of language comes from its use in our forms of life. Actions, or situations involving use of language are the source of linguistic meanings, and therefore pragmatics is more basic than semantics (and subsumes semantics). In a pragmatic theory of semantics, as Kambartel and Schneider have pointed out, 'Language structures are reconstructed throughout as parts of a rational practice rather than as objects'.[3] Activity, rather than substance, is basic.

> [2] *A Wittgensteinian explanation of metaphor subsumes semantics within pragmatics.*

There is in this an important consequence for metaphor. Metaphor as a figure of speech is subsumed by the activity of metaphor making. Metaphor is preeminently 'metaphorising': it is primarily a sort of language use.

3 Kambartel and Schneider, 'Constructing a Pragmatic Foundation for Semantics', 156.

However, this is hardly exceptional as all language use is prior to linguistic expressions as such. The awkward case of metaphor with respect to semantical theories is not the exception that proves the rule but may be seen as the undoing of semantical theories as total explanatory systems. The primacy of language use over language *per se* is thus revolutionary for the relationship between semantics and pragmatics. As it is the living of life which establishes the semantical link, metaphor as an entity is subsumed by metaphor as activity: the activity of metaphor making, or 'metaphorising'; metaphorising as a language-game is prior to its product the metaphor.

This means that an utterance, to be a genuine metaphor, requires a combination of the semantic and the pragmatic features of metaphor. It is the hearer's comprehension or otherwise (not simply the speaker's intention) which distinguishes metaphor from grammatical mistake or nonsense. The hearer relies on context and background knowledge to inform comprehension. Whether a hearer will make the effort to 'rope in' enough information to make sense of an odd utterance depends also on the genre – odd utterances in poems are assumed to be metaphors, but in a story or report they may be more readily seen as typographical errors. Therefore one will work harder to understand the utterance in the poetic situation.[4]

4 Earl Mac Cormac explains the relationship between metaphorising and metaphoric meaning in two different ways: 'locutionary force of language corresponds to semantic meaning. The locutionary aspect of an utterance presents the declarative meaning of the surface language [sentence), whereas the semantic [propositional) aspect presents a deeper structural explanation of the same meaning ... Where the diaphoric [suggestive) quality of a metaphor is great and the meaning perhaps ambiguous, there may exist some difference in meaning between that presented by the surface language (locution) and that presented by a deep structural analysis (semantics). When a contextual interpretation of the metaphor occurs, the hearer combines surface description with deep structural analysis to produce a single meaning'. (Earl Mac Cormac, *A Cognitive Theory of Metaphor* (Cambridge, Massachusetts: MIT Press, 1985), 177–8.) In Wittgensteinian terms, of course, this 'deep structural analysis' is not the mysterious thing it seems: it is simply the intuitive recourse to the (new) language-game in which the 'surface description' (sentence expressing a literally false proposition) is a move.

In this way, metaphorising is a part of the language-game foundation which is basic to our knowing. I will argue later that its role is even more fundamental and comprehensive than this. First, however, how does metaphor as a statement relate to the language-game of metaphorising? If metaphorising is a language-game, what sort of thing is a metaphor in relation to this?

2.1.3. Metaphors and Metaphorisings

[3] *A Wittgensteinian explanation of metaphor understands knowledge as inclusive of 'knowing-how' and not restricted to 'knowing-that'.*

How are the 'knowing-how' activity of metaphorising and the 'knowing-that' statement of the metaphor related? A language-game is no more nor less than its moves which include activities involving the use of language and rule-like entities (propositions, facts, concepts) concerning these uses. Therefore the metaphorising language-game is all of these. It consists of the metaphorising activity, plus its product, the metaphorical statement, plus the rules which make this product a move in such a game.

The various moves of a language-game are internally related. A metaphorical expression predicates, explicitly or implicitly, properties of a subject; it claims to state a fact about that subject. As such it expresses a proposition. According to Aristotle, 'an utterance becomes an assertion ... by asserting something true or false ... And so truth and falsity occur if the speaker affirms or denies something of something'.[5] Any uncertainty about whether this metaphorically expressed proposition is true or false does

5 Aristotle, *De Interpretatione, The Complete Works of Aristotle (2 Vols)*, J. Barnes (ed.) (Princeton: Princeton University Press, 1984), 17a 2f, 22–6. Cited by Eberhard Jüngel, 'Metaphorical Truth', *Theological Essays* (Edinburgh: T. & T. Clark, 1989), 16–71: 34.

not make it any less a proposition.[6] For the moment the concern is with what it means for a metaphorical statement to express a proposition.[7] If it is accepted that what metaphors assert are indeed propositions, whether true or false, then it is possible to establish the relation of a metaphorical expression of a proposition to the proposition it expresses and the relation of both entities to language-games, by establishing what applies to propositions and sentences in general.

Stalnaker understands a proposition to be expressed in a sentence plus its use. 'One of the jobs of natural language is to express propositions, and it is a semantical problem to specify the rules for matching up sentences of a natural language within the propositions that they express. In most cases, however, the rules will not match sentences directly with propositions, but will match sentences with propositions relative to features of the context in which the sentence is used.'[8] It follows that a metaphorical sentence will be no exception to this rule. Its relation to its use in the language-game in which it is a move may be as a 'depiction' or proposition. Yet, as the meaning of a sentence lies in its use, the language-game in which a metaphor plays a part provides its meaning. It is together that they constitute a proposition. It is still possible to understand metaphor on its own as a picturing, or depiction, however this is not a simple isomorphic blueprint, but more like a code.

The later Wittgenstein conceives of a proposition, not so much as a picture as a set of instructions for constructing a picture: 'If you think of propositions as instructions for making models, their pictorial character becomes even clearer'.[9] Because a proposition is the context of a name's meaning, the name-object relation is in fact a part of the sentence-world

6 The issue of metaphor and truth will be addressed in Part Two, Chapter 2, below.

7 It is important not to confuse propositions as such with their expressions. This confusion (which seems widespread) ties a proposition to a single (literal) expression of that proposition. Such a state of affairs is unhelpful to an understanding of how language in general operates, *a fortiori* for the case of metaphor. See the discussion on this point in Part Two Chapter 2 below.

8 Stalnaker, 'Pragmatics', 383.

9 Wittgenstein, *Philosophical Remarks*, II #10.

relation. The view is the same from both perspectives.[10] Thus, from a Wittgensteinian viewpoint, a metaphorical proposition would be a set of instructions for making a picture: that is, a metaphor. The proposition implied in the metaphorical expression is caught up in a reciprocal relationship with the language-game which is its connection with our forms of life. While the language-game is its justificatory ground, the metaphor is the articulation of that ground. As they constitute an inseparable entity, the result is a circularity. 'We cannot get behind the metaphor to the truth of the matter, because without the metaphor we have no matter to consider. We use certain imagery to reflect what happens in our forms of life, and that imagery helps us to understand, to conceptualise certain aspects of that life.'[11]

In her book *Metaphor and Religious Language*,[12] Janet Martin Soskice describes metaphor as 'reality depiction'. While Soskice's account stresses the variation and lack of precision in linguistic picturing of reality, it does not explicitly take account of the role of language-games as language-world links or agents of reference. In an earlier paper, Soskice also understands metaphorical utterances to be a case of Wittgensteinian picturing and sees the language-game in which a metaphorical picture is situated as providing the meaning of the metaphor.[13] This is a clearer statement of the relationship, but it still fails to explain how language-games are involved in the production of metaphors. Neither does it explain the relation of the metaphor as

10 Hintikka and Hintikka, *Investigating Wittgenstein*, 224. It is important for the purpose of this account not to confuse sentences and propositions; a sentence of a particular kind expresses a proposition which is either true or false. Of course, many sentences do not express propositions, at least not directly, although they may imply or presuppose propositions.

11 Ibid. 77.

12 Janet Martin Soskice, *Metaphor and Religious Language* (London: Oxford University Press, 1985).

13 Janet C. Martin (Soskice), 'Uses of Metaphor in Religious Language with Special Reference to Wittgenstein's Views of Language and to Metaphor in the Biblical Writings' (unpublished dissertation submitted as partial requirement for the degree of Master of Arts, The Department of Biblical Studies, University of Sheffield, 2nd September, 1975), 52–3.

sentence or utterance to the metaphor as proposition (although in fairness, this questions are not her concern). However, the metaphor as depiction cannot be separated from the language-game in which it is a move. The danger of such a term as 'depiction' is that it implies that language, as the context of human knowledge, is separate from, and isomorphic to, world.[14] This implies an essentially *Tractarian* view of language.[15]

With the primacy of language-games the idea of the isomorphic depiction of world by language does not actually disappear but it ceases to be primary. Where pictorial relations between propositions and states of affairs are, so to speak, the ground floor of logic in the *Tractatus* – that is, they are foundational, in Wittgenstein's mature thought this ground floor is language-games. In later Wittgenstein there are no longer simple one-to-one language-world relations and this tends to upset the picture idea. If pictures are not primary, then they are constituted by or rest upon the foundation of language-games. 'In the case of verbal propositions, it is the use of the picture that constitutes the method of projection … the blueprint together with an appropriate language-game remains a picture … The "projective relations" constituted by use also have to be incorporated in the "picture" if it is to serve its purpose.'[16] That is, the verbally expressed picture or proposition is now, for Wittgenstein, (as Stalnaker suggests) sentence

14 Patterson, '*Word*, Words and World', 15.

15 See Wittgenstein, *Tractatus*.

16 Hintikka and Hintikka, *Investigating Wittgenstein*, 226–7. It is thus not metaphors alone which refer in an indirect or mediated way, but all language. In his book, *Yesterday and Today: A Study of Continuities in Christology* (London: Darton, Longman and Todd, 1983), Colin Gunton endorses Michael Polanyi's criticism of the 'picture theory' of knowledge as distorted and limited because it requires, first, a 'viewing the mind as external to the world'; second, a restriction of knowledge to a certain kind of knowledge, namely, conceptual knowledge. Instead, 'Words are … not mirrors of reality but the means by which we participate in reality. Language, along with its expression of supposed knowledge of the way things are, is not then discontinuous with other aspects of our experience, an arbitrary imposition of a conceptual structure on reality, but grows out of the human relationship with the world' (144–5). As Gunton observes, Polanyi's insights are seen (in this respect at least) to cohere with those of the later Wittgenstein.

plus use of sentence – that is, language-game. Therefore, language-games must be seen as components of propositions and conversely, the terms which express propositions receive their meaning from the language-games.

Critical realists such as Soskice and Gunton endeavour to rid realism of the notion of a direct and fixed correspondence, or isomorphism, between words and things by maintaining that the ability of words to describe the world is necessarily imprecise and constantly subject to revision. They do not, however, succeed in getting rid of the assumption built into the idea of correspondence, of the separateness of language and world. Gunton prefers to use the scientific terms 'modelling' and 'mapping' to describe the linguistic 'articulation and representation of reality'. This, he considers, avoids the association which the term 'metaphor' has with accurate depiction or mirroring.[17]

Soskice defines a model as 'an object or state of affairs ... viewed in terms of its resemblance, real or hypothetical, to some other object or state of affairs.' While this 'reading off' of the model is in metaphorical terms, the model itself is not a metaphor. Models and metaphors are 'distinct categories'.[18] The exception is in the case of 'theoretical' models which are composed of words only. Here the categories of model and metaphor tend to coalesce and the model may be seen as a sort of compound or extended metaphor. A metaphor, in providing a 'new interpretative web',[19] is expressing in capsule form, in its predication, an implicit, as yet unarticulated, underlying theoretical model or hypothesis which, in another exercise, may be developed into an explicit model. Thus a metaphor is the expression of a tacit model and in turn may itself suggest an explicit model. The 'network of associations' of the metaphoric topic is the implicit model. In metaphor, the vehicle is the words which express the metaphoric combination of thoughts or associations; in a model, it is the thing, or in the case of

17 A map is the means by which selected features of reality are abstracted from the whole and used as a guide to the understanding of that whole. (Gunton, *Yesterday and Today*, 150–3.)

18 Soskice, *Metaphor and Religious Language*, 101–2. While this distinction is valid, the activity of metaphorising is arguably common to both (see below).

19 Ibid. 62.

a theoretical model, the theory, which show these thoughts or associations. If, according to Soskice, a metaphor is 'that figure of speech whereby we speak of one thing in terms which are seen to be suggestive of another',[20] a model is the *showing* of one such in terms suggestive of another. As a *showing*, a model is more developed conceptually than a metaphor: it is really a type of analogy. As the model emerges from its metaphoric 'germ' and becomes explicit, its several parts are structured by analogy and its verbal description or summary becomes a 'conceptual metaphor'.

Gunton suggests that the use of the word 'model':

> Enables us to realize that there is no absolute dividing line between concept and metaphor, reason and imagination. The indirectness of all linguistic expression necessitates that calling into play of metaphors whenever a new insight or discovery is being articulated. As soon as a feature of reality is brought to understanding by means of a metaphor, it ceases to be a 'mere' metaphor and begins to receive systematic employment. As it is indwelt by its user, it becomes more conceptual. Reason, we might say, refines and orders what was at first imaginatively or intuitively grasped.[21]

That is, metaphors gradually come to express 'finished' or 'complete' concepts as repeated use shapes and sharpens their applications. However, the proposition involved in a metaphor may instead remain implicit (acted upon but not articulable within the terms of conventional logic). If it can be said in this case to yield a concept, it is a tacit concept (if this is not a contradiction in terms) which is lived rather than articulated.[22]

If a metaphor may be understood as expressing an implicit model (a proposition as instructions for making a model) – a model which will

20 Ibid. 15.

21 Gunton, *Yesterday and Today*, 152–3.

22 Gillett's work on language-games and concepts may be related to the Hintikkas's understanding of the place of propositions in relation to language-games. On the relationship between concepts and language-games. According to Gillett, 'concepts, for the most part, involve terms and expressions in a natural language and thus, in essence, incorporate distinctive features of the interactions and language-games in which a thinker is engaged. Rules structure his conceptual activity and link his operations with signs to the milieu in which those signs have life in which he is a participating subject'. (Gillett, *Representation, Meaning and Thought*, 179.)

become explicit if the metaphor later comes to express a concept – metaphorising may be seen as the source of both models and metaphors. While models and metaphors may represent distinct categories, they are both products of metaphorising. Thus, as has been noted, metaphorising as an activity has a broader function than the creation of those figures of speech we are accustomed to regarding as metaphors. Jüngel's definition of 'absolute' metaphor as the entry of being to speech is in accord with the wider concept of metaphorising.[23]

While Gunton's alternative descriptions endeavour to avoid the problematic idea that a metaphor mirrors 'reality', the notions of modeling and mapping, as with Soskice's 'depiction', still assume a separation between the representation and the thing or state of affairs represented. Somehow the wrong questions are still being asked. Hausman is closer to Wittgenstein than Gunton in agreeing with Black that 'Metaphors, in a sense, help constitute aspects of reality ... that this claim is no longer surprising if one believes that the world is "necessarily a world under a certain description or a world seen from a certain perspective". Some metaphors can create such a perspective ... metaphors can create if we regard what they create as perspectives ... But if there is only a world "under certain description" or perspective, what metaphors create perspectives on must be more perspectives.'[24]

2.1.4. Inventing Language-Games

[4] *A Wittgensteinian explanation of metaphor as proposition and metaphorising as language-game bypasses or supersedes the traditional categories of realism and idealism.*

23 Jüngel, 'Metaphorical Truth', 56–7.

24 Hausman, *Metaphor and Art*, 84, quoting Max Black, 'More about Metaphor', in Andrew Ortony (ed.), *Metaphor and Thought* (Cambridge UK: Cambridge University Press, 1979), 19–45: 39–40.

It is in practice impossible to separate that which is to be represented from previous representations. The model, map or metaphor is a representation of a reality which is an inextricable mix of new extra-conceptual information with antecedent representations and concepts, as Wittgenstein's later definition of propositions as instructions for model-making (rather than pictures of reality) tends to suggest.

George Lakoff and Mark Johnson consider that the debate over whether metaphors discover or create reality is put in its proper perspective when it is realised that 'many of the similarities that we perceive are a result of conventional metaphors that are part of our conceptual system'.[25] How reality is conceived is itself metaphorically based. What are now construed conventionally as similarities may have started off as a mere association of dissimilars. 'The only similarities relevant to metaphor are similarities *as experienced by people* ... things in the world do play a role in constraining our conceptual system. But they play this role through our experience of them ... Such experiences determine the categories of our conceptual system.'[26] That is, Lakoff and Johnson, like Hausman, refuse to choose between language's being constrained by reality (realism) and language's constraining reality (constructivism) but insist on a simultaneous operation of both processes.

As has been suggested, a novel metaphor expresses a new (explicit or implied) proposition. The expression is indirect, but on a Wittgensteinian view that is the case with all linguistic expression. After a time the expression becomes familiar and its indirectness is overlooked. It has become an idiomatic or literal use.[27] The not-so-new proposition or complex of propositions now is part of the concept the metaphor has become with use.[28] The metaphorical proposition has become the basis of a logical category. As Gillett observes:

25 Lakoff and Johnston, *Metaphors We Live By*, 147.

26 Ibid. 153–4.

27 The issue of metaphor and literality is discussed in Chapter 2 of Part Two below.

28 In the process, as Lakoff and Johnson observe, it has acquired a string of entailments (contingent propositions, both metaphoric and literal). 'Like conventional metaphors, new metaphors have entailments, which may include other metaphors and literal

> The substratum of this experience is the mastery a technique (*PI* 208e). The technique, *inter alia*, enables one to perceive (by actively attending to this and then that) that a figure has certain characteristics. We apply concepts by engaging what confronts us with a structure of uses and practices so that 'seeing it like this' relates the figure to items and features which are part of our rule-governed activity. When we do this we may isolate one feature of a scene as the object of our thought, or assimilate the presentation to some significant type of item marked by the use of a term or sign … The rule governs a way of dealing with things in a variety of situations … They must be public so that others can correct my use of a term by tying it to conditions recalcitrant to my inclinations to use it any old how.[29]

A concept may be understood as a selection made from available world-data, a selection which is subject to correction in terms of the rules of our forms of life but may in fact reflect an alteration in those rules. Concepts categorise. Propositions make fact-claims which categorise. What constitutes a fact about a state of affairs depends on how the situation has been categorised. The category claimed may or may not already exist. An existing category is one for which there is already a concept – in this case the proposition entails knowledge of a concept. However, a new metaphor expresses a proposition which cuts across existing categories, making a claim for the existence of a category hitherto unconceived. As categorisations are rule-governed, in creating a new category the new metaphorising is expressing a new rule: a new language-game.

A proposition and the sentence(s) which express it are both moves in a language-game. As such they are subject to the logic of that game. A metaphor is seen to comprise both a new proposition and its verbal expression. These are new moves in a language-game whose rules they may

---

statements as well [a metaphor-plus-entailments as a maximal proposition]. The network of entailments … form a coherent whole … what we experience with such a metaphor is a kind of reverberation down through the network of entailments that awakens and connects our memories of our past … experiences and serves as a possible guide for future ones'. (Ibid. 140.) By definition, the new proposition expressed by a novel metaphor is inexpressible in terms of existing concepts. By the time the metaphor has grown a string of entailments and has reached the concept stage, some or none of its implied propositions may be articulable within conventional logic.

29 Gillett, *Representation, Meaning and Thought*, 193.

modify. If propositions in general are the products of the prior categorising of concepts, propositions expressed by metaphors are no exception. However, metaphorical propositions make claims which do not fit any category. Instead, the novel metaphor 'violates' existing categories. The proposition expressed by such a metaphor cannot, therefore, make sense within conventional logic although as a proposition it takes the form of logic and employs the (rearranged) content of accepted logical categories.[30]

This is the essential difference between metaphor and analogy. Analogy is the relation according to similarity of one proposition (fact plus the language-game which makes it a fact) regarding (suggesting a picturing, modeling, mapping of) reality to another, where what is related are developed concepts rather than metaphors. As Hausman observes, '[a]n analogy depends for its significance wholly on similarities common to antecedent significances. The point of an analogy is to make a comparison [therefore it]… can be reduced to what was known antecedently [relation or object, or] … expressed as a complex simile'.[31] However, both analogies and similes have metaphorical roots – they began their lives as metaphors[32] (therefore metaphor is prior to analogy). Metaphors may also end their lives as analogies. A metaphor is not able to be interpreted analogically unless or until it has become a concept: 'As frozen, [metaphors] can be interpreted analogically because their fixed significance can be related to other expressions with fixed significance'.[33]

Lakoff and Johnson see metaphors as partial analogies which can be extended to become more complete (except for catachrestic uses which

30 This is why Colin Turbayne has termed them (after Gilbert Ryle) a 'category mistake'. See his *The Myth of Metaphor*, revised ed. (Columbia: University of South Carolina Press, 1970).

31 Hausman, *Metaphor and Art*, 17.

32 Ibid. 17–18. First the suggestion is made (and accepted), then the implications are worked out. What now appears trivial (e.g. 'Stockholm is the Venice of the North', or 'Man is a wolf') is so not only because it expresses a limited or uninteresting idea, but also because all its implications been worked out.

33 Ibid. 19.

tend not to be extended).[34] I would see them more as potential analogies. Mac Cormac has a different perspective: analogy, as an expression of a similarity of type, nature or relation is not a sufficient condition for metaphor; however some similarity is a necessary, if not sufficient condition for metaphor.[35] The important point for the purposes of this discussion is that analogising and simile-making involve a different sort of transfer from that of metaphorising. Analogical transfer occurs within or between existing concepts and categories, where these concepts or categories are preserved intact. That is, analogy operates according to existing logic, whereas metaphorical transfer cuts across existing structures and violates existing logic. The isomorphism of an analogy of relation relies upon the preservation of existing logical patterns; a novel metaphor, if it becomes the basis for a concept, establishes a new logic by altering our understanding of the way things are, or must be.

To return to the argument, the relationship between metaphors and metaphorising may now be seen to be the relationship between a language-game and its moves. Likewise the relationship between metaphors and the new propositions they express can be seen to be that of different kinds of moves in a language-game. The language-game of metaphorising may be observed to produce ultimately (although not in every case) new language-games with moves which constitute new concepts. It is paradoxical that the metaphorising activity which produces metaphors and ultimately new concepts and categories both depends on (is parasitic on) existing concepts and expresses no known concept. How this can be explained will be explored in chapter 2. First, however, an excursus.

34 Lakoff and Johnston, *Metaphors We Live By*, 52.
35 Mac Cormac, *A Cognitive Theory of Metaphor*, 10–11.

2.1.5. Wittgenstein's View of Metaphor

Wittgenstein, while firmly within the pragmatic tradition, seems virtually to disregard metaphor. His stated concern is with ordinary language. According to Gerry H. Gill, 'It seems clear that Wittgenstein had no explicit theory of metaphor. It is just as clear, however, that his writings contain an implicit view of the nature and significance of metaphorical speech.'[36] While Wittgenstein's theory of language in the *Tractatus* left no room for metaphor, it is evident that in it he nevertheless made considerable use of metaphor. Gill thus sees Wittgenstein's view of meaning as use as consistent with his employment of metaphor. In his use of metaphor, he demonstrates the role of metaphors in language.[37]

Wittgenstein appears here and there to class metaphor as a special use of language. As Gill sees it, the question: 'what does Wittgenstein mean by "ordinary language"?' may be answered by observing his own use of language: Wittgenstein has an implicit theory of metaphor which is revealed in his use of metaphor. On this basis it seems evident that Wittgenstein regarded metaphor as a part of ordinary language. Yet, at no point does he make explicit mention of the language-game of metaphorising or its fundamental role in our acquisition of language as related to the concept of training (a role which will be explained below). I will argue that this also is implicit in his philosophy.

Independently of Wittgenstein's own view, it is reasonable to argue on empirical grounds (as do Cohen and Margalit) that metaphor should be included in the semantics of natural language and not be regarded as an anomaly. Cohen and Margalit note, first, that metaphor is naturally integrated in ordinary speech; second, that it is known to be an agent of semantic change (the death of a metaphor can be seen as a 'boundary shift' within language regardless of the point at which this death is deemed to

36 Jerry H. Gill, 'Wittgenstein and Metaphor', *J Phil. and Phenom. Research* 40 (1979–1980) 272ff: 272.

37 Ibid. 281, 284.

have taken place; that is, whether idioms and the like are included within metaphorical or literal utterances); and third, that metaphorical language is no more nor less sophisticated or easily learned than literal language.[38] More than for simply these reasons, metaphor's sheer pervasiveness and ubiquitousness should qualify it for 'ordinariness' according to the normal use of the term.

2.1.6. Summary

1. If language-games are basic and metaphorising is a language-game, the activity of metaphor-making is ontologically prior to the metaphorical statement itself. Metaphorising as an activity has a wider function than the production of figures of speech and may be seen as the production of a new language-world connection.
2. Metaphorising gives rise to metaphorical statements which express propositions. Metaphors in turn give rise to concepts.
3. With both metaphors and concepts, the proposition involved may remain implicit (acted upon but not articulable within the terms of conventional logic).
4. While Wittgenstein has not addressed the issue of metaphor as such (and his occasional remarks in passing imply a traditional, non-incremental view), I suggest that it is consistent with his philosophy to treat metaphor as a part of ordinary language and as such subject to the same working rules.

38 L. J. Cohen and Avishai Margalit, 'The Role of Inductive Reasoning in the Interpretation of Metaphor', in Harman and Davidson, *Semantics of Natural Language*, 722–40; 722.

CHAPTER TWO

Metaphorising

2.2.1. Metaphorising the World

[5] *A Wittgensteinian explanation of metaphor shows how metaphorical activity is part of the totality of language-games and yet effects an increment to knowledge as understood in terms of that totality.*

It has already been argued that metaphorising as a language-game shares in the basicality of language-games in general. It is arguable that there is, however, a sense in which this particular language-game is more basic than others: metaphorising, in creating new uses of language, is a language-game which brings new moves in other language-games into being. If language-games are basic, the metaphorising language-game is basic to the development of other language-games.[1] Gill comes close to this conclusion when he notes, first, that 'The key … is to acknowledge the bedrock character of metaphoric expression and to develop an account of language and its relation to reality which is in harmony with it in general, and which leaves room for it in particular'.[2] And then, that

1 See Patterson, '*Word*, Words and World'. A reminder that while specifically metaphor will be referred to in this chapter and elsewhere, the process of metaphorising is not restricted to the making of figures of speech alone but may be said to include all ways in which new knowledge is arrived at by means of a recombination and reassignment of the old. While it is obvious that metaphor as such requires the involvement of words, metaphorising is rather broader in its scope, including actions and other forms of communication as well as words, models as well as figures of speech.

2 Gill, 'Wittgenstein and Metaphor', 274.

> new expressions and language-games are continually being incorporated into language while others are continually being left behind. Thus innovation and obsolescence are important features of any natural language. One of the primary bearers of innovation is metaphor, for it often takes the form of combining two fairly well-established meanings to produce a fresh one. It is this feature of innovation which goes unaccounted for in the *Tractatus*, even though it itself is clearly dependent upon it.[3]

Gill seems to be referring implicitly to language-games when he writes of Wittgenstein (in *On Certainty*) as

> [E]mphasizing that there is a tacit level of understanding and knowing which underlies, indeed which makes possible the more explicit level ... at this bedrock level the kind of knowing which takes place is not best described as inferential in character. Rather, the term 'integrative act' better characterizes the fundamental knowing experience in which the particulars of a situation are interacted with in such a way as to give rise to an awareness which provides the framework within which more explicit knowledge is possible. The sort of justification that can be offered for such 'protoknowing' is not that of inferential reasoning, but is rather the simple efficacy of the whole pattern of our existence, the very weave of our particular way of being-in-the-world.[4]

Leaving aside Gill's tendency to think of knowledge in terms of levels or layers (tacit, explicit),[5] there is here an implicit (at least) understanding of language-games in general as basic and of metaphorising as *a fortiori* basic. While Gill continues to talk simply of 'metaphor' without attempting to distinguish the product from the process (metaphor is tacit yet expressible as the 'shown' foundation of knowledge – 'a necessary primordial feature of the whole linguistic-cognitive enterprise'[6] – be that as it may, for Gill metaphor as 'integrative act' is epistemically basic. '[A]t the fundamental level reality and practice are symbiotic ... The bedrock nature of certain ways

3 Ibid. 277.

4 Ibid. 279 (c.f. Wittgenstein, *On Certainty*, #110, #599).

5 This reflects Gill's Polanyian metaphysics – see, for example, Jerry H. Gill, *On Knowing God* (Philadelphia: Westminster Press, 1981).

6 Gill, 'Wittgenstein and Metaphor', 279.

of thinking and behaving in no way implies that they are arbitrary or irrational. Rather, they are themselves the necessary conditions of rationality.'[7]

2.2.2. Metaphorising and Verification

If the metaphorising language-game (being the source of new moves in other language-games) is basic with respect to all other language-games, then the metaphorising process itself will not be subject or accessible to verification. Nevertheless, individual metaphorical expressions are subject to two sources of verification: for their verification as metaphors they are dependent on the metaphorising language-game, whereas for their verification as propositions they are dependent on the language-game(s) in which they are a new move.

What sort of a proposition is a metaphor? Given agreement with Aristotle that metaphor is an assertion and as such either true or false, is the proposition expressed by a metaphorical statement true or false? It is not uncommon for theorists to talk about metaphors as creative and in the same breath to say that they are partially true.[8] I consider that any talk of partial truth in any context is confused; by definition truth cannot be partial. Such confusion arises from mistaking the 'is-is not' nature of the metaphorical statement for the new proposition this statement is endeavouring to express in terminology borrowed from other, antecedent uses.

What does it mean for a metaphor to express a true proposition? This question may be rephrased as: how may a new proposition be verified? It is a question about reference.[9]

7 Ibid. 279; (Wittgenstein, *Philosophical Investigations*, ##241–2).

8 For example Mac Cormac, *A Cognitive Theology of Metaphor*.

9 As I suggested in Part One, it is stretching the concept of reference somewhat to use it in connection with the verification function of language-games. Yet there is some value in doing this here because it allows the Wittgensteinian and semantic-metaphoric paradigms to find some common ground.

The verification of literal propositions is assumed by 'the man in the street' to be straightforward. The facts speak for themselves – or seem to. Yet this is a deception visited on us by a worldview in which the world and its linguistic representations are construed as isomorphic. The later Wittgenstein's insight is that the correspondence of the linguistic and the nonlinguistic does not operate like this.[10] All correspondence is indirect, reference being effected by means of language-games in which the linguistic and the nonlinguistic aspects of reality are inextricably interwoven. This puts metaphor on a par with literal language with respect to reference. If no reference is straightforward but all language-world links are effected by language-games, then the problem of the verification of metaphors is no different from the problem of verification of propositions in general. This does not necessarily mean that there is no difference between the way literal and metaphorical statements refer, merely that the difference is not as simple and obvious as might have been thought. This issue will be discussed below.

The problem of verification is the difficulty of how the fittingness of a statement is assessed when, as Black says, all that is possible is a perspective on a perspective – a 'world under certain description'.[11] Creative metaphors may create new insights by designating new referents but what constitutes the referent in a Kantian world which is 'world-plus-concept of world'? 'Does it obviously make better sense to speak of accommodating language to the world than of accommodating the world to language?' asks Hausman, 'Or is the way of talking that creates that distinction itself illusory? Is what we refer to as the world perhaps a product of a mutual accommodation between experience and language?' How does experience differ from world? Are our experiences independent of language? Introducing experience just seems to shift the problem and a vicious regress threatens. 'Nevertheless, [he concludes,] Kuhn's conception of an interaction between language

10 While propositions are 'instructions for making models' these instructions are too complex to be compared directly with the world, hence the need for mediation by 'certain rule-governed activities'. (Hintikka and Hintikka. *Investigating Wittgenstein*, 238.)

11 Black, 'More about Metaphor', 39–40. See Part Two, Chapter 1.

and something extralinguistic (whether the world or experience) is the only way I can see of attacking the dilemma, even if this is not to resolve it'. Hausman sees metaphor as creating Peircean intentional objects which, while 'constituted of imposed meanings or intelligible senses ... [are] also under the constraints of the objects to which they are apt'. Therefore a metaphor may be both creative and appropriate. 'There is an experiential encounter ... that signals more than cultural consensus that provokes the recognition of some metaphors as faithful and others as less faithful or inappropriate'.[12] (The Peircean ontology thus again is seen to resemble the idea of language-games.)

It is not surprising that the explanation of the fittingness of an expression emerges as a difficulty only in the situation where existing language-games do not provide any rules, where the new language use and its expression have arisen from a new patterning of language-world in which the old categories do not fit.[13] Metaphorical language is in this respect, by definition, *unfitting*. In the metaphorical instance, the assessment of fittingness (or faithfulness to reality) cannot rely on established convention and must be made intuitively and blindly. However, what is overlooked is that, on a Wittgensteinian view, judgments regarding literal uses of language are also made intuitively because they are made with respect to language-games. It is not as if literal statements are amenable to checking from an 'eye of God' perspective whilst metaphorical expressions are not. (In this respect at least there is no difference between literal and nonliteral, and theories of metaphor which depend on this means of distinction must lack explanatory power.) The evidence of fittingness is lived, and lived anew. Any conceptions one might have of fittingness are *post hoc* rationalisations of prior intuitive leaps.

In the case of a new, metaphorical, use there is no *post hoc* rationalisation available. The intuition of the faithfulness of the metaphor to the new

12 Hausman, *Metaphor and Art*, 97–100. Hausman cites Thomas Kuhn, 'Metaphor and Science', Ortony, *Metaphor and Thought*, 409–19.

13 Conventions of use (that is, existing language-games) have provided rules for the application of existing concepts and categories. The language-world link itself determines what is considered fitting as language use.

language-world link which is its move in the language-game, cannot be thus rationalised but is no less reliable for that. As I sought to demonstrate in Part One, 'knowing-how' is just as much knowledge as 'knowing-that'.

What conditions the fittingness of a new insight needs to be something in the world that is not identical with these perspectives. The special turn that the appropriateness issue takes with creative metaphor suggests that when metaphorical experiences are perceived as creative, they are viewed as being at the cutting edge of language as a whole. Thus the linguistic-conceptual proposal to regard the system of linguistic conceptual data as the ground of cognitive conditions poses a special problem in the case of metaphorical expressions.[14]

Lakoff and Johnson accordingly see a metaphor's aptness as established pragmatically. It is the fit of a metaphor with our experience which makes it apt; at the same time the metaphor shapes that experience and becomes foundational for further actions and understanding of our experience. Thus metaphor cannot be simply a matter of mere language. On a pragmatic view, the aptness of metaphors may well have survival value in determining what view of reality we act upon.[15]

What, then, are the implications of saying that a new proposition (such as a metaphor) is true? Hausman argues that metaphorising both creates and discovers a new reference and thereby a new sense.[16] A new language-world link is formed as metaphorising invents a new move in a language-game.[17] 'Creative metaphors take a fundamental responsibility for language as a whole, making language responsible to something independent of itself, at least as it is constituted at the moment of creation.'[18] Mac Cormac's pragmatic opinion is that if metaphors fix new referents then they must have

14 Hausman, *Metaphor and Art*, 85.

15 Lakoff and Johnston, *Metaphors We Live By*, 142–5.

16 Hausman, *Metaphor and Art*, 82. The traditional dichotomy of creation and discovery is dispensed within a Kantian perspective; see Part One.

17 It is important to recognise that his new move doesn't stand alone, but in establishing a new language-world link or renovating an old one, takes the whole language-game along with it.

18 Ibid. 88.

a truth-value.[19] Because of this, some theorists have classed metaphors as performative utterances. Mac Cormac notes that John Searle has classed them as 'declarations' because they bring something into being 'and they have the force of instructions to recognise what they create and pick out ... Declarations are peculiar because "the performance of a declaration brings about a fit by the very fact of its successful performance"'.[20] This has to do with the social or institutional credibility of the declarer. According to Searle, declarations are made by 'representatives' of institutions or conventions. A poet is a representative of literary institutions or conventions, hence a metaphor uttered by a poet will have more credibility than one uttered by a child.[21] The non-authorised utterer of a metaphor is more likely to be dismissed as talking nonsense. From a Wittgensteinian viewpoint, of course, issues of credibility and representativeness (with their social criteria) are subsumed within the playing of language-games in forms of life; it is they that determine what is credible and representative.

If reference is the function of language-games, how do language-games refer? What is reference? According to Hausman, 'Reference is a relation in which there are two relata and one of them is directed from itself to the other. One relatum functions as a sign: that is, it leads to, or directs attention to, the other relatum, and the second relatum is the object to which the first relatum leads. The second does not lead to the first, at least in the same respect that the first leads to the second ... Even natural signs refer in this asymmetric way'.[22] However, as has already been suggested, metaphor just does not seem to fit traditional realist theories of reference.[23] In

19 Mac Cormac, *A Cognitive Theology of Metaphor*, 111.

20 Ibid.

21 Ibid. 112–13. In the same way, Charles Travis's notion of 'reasonable judges' takes in the credibility of the utterer – which is a matter of whether that person can be taken to be both representative and knowledgeable. See Charles Travis, *The Uses of Sense: Wittgenstein's Philosophy of Language* (London: Oxford University Press, 1989).

22 Hausman, *Metaphor and Art*, 91.

23 The so-called 'causal' theories of Saul Kripke and others do not pose the problem of fit so much as of explanatory power. On its own, the property of being the causer of a particular sensation or experience or event, while it may be sufficient for the purposes of pointing out or stipulating a referent, is not sufficient to describe it.

so far as successful metaphors are a fact of life (that is, are found, in spite of this, to be meaningful and thus apt), their success must raise questions about the adequacy of these theories. 'Primitive' or 'naïve' realist theories, assuming as they do a one-to-one naming relation, require that linguistic description be based on some sort of independent knowledge of a completely extralinguistic referent.

Yet, if metaphorising creates (and the metaphorical statement constitutes) new uses of language,[24] and at the same time reference is understood to be not simply to an extralinguistic referent but to a prior conception of that referent, such knowledge is denied twice over. The extralinguistic referent cannot be conceived independently of language and any prior (to the new use) conception available does not match the new use. On a naïve realist view, metaphorising is simply a process of discovery and description. Yet metaphorising as a language-game does not merely discover that which lies outside of language but can be said to create or invent a new situation of use, a new combination of words and world which cannot be disentangled into referent and reference in the old way, but which nevertheless effects a reference (insofar as it is still possible from such a perspective to use this term).[25] The creation of the new reference entails the creation of those moves in the language-game which are metaphorical statements.[26] Jaakko Hintikka contends accordingly that the distinction between meaning and reference is simply misleading. 'All that is needed to grasp the information

While Kripke never claimed that it was sufficient, such a reference seems devoid of information or interest. See Saul A. Kripke, 'Naming and Necessity', in Harman and Davidson, *Semantics of Natural Language*, 253–355.

24 It is important to distinguish between *uses* of language (for example, metaphors) as moves in language-games, and the practices involving these uses as the language-games themselves.

25 Under a Wittgensteinian perspective, the term 'reference' becomes virtually unusable, saddled as it is with a baggage of isomorphic correspondence connotations.

26 But because the language-game is prior to its moves, awareness and articulation of the new move precedes awareness that a new concept has been created (precedes articulation of such concept). A metaphor only becomes a verbalised concept in some cases.

that a sentence of such a language is given by the rules that determine the references of its terms, in the usual sense of the word'.[27]

This 'Wittgensteinian' view of metaphor and reference may be compared with those of other writers on metaphor. Hausman's reading of Ricoeur suggests that while all instances of language have reference, metaphorical reference is qualitatively different.

Following Roman Jakobson, Ricoeur adopts the expression 'split reference' which is the basis of a tension between two fundamental functions of the copula in metaphors ... consisting of an interplay between identity and difference ('is' and 'is not') ... And the verb to be (which in metaphors is existential as well as relational between terms [i.e. creates referent)) has a split function. Thus reference is split and metaphorical truth is tensional.[28]

27 '[It] seems to me ... completely hopeless to try to divorce the idea of the meaning of a sentence from the idea of the information the sentence conveys to a hearer or reader, should someone truthfully address it to him ... in the case of a first-order language these truth-conditions cannot be divested from the references of singular terms and from the extensions of its predicates. In fact these references and extensions are precisely what the truth-conditions of quantified sentences turn on. The truth-value of a sentence is a function of the references (extensions) of the terms it contains, not of their "meanings". Thus it follows from the above principles that a theory of reference is for genuine first-order languages the basis of a theory of meaning'. Jaakko Hintikka, 'Semantics for Propositional Attitudes', *Reference and Modality*, Leonard Linsky (ed.) (London: Oxford University Press 1971) 145ff: 145–7.

28 Hausman, *Metaphor and Art*, 105 [Paul Ricoeur, 'The Metaphorical Process as Cognition, Imaginaton and Feeling', in *On Metaphor*, Sheldon Sacks (ed.), (Chicago: University of Chicago Press, 1979), 153–9; Paul Ricoeur, *The Rule of Metaphor*, Robert Czerny et al. (trs.) (London: Routledge, 1978), 224–5, 248]. Hausman says about Ricoeur's theory: 'The "is not" side of the split reference ... should be understood in terms of the internal tension between subject terms ... in the metaphor ... [T]his "is not" is existential as well as relational. It is a referential function of the metaphor. Yet it is impossible to apply; it is "implied in the impossibility of existential interpretation"'. (105), (Ricoeur, 'Metaphorical Process', 153). 'But if application is impossible, there can be no referent for the metaphorical copula in its negative ("is not") function ... [Instead, the "is not" (falseness of the literally expressed proposition)] thrusts meaning toward the new reference'. (Hausman, 105–6.) However, it must be asked: what proposition (cf. sentence) are we dealing with here? Are we

Mac Cormac in his turn suggests that Ricoeur sees the picturing function of metaphor as providing an additional reference over and above the ordinary reference of its terms to the physical world.[29] According to Mac Cormac, Ricoeur's idea of metaphor as 'icon' relies on Wittgenstein's notion of 'seeing as' as applied by Marcus Hester.[30] What the metaphor 'pictures' is not the physical world but a world of its own invention which constitutes a new hypothesis about the actual world. Mac Cormac considers that metaphors may, as Ricoeur suggests, have two types of reference to two types of reality: the (descriptive or literal) denotative and the (iconic) non-denotative. However, as Hausman notes, in appearing to express a false proposition the former (literal) reference self-destructs and only the latter seems upheld. Thus the two references reduce to one.[31]

The problems with the idea of picturing have already been discussed. The difficulty here again seems to be with a confusion of propositions with their verbal expressions. While the metaphor appears to express a false proposition, in reality it may express a new (true) proposition which is ahead of antecedent logic: that is, it is a move in a new language-game which changes the way we understand the world.[32]

---

not ruling out the overt but false ('is not') proposition in favour of the covert ('is') proposition contained in the metaphor?

29 Hausman, *Metaphor and Art*, 193–7.

30 Marcus Hester, *The Meaning of Poetic Metaphor: An Analysis in the Light of Wittgenstein's Claim that Meaning is Use* (The Hague: Mouton & Co., 1967).

31 Mac Cormac, *A Cognitive Theory of Metaphor*, 193. Mac Cormac employs Langer's notion of 'virtual worlds': '... the virtual world exists apart from the actual world and its laws are those of its own genre, but the virtual world employs material from the actual world and these materials are, in the case of words, their ordinary meanings'.

32 Mac Cormac may be saying something similar to this when he writes that both these references presume 'the semantic associations of the referents at a deeper level of explanation'. (Ibid. 199.)

2.2.3. Pragmatic Parasites

Given that the metaphorical-literal distinction is one which is meaningful and employed on a regular basis, what light does a Wittgensteinian view of language bring to bear on this issue? Lakoff and Johnson work with a broad concept of metaphor which includes 'literal' metaphors. Some metaphors restructure what we already know; others introduce new knowledge (a new understanding of experience [or an articulation of new experience]) and add to our conceptual structure.[33] Novel metaphors work in the same way as conventional ones, creating a structure which highlights some aspects of experience and hides others.

What are the implications of the present discussion for the traditional literal-metaphorical distinction? Is this distinction preserved and if it is, do the meanings of these terms change? Can the concept of 'literal' survive if its claim to a monopoly on truth is challenged?

To begin with, this distinction is subject to two common misconceptions. First, it is a mistake to think that metaphors may be distinguished from literal utterances on the grounds of metaphor's dependence on similarity. Searle makes the important point that metaphorical similes do not rely on similarities any more than do metaphors. Similes are no closer to literal similarities than metaphors are – that is, the assertion of likeness is just as discrepant from the literal facts as the metaphorical predication: 'So deeply embedded in our whole mode of sensibility are certain metaphorical associations that we tend to think there must be a similarity, or even that the association itself is a form of similarity'[34] The question 'How do metaphors work?' is like the question, 'How does one thing remind us of another thing?' There is no single answer to either question, though

33 Lakoff and Johnston, *Metaphors We Live By*, 139.

34 John R. Searle, 'Metaphor', in Ortony, *Metaphor and Thought*, 92ff: 105, 109.

similarity obviously plays a major role in answering both. However, metaphors cannot employ more than partial similarities or they become literal statements.[35]

Nor should it be assumed that 'metaphorical utterances (as distinguished from literal utterances) are dependent on the context for their interpretation' as both of these are also true of 'literal utterances' and therefore are not distinguishing features of metaphors. A metaphor depends upon a particular context and cluster of hearer-associations without which the metaphor has no meaning (and is not therefore a metaphor). The expression becomes more 'portable' (rather than more fixed as Mac Cormac contends[36]) as the context and associations become habitual enough to be assumed. They are still inseparable from the statement (that is, they are assumed in the particular sense of the expression which has become its most conventional meaning). Yet their presence has become invisible. They are taken for granted. There is, therefore, no real difference between metaphors and literal expressions regarding degree of dependence on context.

Jerrold Sadock makes the important point that the literal-metaphorical distinction is a continuum: 'the pragmatic effect of numerous figures of speech is on the way to becoming part of the conventional content of the expressions that are used to convey them. But this process occurs by stages so that in most cases the communicative value of an expression that began life as a metaphor … is partially conventional and partially not'.[37] However, if metaphorising is to be included among ordinary language-using activities, this seems to preclude the easy option of equating literal language use with what is conventional. A novel metaphor is the growing tip of language where nonsense and meaning meet. What is considered an unconventional move at one time and place has become conventional by

35 Ibid. 113.

36 Mac Cormac, *A Cognitive Theology of Metaphor*, 206.

37 Jerrold Sadock, 'Figurative Speech and Linguistics', in Ortony, *Metaphor and Thought*, 46–63: 63.) agrees. For Fraser metaphor is a continuum from live to dead. Dead metaphors are idioms (idiosyncratic conventions of the language). They do not require a context or creative effort of understanding (because, I contend, their contextual associations are taken as read), whereas live ones do. (Ibid. 173.)

another. The actuality of our forms of life is 'at the still point of the turning world',[38] a point of dynamic equilibrium where new language uses are gained and old ones lost.

Moreover, the distinguishing of metaphoric from literal expressions cannot be done on the grounds of veracity or faithfulness to the facts or to the way things are. The first objection is logical. Conventionality-unconventionality and literality-non-literality are not discrete categories but come in degrees, whereas truth and falsity are dichotomous: something either is so or it is not. Therefore there can be no simple equation of either convention or literality with truth, however literality and truth might be conventionally associated.[39] The status of these categories must be determined in some other way. The second objection is also logical. On what grounds is it possible to deny metaphors the function of expressing true propositions? How is a proposition assessed in terms of veracity?

This objection again questions (this time from a different angle) the very idea of a linguistic expression's corresponding to a fact or a state of affairs. Literality, in purporting to have something to do with reference (but as the term 'reference' connotes, an understanding of literality based on reference) implicitly depends on a traditional realist correspondence theory of truth. While on a traditional classical reckoning, literal statements are non-fictional (factual, truth-bearing) whereas metaphorical statements are fictional (non-factual, 'literally' false),[40] on a Wittgensteinian view, the verification of a proposition (and its verbal expression, metaphorical or

38 T. S. Eliot, 'Four Quartets: Burnt Norton', *Collected Poems: 1909–1962* (London: Faber and Faber, 1963), 194.

39 However, Jüngel's contribution to this debate is the insight that the idea of literality is inextricably caught up with truth. The traditional opposition of metaphor and literal speech is based on the assumption that metaphors are non-truth stating. If this assumption is abandoned and metaphors are accepted as expressing true propositions, the distinction between the metaphorical and the literal must break down. Therefore, metaphor is 'a particular mode of literal speech'. (Jüngel, 'Metaphorical Truth', 67.)

40 See ibid.

not) is provided by the language-game in which it is a move.[41] The virtue of the language-game concept is that it offers 'a pragmatic explanation of how one grasps the truth-conditional content of a sentence' while at the same time the language-game is that very truth condition. 'The sentence-world relation which gives the sentence its content and makes it true'.[42]

On this view, a metaphorical proposition contains its own verification in the form of the language-game in which its assertion or expression is a move.[43] For Wittgenstein a sentence (metaphoric or literal), as a move in a language-game and as a proposition, is expressed not simply by a sentence but also by the language-game in which the sentence is a (metaphoric or literal) move. What, on this basis, can it mean to say that an expression is apt or a proposition is true? What is the metaphorical or literal expression true *to*? On a Wittgensteinian view, what it is true to is what a form of life says it is true to: the proposition in which it (and the language-game in which it is a move) are embedded. Metaphor thus poses no problem for a Wittgensteinian theory of reference, but such a theory provides no way of distinguishing literal from metaphorical truth.[44]

Is it necessary on this count to give up the literal-metaphorical distinction? Mac Cormac thinks not. In his view, it is not the way reference is

41 This does not mean that Wittgenstein intended the language-game to supplant or abolish the standard notions of truth and reference. The language-game is simply a recasting of these ideas in a new perspective.

42 Jaakko Hintikka, 'Jaakko Hintikka's reply to Barry Richards', in *Profiles 8*, 295f.

43 This understanding of truth is necessarily relativistic (its ultimate adequacy will be tested in Parts Three and Four). As such it has some affinity with that of Lakoff and Johnson, for whom truth must be relative because 'Truth is always relative to a conceptual system that is defined in large part by metaphor'. They warn of the 'danger of mistaking the culture-relative truth for the absolute'. This relativism is inevitable when experience is taken as basic. (Lakoff and Johnston, *Metaphors We Live By*, 159–60.)

44 For Wittgenstein, truth is a function of the givenness of forms of life as constituted by language-games. On this view, the acceptance of a metaphor as apt is therefore all the confirmation of its truth that is needed. It is contended here (below) that the obvious circularity of Wittgenstein's position is not redeemed by a simple doctrine of 'givenness' but requires a theological remedy.

effected which distinguishes the literal from the non-literal but, in the main, metaphor's incongruence with existing concepts.[45] This operates together with the presence of two 'key meaning units' which mutually interact and together 'anchor' the metaphor to the present linguistic structure, along with metaphor's ability to express a whole in terms of an aspect without the aspect losing its integrity with the (other) whole of which it is an aspect.[46]

Psychologist Zenon Pylyshyn suggests that the metaphorical-literal distinction is not semantic but pragmatic in terms of 'stability, referential specificity and general acceptance of terms' and the 'perception shared by those who use the terms, that the resulting description characterises the world as it really is, rather than being a convenient way of talking about it, or a way of capturing superficial resemblances'.[47] This, however, merely seems to be another way of equating the literal with the conventional. On the other hand, Nelson Goodman, like Mac Cormac, does not simply equate literality with convention: 'Realistic representation depends not upon imitation or information, but upon inculcation'.[48] Literality is pragmatically determined. Nevertheless, there is a grey area where a degree of novelty overlaps with convention: the idiom or idiosyncratic use. Conventions are local before or until they become universal. Some never achieve universal-

45 Mac Cormac, *A Cognitive Theory of Metaphor*, 20. Mac Cormac considers that deviance theories offer a 'viable way of distinguishing between metaphor and non-metaphor' but admits that this relies on a separation between ordinary rule-governed language and metaphorical rule-breaking language (ibid. 32). This in effect reduces the distinction to one of convention or normative-ness. Deviance alone cannot account for metaphor; as Ricoeur suggests, it is only its beginning moment.

46 Ibid. 59–72. Mac Cormac concludes his quest for the key distinguishing factor between metaphorical and literal uses of language by observing that 'Metaphors force us to wonder, compare, note similarities and dissimilarities, and then seek confirmation or disconfirmation of the suggestions posed by metaphor. Literal language rarely forces us to do any of these things'. (Ibid. 76.) That is, what distinguishes metaphor seems to be the greater degree of effort required for its comprehension. This criterion does not, however, distinguish it from merely unconventional speech.

47 Zenon W. Pylyshyn, 'Metaphorical Imprecision and the "Top-Down" Research Strategy', in Ortony, *Metaphor and Thought*, 420ff: 434.

48 Goodman, *Languages of Art*, 38.

ity. Local conventions are novelties elsewhere. These are the idioms which resist translation into another dialect or subcultural jargon, or language. Not every novel use is metaphorical.

There has to be a certain degree of disparate-ness from the literal for a use of language to qualify as metaphorical. Goodman concludes: 'Where there is metaphor there is conflict ... application of a term is metaphorical only if to some extent contraindicated.'[49] This resembles Mac Cormac's (and Ricoeur's) incongruence factor. While I not see this is as a sufficient condition for a metaphorical-literal distinction, I agree with Goodman that 'The question why predicates apply as they do metaphorically is much the same as the question why they apply as they do literally', and that '[d]ifficulties in determining truth are by no means peculiar to metaphor'.[50]

Another seemingly plausible way of distinguishing metaphoric and literal is on the basis of precision or exactitude. By this reckoning literal language is precise or exact while metaphorical language is vague or ambiguous. However, as Mac Cormac points out, metaphors are neither vague nor ambiguous: their meaning is quite definite – it is merely inarticulable as the proposition expressed by the metaphor is too new to be conceivable.[51] Moreover, literal uses of language also fail to be precise or exact. Exactitude in language is a myth. As Jüngel observes, language of any kind, literal or metaphorical, is a translation from being to speech. As no translation can be exact, this is not a basis for distinguishing between literal and metaphorical. Of course, from a language-game viewpoint, what is taken to be exact is a matter of convention. The debate seems to have travelled full circle.

I have already suggested that Wittgenstein's great contribution to the literal-metaphorical debate is to demonstrate that no reference is direct: all of our knowledge of reality depends upon language-games. How can this insight, which appears to iron out the distinction between literal and metaphorical, be of use here? While a distinction on the grounds of reference is a solution which has already been discounted, it contains the seeds of a more satisfactory idea.

49 Ibid. 69.

50 Ibid. 78, 80.

51 Mac Cormac, *A Cognitive Theory of Metaphor*, 73.

Ricoeur distinguishes the literal from the metaphorical on the grounds of directness of reference. Ricoeur suggests that it is not that nonliteral uses of language do not refer to reality; it is that they do not refer directly, but do so

> by the means of a complex strategy which implies, as an essential component, a suspension and seemingly an abolition of the ordinary reference attached to descriptive language. This suspension, however, is only the negative condition of a second-order reference of an indirect reference built on the ruins of the direct reference. This reference is called second-order reference only with respect to the primacy of the reference of ordinary language. For in another respect, it constitutes the primordial reference to the extent that it suggests, reveals, unconceals – or whatever you say – the deep structure of reality to which we are related as mortals who are born into this world and who dwell in it for a while.[52]

In the same way as the metaphorical sense not only abolishes but also preserves the literal sense, 'the metaphorical reference maintains the ordinary vision in tension with the new one it suggests'.[53]

While directness of reference has already been refuted as a discriminator between metaphorical and literal uses, if one reads 'language-game' where Ricoeur has 'reference', the language-games in which new metaphors are moves may be seen as instances of Jaakko and Merrill Hintikka's secondary uses (secondary language-games) which are 'parasitic' on primary uses of terms. While the system of language-games as a whole is basic, not all language-games within it are basic. In the distinction the Hintikkas make between primary and secondary language-games, the secondary games are built on primary ones. It is the moves in the primary games that have to be taken as incorrigible. If they were not so, they could not serve as the basic language-world links. 'Since primary language-games are what mediates the relation of language to [nonlinguistic] reality, there is not, and cannot be, any way of challenging what happens in such language-games. For such a challenge would presuppose an independent link between one's language and the world, a link that would bypass these language-games. But then

52 Ricoeur, 'The Metaphorical Process', 141ff.

53 Mac Cormac, *A Cognitive Theory of Metaphor*, 151–2.

they would no longer be the primary vehicles of our semantics.'[54] Primary language-games include physiognomic, physiological and perceptual activities and those associated with colour.[55] Their activities are first order and their terms are concrete whereas the secondary games which depend on them for meaning employ less concrete terms. The secondary games take their meaning from the primary games, therefore their relation is semantical; this semantical relationship involves the two games as wholes. 'Many important concepts can be used only in a suitable secondary language-game. They include knowledge, belief, doubt, correctness and mistake.'[56] Unlike primary games, secondary games are corrigible, depending for their reference and justification on the foundational primary games. In this way the meanings of metaphors depend on the uses of the same terms in primary or other secondary games.

The Hintikkas regard this distinction as essential for the stability of meaning. If all shifts in language use brought about a corresponding shift in meaning, the sheer multiplicity of language-games would eliminate all hope of stability in meaning and make the transfer of knowledge from one situation to another impossible. The only solution to this dilemma seems to be to suppose that words acquire their uses in some language-games only and that this use is duplicated in others – that is, that there are use-creating and use-utilising or confirming language-games.[57] I suggest that perhaps there are subtle shifts in use between language-games but an inertia factor favouring the nearest existing use means that a more than subtle shift in use is required to change meaning – that is, for the construal of a lack of identity in meaning. This argument would tend to support a 'cluster' theory of shifts in language-use.

54 Hintikka and Hintikka, *Investigating Wittgenstein*, 279.

55 Ibid. 277.

56 Ibid. 274.

57 On this issue see also H. E. Mason, 'On the Multiplicity of Language-Games', Elisabeth Leinfellner et al. (eds), *Wittgenstein and his Impact on Contemporary Philosophy (Proceedings of the Second International Wittgenstein Symposium), 1977, Kirchberg/Weschel, Austria*, Vienna: Holder-Pichler-Tempsky, 1978, 332ff: 333.

The relation of secondary to primary is that of superimposition. The primary provides the reasons for the secondary; that is, secondary language-games need criteria whereas primary ones are self-authenticating.[58] While secondary language-games may function independently of the primary ones from which they have arisen, they may not mean the same when they operate independently. Thus Wittgenstein: 'When children play at trains their game is connected with their knowledge of trains. It would nevertheless be possible for the children of a tribe unacquainted with trains to learn this game from others and to play it without knowing that it was copied from anything. One could say that the game did not make the same sense to them as to us.'[59]

While in these language-games the primary uses are assimilated in the new secondary use, they nevertheless somehow retain the suggestion of their primary use in the new situation of use until (or unless) habituation through frequency of use entirely obliterates the derivation of the secondary from the primary. The progress here is from metaphor through idiom to literal expression. When the contact with its primary games is finally lost, it no longer means the same; its sense has altered. It has become an idiom or literal use; its context is taken as read. However, the metaphorising language-game itself is in a sense in a category of its own in being responsible for the transfer of terms from primary to secondary use. It is to be distinguished from the secondary language-games it creates (or makes possible) by employing the content of primary games.

I suggest, therefore, that a case may be made for a 'double-language-game' – or 'two-stage-verification' (rather than 'split reference') explanation of the distinction between literal and metaphorical uses of language. According to this understanding, indirectness of reference (if the term can still be used) is, in the case of a new use of language, doubly indirect: reference is neither isomorphic (being mediated by language-games) nor simply effected by one language-game as the new secondary (to begin with) use relies on primary uses for its meaning. The way in which this process operates to increase our access to and comprehension of reality will be examined in the next chapter.

58 Hintikka and Hintikka, *Investigating Wittgenstein*, 281, 285.

59 Wittgenstein, *Philosophical Investigations*, #282, quoted in ibid. 301–2.

2.2.4. Summary

1. As I argued in Chapter 1 of Part Two, metaphorising is a language-game and therefore what applies to language-games in general applies to metaphorising. If language-games in general are epistemically basic, so are metaphorising language-games. A language-game is no more nor less than its moves which include activities involving the use of language and rule-like entities (propositions, facts, concepts) concerning these uses. Therefore the metaphorising language-game is all of these: the metaphorising activity plus its product (the metaphor or model) and the rules which make this product a move in such a game.
2. Yet, at the same time, it may be seen that metaphorising is a language-game which creates new moves in other language-games. The metaphorising language-game is thus a source of new language-world links and thereby of new knowledge. Therefore non-metaphorical (so-called 'direct') reference may develop from a prior metaphorical (so-called 'indirect') reference.
3. The metaphorising language-game, in being primitive to the language formation process, is not itself susceptible of verification. Nevertheless, individual metaphorical statements depend for their verification on both metaphorising and 'ordinary' language-games.

The question which may now be asked is: *how* does metaphorising produce new language-world links as new moves in language-games and thus effect a gain to knowledge?

CHAPTER THREE

Inventions and Inculcations

2.3.1. Metaphorising as Invention

Having established that metaphorising is a 'given' upon which much if not all knowledge rests, it remains to be seen how metaphorising is a source of knowledge. How does metaphorising effect an increment in existing conceptual knowledge while still being dependent upon existing conceptual knowledge? The question of whether metaphorising creates or simply discovers new language-games is not simply one of realism versus idealism; it also relates to the way in which metaphorical subject and predicate interact. Why, Samuel Levin asks, should metaphorising be restricted to the modification of subject by predicate? Levin sees this error as creeping in because of the tendency to think in terms of explicit predicates. This biases the direction of the construal (and also tends to turn the subject-predicate relation into a comparison. However, as Levin points out, it is not comparison that effects the construal (although it may be the basis for the construal); the construal is achieved by a process of 'transfer and amalgamation, where from the total range of elements associated with one term of the comparison a subset is selected that is compatible or viable with elements of the other term'.[1]

If metaphorising creates new moves in language-games (which include new propositional rules), metaphorising effects a gain to knowledge in

1 Samuel R. Levin, 'Standard Approaches to Metaphor and a Proposal for Literary Metaphor', in in Ortony, *Metaphor and Thought*, 124–35; 128–9. While this chapter will mainly refer to metaphor, this is not to be taken to imply an abandonment of the wider application of metaphorising advanced in the previous two chapters.

the broad sense which includes 'knowing-how' as well as 'knowing-that'. According to Jüngel, this is accomplished through the way

> [m]etaphorical language specifies by working with the dialectic of familiarity and strangeness. It makes language both a state of affairs and a pattern of use strange by employing an unusual word [or relation of words) to signify a state of affairs in an unusual way … In a metaphorical statement, a word functioning as a predication is used in such a way that in this instance it loses its usual relation to the state of affairs which it signifies (i.e. its usual meaning) although the meaning which is lost is still presupposed.[2]

The process of assimilating new information by relating it to things already known is known as apperception. Metaphor is a challenge to apperception.[3] However, if comprehension depends upon our being able to slot new information into a ready-made context, how is it possible for these contexts themselves to change if we do not already in some way have the new context? Otherwise our learning of something would appear quite arbitrary. Educationalist Hugh G. Petrie considers that 'metaphor is one of the central ways of leaping the epistemological chasm between old knowledge and radically new knowledge'. Metaphor provides a rational bridge from the known to the unknown from one context of understanding to another. This is because metaphors (paradoxically) 'invite the use of a familiar, rule-governed device for dealing with the material to be learned in ways which require the bending or even breaking of the familiar rules'.[4] It is perhaps metaphor's ability to create similarities, or to express similarities

2 Jüngel, 'Metaphorical Truth', 68.

3 George A. Miller, 'Images and Models, Similes and Metaphors', in Ortony, *Metaphor and Thought*, 240ff: 248.

4 'The belief that there is such an epistemological chasm depends upon certain presuppositions … First, experience is never directly of the world as it is, but is always in part constituted by our modes of representation and understanding … Second, most learning consists of processing that which impinges on us in terms of a context of rules or schemata. These contexts of rules form our modes of understanding. Much learning is thus being able to experience in terms of context … Third, on some occasions we learn by actually changing the contexts of understanding. The result of changed structures of understanding is … radically new knowledge … (Piaget).

which are not antecedently known but which inhere in the reality (here Ricoeur's combining of the notions of creating and discovering in 'invention' is perhaps the best solution) which enable it to be a bridge.[5] In other words, the metaphor creates a category which, while new, is similar enough to some other familiar category to enable us to relate new information to the old categories.

Metaphor creates by juxtaposing referents combining familiars in unfamiliar fashion, which leads to the location of previously unknown similarities and the possibility of transformation of the dissimilarities into similarities.[6] This process is saved from the circularity of an arbitrary creation of categories by the interweaving of language-world.[7] According to Hausman, metaphorising is both the creation (of a new description of a 'world under a certain description') and the discovery (being the establishment of a new language-world link) of a new reference which extends the

---

During assimilation, we learn by changing our concepts and modes of understanding to fit our experience.' Hugh G. Petrie, 'Metaphor and Learning', in ibid. 438–61; 440–1.

5 Ibid. 442. (See also Mac Cormac, *A Cognitive Theory of Metaphor*, 127.)

6 Mac Cormac, *A Cognitive Theory of Metaphor*, 50. As Mac Cormac observes elsewhere, '[m]etaphors allow us to extend our knowledge by juxtaposing normally unrelated referents and by suggesting that some of the attributes of each referent are similar. Other attributes of each referent remain dissimilar ... Both the production and the recognition of a metaphor demand the ability to link attributes of normally unrelated referents. The more difficult the comprehension of the linkage, the more suggestive the metaphor'. (Ibid. 17–18.)

7 Ibid. 21. As has already been noted, on a conceptual-realist view, metaphoric creation is at the same time both creation and discovery. We discover new language-world links at the same time as we create new concepts; neither is possible without the other. 'Seeking natural categories about the unknown requires extension of our existing categories, but how should we extend them? There exist almost infinite possibilities for extension ... Metaphors that juxtapose often unassociated categories creating semantic anomaly offer one method of seeking the proper categories that might be prototypical and natural. Diaphors become epiphors when confirmation of a suggestive hypothesis is found. If the confirmation occurs over and over again, then a new category arises from the combination of the two categories previously not associated'. (Ibid. 76.)

scope of language-world. 'A metaphorical expression functions so that it creates its significance, thus providing new insight through designating a unique, extra-linguistic and extra-conceptual reference that had no place in the intelligible world before the metaphor was articulated … [I]n being creative, a metaphor must meet two conditions that the adopted concept of reference makes fundamental: uniqueness and extralinguisticality.'[8]

Hausman posits three levels or stages of metaphor: first, literal but incongruous meaning (the 'antecedent meaning' stage); second, the stage of 'deeper' meaning where the metaphor is seen as more than its incongruous constituents; and third, the advance of intelligibility beyond the level prior to the metaphor (the 'consequent meaning' stage). It is a mistake to equate the consequent meaning of the metaphor with the antecedent meaning of either of its key terms – one term hasn't simply come to mean the other; both terms have changed in use. 'It is the transformation of terms into constituents and their unprecedented functions as consequent meanings that is the metaphor's creative achievement.'[9]

For Ricoeur, as with Hausman, discourse is defined by its relation to extralinguistic reality.[10] This link is required because convention alone cannot account for a sense of rightness or fittingness, but how is discourse seen to fulfil this function without falling back on some notion of isomorphism? Ricoeur develops a 'double invention' concept of metaphor as organiser and organisee of reality: 'What it creates it discovers; and what it finds it invents.'[11] Ricoeur's insight regarding the pervasiveness of

8 Hausman, *Metaphor and Art*, 94. (Hausman's language here at least suggests a position which is somewhat direct-correspondence realist.) Similarly Jüngel: 'Since metaphorical predications work with the strangeness both of the state of affairs about which a statement is made and also of the word with which a metaphorical predication is accomplished, they presuppose familiarity with both this state of affairs and the original meaning of the word. If this familiarity is not present in a natural way, it must be created through narration. Metaphors expand and specify the narrated world.' (Jüngel, 'Metaphorical Truth', 68.)

9 Hausman, *Metaphor and Art*, 74–7.

10 Ricoeur, *The Rule of Metaphor*, 124.

11 Ibid. 239. 'This ontological vehemence [of the 'referential character of metaphor' announced in the copula ('is'/'is not')] cuts meaning from its initial anchor … But

language leads him to an important insight regarding metaphor. As we must operate within an existing language order, metaphor's creation or discovery of a new order must be by way of creating rifts in the old order which was itself created in the very same way. Ricoeur posits an 'initial polysemy' in which a word has several common uses.[12] These established uses in the language-games in which they feature are a 'sea anchor' which is 'dragged' by metaphor. Metaphor makes an assertion which confounds those uses.[13] Semantics are thus created by metaphor in the violation of existing categories 'Order itself proceeds from the metaphorical constitution of semantic fields' and is in turn transgressed by the constitution of a new field. Thus the concept constantly evolves from the metaphor in a circular (or more accurately, a spiral) process.[14] In this way metaphor can be seen to break the circularity of verification between expression of proposition and language-game in a form of life through the revelation of a use which has not hitherto been recognised as a move in any existing language-game.

It may be deduced from this that '[c]reativity lies in the selection of the proper referents producing enough similarity for recognition and enough dissimilarity, and the right kind of dissimilarity, to generate a hypothetical

---

in order to declare itself this ontological vehemence makes use of mere hints of meaning, which are in no way determinations of meaning. An experience seeks to be expressed ... Its anticipated sense finds in the dynamism of simple meaning ... a sketch that now must be reconciled with the requirements of the concept'. (Ibid. 299–300.)

12 Ibid. 121–2, 131.

13 Ricoeur notes that traditional theories of reference can be only speculative, as they require a standpoint outside of language if the language-world relation is to be known. But his answer to this problem seems to be the positing of a meta-language: 'Speculative discourse is possible, because language possesses the reflective capacity to place itself at a distance and to consider itself, as such and in its entirety, as related to the totality of what is. Language designates itself and its other ...' (Ibid. 304.) This is undoubtedly convenient, but is it coherent? Of course speculative discourse is possible but can it be other than heuristic? How can language alone express the language-world link?

14 Ibid. 22–4.

possibility.'[15] Whether or not this hypothetical possibility is accepted as in some sense real or true depends on the context of understanding within a particular milieu. But whence comes this communal decision regarding the success of a metaphor? – of the application of the term in the primary game (in this sense always, to begin with, catachrestic, plugging a gap in terminology, defining an unknown)? – and of the transfer of the term in the secondary metaphorical (combining of primary games) game? 'Describing how this process of reconceiving through the creation of new forms of language takes place remains almost inconceivable'.[16] Theories of metaphor cannot answer these questions. They can only point to the mystery.

To conclude, then, paradoxically, metaphors violate old conventions to make new ones. While training in metaphorising may be given, the quality of the metaphors such training produces is another matter.[17] If there is a rule governing the selection of metaphorical referents, it lies in the whole language-game of metaphorising, not in a set of articulated formulations.

2.3.2. Metaphorised Inculcations

I have maintained that logically language-games cannot be separated from their moves. Metaphorising must therefore bring about a new interweaving of language-world in human activities. At this point it enables us to 'see' something in terms of something else. A transfer of previous learning (training) reveals what we have not seen before.[18] The unfamiliar is thus born in the midst of the familiar. The utterance cannot be separated from the language-game any more than the metaphorical vehicle can be separated

15 Mac Cormac, *A Cognitive Theory of Metaphor*, 148.

16 Ibid. 136.

17 Ibid. 137–40.

18 For further discussion on the material in this section see chapter 4, 'The Anatomy of Language-Riddenness' in my book, Patterson, *Realist Christian Theology*, 73ff.

from its topic. Thus, while metaphor is essentially verbal, it is not entirely so but depends upon a mix of the verbal and nonverbal, the linguistic and the nonlinguistic in the activities of our forms of life. Therefore truly novel metaphors do not involve simply a deliberate superimposition of concepts that are seen to have a common element. Such conceptual metaphors, which are more like similes or analogies, are the later products of novel metaphors. How then does metaphorising create new moves in language-games? And what sort of language-game is metaphorising?

Wittgenstein describes the process of learning language-games as 'training'. How does the activity of metaphorising relate to training in a language-game? According to Gillett, 'When Wittgenstein discusses perception he spends a great deal of time on "seeing as" or "aspect seeing" ... The fact that we see some things now as this and now as that suggests that we do so by means of representations which are distinct from those things. Thus we can approach this more general question by discussing whether a valid reading of "perceiving x as y" substitutes a "percept" or similar for x and something in the world for y.'[19] Psychologists Thorndike and Woodworth have established empirically that training is a fundamental part of learning. Where the performance is associated with words, training in that performance will facilitate the learning of those words in that context.[20] While Wittgenstein does not explicitly mention transfer of training, his notion of 'seeing as' leans in that direction. 'Seeing as' can be given a wider application than perception. When the learner encounters a situation or activity which in some way resembles what has been learnt, the new situation will be 'read' in terms of the old: the novel activity acquires meaning through application of the familiar. Now we know how to go on.

19 Gillett, *Representation, Meaning and Thought*, 189.

20 E. L. Thorndike and R. S. Woodworth, 'The Influence of Improvement in One Mental Function upon the Efficiency of Other Functions (I); II The Estimation of Magnitudes; III Functions Involving Attention, Observation and Discrimination.' *Psychological Review* 8 (1901), 247–61, 384–95, 553–64; cited by Charles E. Osgood, *Method and Theory in Experimental Psychology* (New York: Oxford University Press, 1953), 524.

Here 'seeing as' can be understood as a perceptual metaphor for the entire process of generalising what we already know to an unfamiliar situation.

Hester suggests that metaphor may be explained in terms of 'seeing as', as it appears to come into the category of ambiguous entities characterised by Wittgenstein in *Philosophical Investigations* by Jastrow's duck-rabbit. Here 'seeing as' is a matter of selecting one of several aspects.[21] In metaphor, as in the duck-rabbit, seeing an aspect confers intelligibility on the whole; the aspect is selected from the context. Black also observes that the metaphor serves to focus attention on the particular aspect of its context which gives it meaning. In Black's 'Interaction' theory, extra-utterance associations (which need not be extralinguistic) are the 'associated commonplaces' which combine to make the metaphor a unit of new meaning. These subjects then 'draw out and emphasise certain implications of each other while suppressing other irrelevant qualities'.[22]

As has already been noted, Lakoff and Johnson also understand metaphorising as creating new categories by way of highlighting some properties and downplaying others. Categories focus on a particular aspect of reality. Statements relating to a given category are true relative to that focus in that our understanding is category-dependent. With new metaphors, other (not so new) metaphors act as mediators.[23] That is, metaphorising creates the means of interpretation (the language-game) for the metaphor. In a local context 'we understand a statement as being true in a given situation when our understanding of the statement fits our understanding of the situation closely enough for our purposes'.[24] Here a novel metaphor rearranges an existing scheme to invent a new one. Thus metaphorising is more than mere recognition of natural categories (unconditioned regularities

21 Hester, *The Meaning of Poetic Metaphor*, 170. See also my '*Word*, Words and World'.

22 Max Black, *Models and Metaphors: Studies in Language and Philosophy* (New York: Cornell University Press, 1962), 44–5.

23 Lakoff and Johnston, *Metaphors We Live By*, 163–4, 175–7.

24 Ibid. 179–80.

that are simply 'out there'). It also involves their assessment in terms of existing categories.[25]

Metaphor, then, may be described as the articulation of the seeing of an aspect, the articulation of a particular 'seeing as' which is a new move in a new or existing language-game. A new language-language link gives rise to a new language-world link. While there might appear to be a distinction between 'ordinary' instances of 'seeing-as' which are perceptual (primary) language-games and metaphorical 'seeings-as' which are secondary language-games in that we deliberately and articulately 'see' (conceive) something as something else, this distinction is blurred by the involuntary metaphorising performed by children (and recognised as either category mistakes or metaphors by adults) when they apply what they have learned in one situation to another situation. Yet their recognition as metaphorical makes them moves in the secondary language-game of metaphorising.[26] In the case of children's learning of existing uses of language, this conflict of interpretations does not usually arise. Yet what is there to distinguish this situation from the one in which there is no existing use which exactly fits the state of affairs to be described or expressed? This is in effect the child's situation where the child does not know what the adult knows: that there is an established terminology for a given situation, and has to fall back on the closest-fit aspect of what it already knows. Here there is no simple judgment of rightness or wrongness of use; the decision must rather be made according to congruence with the general (unarticulated) experience of the hearers. Truth or falsity here is therefore intuitive yet rule-governed, as Gillett observes:

25 'The process of creating new concepts in metaphors differs from that of recognising prototypical categories in that when confronted with a metaphor, the hearer must consider the ways in which the referents are similar and ways in which they are dissimilar.' (Mac Cormac, *A Cognitive Theory of Metaphor*, 76.)

26 See Chapter 2 of Part Two above. All metaphors are moves both in the metaphorising secondary language-game and in the primary perceptual 'seeing as' language-game where their 'seeing-as' creates a new language-world link.

> Although most of the time what I perceive is what is there (this is entailed by my grasp of the meanings of words), at times I can perceive an aspect of something which involves assimilating that object, in an imaginative way, to other (equally public) objects of experience. By so doing, I forge an internal relation (based on the practices in which a term is used) between the x I am seeing and y. The assimilation essentially involves the application of a term with meaning, marking the concept <y>, to x so that we see it as y. When I see an aspect, I locate what I am seeing in a conceptual practice the specifications of which involve concrete situations and what people say and do in them. To see an aspect is thus to draw upon a technique (or rule-governed habit or custom) which ties sensory contact to action and discourse.[27]

While metaphorising cannot simply be seen as a kind of perception (needing first to 'see' or describe something as something else and then be seen as metaphorising), Gillett's comments nevertheless are pertinent to metaphor conceived more broadly, where 'seeing' becomes itself a metaphor for the various types of metaphorical construal and description. Thus a Wittgensteinian view of metaphorising reasonably begins with 'seeing-as' but goes beyond perceiving of aspects.

When Wittgenstein describes the process of learning language-games as 'training', what is meant by 'training'? Training is ordinarily understood to be 'any activity designed systematically to improve job knowledge skills and/or abilities of individuals'.[28] As the concept of training is traditionally narrower than that of learning and more specific and practical in scope, Wittgenstein's use of the term to describe the learning of a language-game is appropriate in view of this emphasis on the acquiring of specific practices. Yet the primacy Wittgenstein accords to language-games arguably has the effect of subsuming all acquisition of knowledge under training. In the same or similar way that a primary language-game is learnt in the first instance by training, so subsequent new applications of language are learnt by transfer or generalising of that training. These are then themselves inculcated by means of training.

27 Gillett, *Representation, Meaning and Thought*, 194.

28 See Rom Harre and Roger Lamb (eds), *The Encyclopaedia Dictionary of Psychology* (Cambridge, Massachusetts: M.I.T. Press, 1983).

> [T]he child must become adept in the use of a series of terms which, by virtue of their role in the activities he shares with others, enable him to pick out and think about various features of his world. Winch remarks: 'It is only in the context of forms of life that we can make any sense of the idea of their being objects of a particular category and in making sense of such an idea we also grasp the sort of 'combination' with a 'name' that goes along with such an object ... Categories of objects, individuating conditions over time and different types of encounter, and what counts as this or that all have to be learnt. They are learnt as the child latches on to the ways in which 'names' (or more generally terms) are applied to 'objects' (or situations and their elements). In that this learning involves the meanings of terms, which I have assumed must be objective and intersubjective, it implies that the (repertoire of) concepts is developed in a language-related set of activities.[29]

If training is indeed fundamental to the process of learning, training theories may have a broader scope than they have enjoyed traditionally. Of particular interest in the present context is the educational psychological theory of transfer of training developed by Thorndike and Woodworth.[30] Transfer of training (also called transfer of learning with a slightly broader application) is considered to have occurred when some aspect of previous experience is seen to affect subsequent performance. When such an influence occurs, it can consist of either positive transfer (which enhances ability) or negative transfer (which impedes performance). Transfer may be specific, as when the same knowledge is applied in two situations, or it may result from generalisation where the second task is similar to the first in some way; or it may be more abstract or conceptual in that performance on the second task is based on some general principle or rule which the two tasks share. Transfer may also depend on inference, previously learned material being combined with new information to general novel behaviour.

Transfer of training is commonly observed in motor and verbal learning. While transfer of training as traditionally conceived relates to learning facility rather than learning content, what is interesting for the present argument is that a transfer of previous experience is involved. A previous

29 Gillett, 'Learning to Perceive', 608 (quoting Peter Winch, *Ethics and Action* (London: Routledge, 1972), 125).

30 Thorndike and Woodworth, 'The Influence of Improvement', 247–61.

activity or performance has been utilised to the benefit or detriment of a new activity. It can be said that the old activity has become transferred to and mixed up with the new one.

When Wittgenstein recognises the crucial role language-games play in language learning ('The connection between words and things is set up by the teaching of language'[31]), although he does not yet see the language-game as prior to its rules, he nevertheless is able to see language-games as 'complete systems of human communication'.[32] Learning of language in general is a matter of training to master language-games, not instruction in formulations of rules: 'one takes one's directions from the sign-post only insofar as there exists an established use, a custom'. That is, the drill makes the sign comprehensible.[33] Metaphor may be seen as an instance of where, in the absence of other directions to where we are going, one needs to read the sign differently. That which the sign now represents is a different thing; therefore, neither the sign nor the signified are the same any more: both have undergone a process of transfer.

Jacob Joshua Ross expresses a similar viewpoint:

> Wittgenstein's notion of 'language-games' which are rooted in 'forms of lite' can be interpreted as being meant (at least partly) to provide a solution to this problem [of how we learn language]. The root idea embodied in this theory is the idea of language as a tool or instrument of communication. The need for communication precedes language … Our common needs and wants provide the basis for the agreement in judgments which according to Wittgenstein (PI #2421) enables communication. Once there is such agreement we have what Wittgenstein calls 'forms of lite' which are significant modes of human activity. There are many such models … [E]xpressions of ours are the counters with which we participate in a given mode of activity. When they are introduced as part of these activities, we have 'language-games'. The meaning of an expression is connected with its use in a particular 'language-game' (PI #43). Hence, as Wittgenstein puts it '… to imagine a language is to imagine a form of life' (PI #19).[34]

31 Ludwig Wittgenstein, *Philosophical Grammar*, Rush Rhees (ed.), Anthony Kenny (tr.) (Oxford: Blackwell, 1974), IV #56.

32 Hintikka and Hintikka, *Investigating Wittgenstein*, 192.

33 Ibid. 200; Wittgenstein, *Philosophical Investigations*, #198.

34 Jacob Joshua Ross, 'Wittgenstein on the Learning of a Language', Leinfellner et al., *Wittgenstein and his Impact*, 398ff: 459.

According to Ross, Wittgenstein sees the process of learning as proceeding from the simplest, most primitive language-games to the more sophisticated ones. In this process noises (and, it should be added, gestures, postures and grimaces) are replaced (or rather supplemented) by articulations.[35] But how does this happen? Ross agrees with Toulmin[36] that Wittgenstein seems to employ a gestalt-type of learning theory. 'A child learns individual language-games, not a whole system of language (as Chomsky would maintain). Once the child knows the more primitive games, these can form part of more complicated games. We absorb language-games in a holistic way as we are capable (maturationally), exposed (contextually) and motivated (involved). "Light dawns gradually over the whole".'[37] The Hintikkas would maintain that Ross is correct to see that language-games are constructed from other language-games; some language-games are parasitic on others. Ross suggests that this may be a sort of transfer process. However, I do not consider that gestalts are simply equatable with language-games. To equate them thus is to limit the scope and operation of language-games in the learning of language.[38]

The concept of transfer of learning has an affinity with Lakoff and Johnson's insight that in metaphor we use the concrete or simple to describe the less so. In this way experience is able to take on conceptual form. Because we acquire the former first, as children, this is the learning, or training (in playing the games associated with these uses), which we have available to transfer. With time we are able to transfer more complex learning.[39]

35 Wittgenstein, *Philosophical Investigations*, ##5, 7, 25; *Blue Book*, 17, 81; Ross, 'Wittgenstein on the Learning of a Language', 459.

36 Stephen Toulmin, 'Ludwig Wittgenstein', *Encounter* 32 (1969), 58–71.

37 Ross, 'Wittgenstein on the Learning of a Language', 460–1.

38 To say that becoming trained in the playing of a language-game is tantamount to absorbing or assimilating a gestalt is to say that playing a language-game is the same as learning a proposition – or perhaps not quite the same. See section 2.3.3.

39 'Normally speaking, the process of language comprehension and production for a young child not fully familiar with the conventional range of application of a term must proceed through a process of fitting the aspects of the current situation into the closest lexical concept already available'. (David E. Rumelhart, 'Some Problems with the Notion of Literal Meanings', in Ortony, *Metaphor and Thought*, 78–91:

Likewise, transfer of learning (or training) is employed when we use physical object language to refer to internal sensations. Such language is inevitably metaphorical (for instance, a pain is described as 'stabbing' or 'throbbing' or 'sharp'). Such avowals or internal states can only be expressed metaphorically. Later these form the basis of (true) propositions about these internal states. Of course, the language employed is not simply physical object language but social, form-of-life language, because we have been trained in its primary (immediate) use by a community of trainers, which establishes the conventions of use. Accordingly, metaphorising may be understood as a language-game of transfer of both learning, as in the case of a learner, and also training, as the product of a community of trainers.

New concepts or propositions may thus be seen to be acquired through a transfer of learning at language-game level effected through a combination of language-games. Here Gillett's work on the generalising of concepts adds a philosophical perspective to the psychological work on transfer of training. Gillett understands the generalisation process as a linking of language-games by means of common features: 'Concepts, *inter alia*, group objects as to whether they count as instances of this or that. Therefore they link different experiences by capturing common features, such as the occurrence of <red> or <dog>.'[40] It could be said that transfer of training in the practice of natural language, when not artificially induced by psychologists or teachers, is evidenced by conceptual linkages. We are used to thinking of concepts as simply instances of explicit 'knowing that'. However, here conceptual knowledge is portrayed as including 'knowing-how': 'to grasp a concept is to understand how to group certain objects in a principled way and to be able to reason about that grouping'. Moreover, 'a subject grasps a concept when he can judge whether a meaningful term can be applied to something presented to him … [T]he grasp of a concept is an

---

79–81.) Sometimes this application will fit conventional usage, sometimes it won't. The same goes for comprehension. The child has to use its existing concepts and transfer (generalise) them to new uses. Thus metaphor is inherent in the learning of concepts and language. It is not that this is so remarkable as such as that the traditional view of meaning and metaphor makes it remarkable.

40 Gillett, *Representation, Meaning and Thought*, 6.

ability to respond to an item in a rule-governed way (the ability may be well or ill-developed).'[41] Therefore, knowledge consists of a series of concepts about what things go with what, concepts which are determined by the language-games in which the things in question receive their meaning.

It is because we are able through discovery of common elements to make links between and within situations that we are able to generalise our experience and thus form concepts.[42] I argue that this linking is the function of metaphorising. Each metaphorising, as production of a link, produces a metaphor. Further reinforcement of the link turns the metaphor into a concept. Therefore 'to grasp a concept is to grasp a rule that allows one to generalise from one situation to another'[43] where this rule is the metaphorising language-game which effects a transfer which is tantamount to a transfer of training. Thus a new metaphor is not yet concept (or perhaps more accurately, the product of the metaphorical generalisation, the novel concept underlying the metaphor, is not yet grasped) because its generalisability is not yet established: 'manifestability is [also] an essential feature of the grasp of a concept'.[44] What makes a concept manifest is the appreciation of its meaningfulness for our forms of life. The formation of a concept may thus be seen as the result of the metaphorical selection process: to metaphorise is to select an aspect of one individual or situation or relation which may be linked to another individual, situation or relation.[45]

As has been seen, it is the norms of our forms of life, as expressed in their various language-games, which determine both our judgments as to the aptness of a metaphor and as to the rightness or wrongness of the ensuing

41 Ibid. 10–11.

42 Ibid. 12. Gillett calls this the 'Generality Principle'. Gillett also makes use of Gareth Evans's similar idea of the 'Generality Constraint'. [See also Gillett, 'The Generality Constraint and Conscious Thought', *Analysis* 47 (1987): 20–4.]

43 Ibid. 13.

44 Ibid. 14.

45 Hence, 'The aspects picked out have a form determined by links to other experiences which articulate one's conceptual repertoire. To appreciate something as being thus and so is, therefore, to judge that it is both like and unlike other things in certain respects. This gives conscious experience both form and structure and allows the conscious subject to make inferences based on connections in experience'. (Ibid. 15.)

concept. Human forms of life as expressed in their practices provide the verification of a given content. To judge a given content to be veridical is to commit oneself to thinking in a particular way about that content,[46] which entails a commitment to other judgments in turn. Grasping these entailments is part of grasping the concept.[47] The generalisability of what is grasped in this instance means that novel situations can also provide grounds for the acceptance of a given content. Gillett suggests that this is why 'some concepts just "click" or are, as it were, grasped in a flash of insight. Links to an already existing repertoire can be exploited when a rule or principle of grouping marked by a novel term can "tap in" to the system in a way that is potentiated by the subject's extant abilities'.[48]

The relation of metaphorising to generalising of concepts thus has the following result: an existing concept is generalised to a new application. If the new application is apt (is congruent enough with what is normative for our experience, which is not necessarily the same as being in tune with the concepts linked with our experience – hence the intuitive nature of this judgment), it is reinforced by repeated applications. In this way a strong enough link is established to enable the transfer of the entire link

46 'A concept is a normatively constrained function of judgment in and across different experiences. To grasp a concept is to appreciate what it is to respond in this principled way. And this appreciation, inter alia, includes the realisation that there is a way of going right and wrong. To master a concept is to be able to exercise such an ability with assurance in a sufficient range of cases'. (Ibid.)

47 'Conceptual connexions between states of affairs are better thought of as "links" than as "grounds" or "commitments" because they may not rest on strict logical entailments. There are usually many links, all defeasible, which, in different combinations and context, warrant any judgment.' (Ibid. 20.)

48 Thus 'the subject selects from the feature (not necessarily perceptual) of any situation those which ground the use of certain concepts in judgments about that situation. His judgments link the situation about which he is thinking with practices in which he has grasped the relevant concepts. In those practices rules for the application of the concept have found some "bite" on his performances or propensities'. However, the foundationality of language-games does not result in a rigid determinism: 'the concept-using subject shows a flexible and interest-directed capacity to respond to various aspects of any situation. Thus it may be difficult to say just when a subject first intelligently applies a concept'. (Ibid. 19–20.)

to another situation. At this stage it can be said that the metaphor has become a concept.

However, a theory of metaphor as transfer of training, no matter how satisfactory in other respects, cannot explain how it is that we manage to transfer our knowledge of one language-game to another. Nor can it explain how we decide which transfers are appropriate. How might this be achieved? There have been in recent studies two main hypotheses, one Wittgensteinian and one psychological (cognitive), which sometimes appear in synthesis. These are the family resemblance and clustering (gestalt) theories.

2.3.3. The Fittingness of Transfers

The linking of common elements in concept or category formation has been seen by a number of philosophers as conforming to Wittgenstein's notion of 'family resemblance'. This is a no-common-threads thesis which holds that 'there is no set of features running through all cases of what a given predicate or concept applies to – all cases of what would fit the concept, or what would be as the predicate says a thing to be'.[49] While Mary Hesse observes that 'not all members of a category are equally representative of it; there are no necessary and sufficient conditions for membership of a category; and the boundaries of a category are not uniquely determined',[50] Clara Seneca suggests that

> there has developed over the years the need for more flexible criteria in determining the relationship between the meaning and reference of terms ... According to Wittgenstein, one word can have a 'family of meanings'. The application of one word to different objects ... is possible because the referents to which the word applies

49 Travis, *The Uses of Sense*, 285.

50 Mary Hesse, 'Theories, Family Resemblance and Analogy', in David H. Helman (ed.), *Analogical Reasoning* (Dortrecht: Kluwer, 1988), 317–40: 323.

> share certain properties … which 'criss-cross and overlap' like the physiognomic characteristics of a family … Wittgenstein explicitly points out that we are not to look for some common element among the members of a class designated by a general terms, but rather that in considering the meaning of a word such as 'game' we are to consider its use.[51]

That is, for many, if not all, words meaning is a function of use. Seneca suggests that Wittgenstein is here primarily concerned with general terms – that is, 'terms whose meaning cannot be exhausted by a single ostensive definition'.[52]

Hesse considers that family resemblance operates in a clustering way: 'although species are not discrete, and do not form a unique system with definite boundaries, it must be presupposed that there is some clustering of objects and properties in the world, so that not every combination has equal probability of occurrence'.[53] Elsewhere she suggests that 'Members of a class … are loosely grouped by relations of similarity and difference into fuzzy, overlapping, and temporarily defined classes whose boundaries change with experience and cultural convention'.[54] This, as Hesse says, is 'a model that goes "horizontally" from particulars to particulars'. Objects or properties are more likely to be related if they are similar and they are more likely to be related in ways which are already familiar rather than in ways which are unfamiliar. This is hardly surprising. Its significance for metaphor is that the novel metaphor, which does not depend on previous recognised similarity for its aptness, is really going against the grain of more-of-the-same which appears to characterise the way we think.[55]

51 Clara Seneca, 'Family Resemblance and Partial Interpretation', in Leinfellner et al., *Wittgenstein and his Impact*, 277ff: 277 (Wittgenstein, *Philosophical Investigations*, ##66, 71.)

52 Ibid. 278.

53 Hesse, 'Theories, Family Resemblance and Analogy', 324.

54 Mary Hesse, 'Texts without Types and Lumps without Laws', *New Literary History* 17 (1985–6), 31ff: 38.

55 It must be remembered that concepts, and hence metaphors, are not private but are the product of social interaction in forms of life. (See ibid. 10.)

Lakoff and Johnson take a 'cognitive cluster theory' approach to metaphor. In so doing they also typify a particular trend in metaphorical theories to use a phenomenological paradigm.[56] Lakoff and Johnson see basic human experience (to which they see concepts as reducible) as perceived by us in clusters or gestalts, which, while stable, have fuzzy boundaries. There are simple gestalts and there are complex gestalts, 'multidimensional structured wholes' which are structured in terms of other, simpler, gestalts. 'These are metaphorically structured concepts'. However, they concede that our experiences are structured in turn by our concepts and that we understand one concept in terms of another – the more abstract and complex being understood in terms of the more concrete and simple.[57]

The idea of metaphor as a gestalt, a natural prototype of a category, or a 'fuzzy' schema for concept formation,[58] may be related to the Wittgensteinian notion of 'seeing as' as the basis for metaphorising. For the comprehension of the unfamiliar, abstract or complex in terms of the familiar, concrete or simple, prototypes are 'borrowed' from the latter to use as 'explainers' or describers of the former. Here a prototype is a model or picture (proposition as instructions for making a model) that we look

56 To reiterate, on a Wittgensteinian view, the use of phenomenological terms to explain a linguistic or partially linguistic entity such as metaphor or metaphorising is circular. The paradigm itself is a compound metaphor or analogy, relying as it does on physical object-language.

57 Lakoff and Johnson, *Metaphors We Live By*, 71–2, 77, 81–5, 112–15. Mac Cormac points out that the conceptual system of Lakoff and Johnson requires 'a direct bodily interaction with the physical environment'. The physical is primary, prior to the cultural (although they interact). Spatial concepts are used as a primary example of the 'direct emergence' of concepts from physical experience. It is not clear how one is to delineate the spatial without recourse to cultural input. 'Does the language possess an implicit intuitive knowledge of the directness and nonmetaphorical character of spatial concepts?' (Mac Cormac, *A Cognitive Theology of Metaphor*, 66–8.) It can scarcely be denied that spatial concepts are also metaphorical and vary from culture to culture.

58 Lakoff and Johnson, *Metaphors We Live By*, 73. For this theory Lakoff and Johnston are endebted to Rosche and Mervis, 'Family Resemblances Studies in the Internal Structure of Categories.' *Cognitive Psychology* 7 (1975), 573ff.

through or understand through.[59] As such it is a proposition, therefore I cannot agree with Ross and equate gestalts with language-games. Playing a language-game involves the learning and accepting of propositions but this does not mean that language-games are no more nor less than propositions. The particular type of proposition or quasi-proposition, which is the gestalt or prototype, arises from the language-game of 'seeing as'. It may be defined in terms of the physicalist paradigm as a predicated compound property some of whose parts (aspects) fit the subject (are exemplified by S) and some of whose parts/aspects do not fit.

This view may be related to Lakoff and Johnson's understanding of metaphor as emphasising some aspects of experience at the expense of others. In the metaphoric subject-predicate relation each serves as prototype for the other and highlights some aspects of the other.[60] Schemas become prototypes when transferred to a new context; while at the same time the new context itself acts as a schematic prototype. But the extent of symmetry is affected by the degree of abstractness, vagueness, familiarity of the subject. At the concrete, precise, familiar end of the continuum, subject and predicate are alike in these respects; at the other the metaphorical predication performs a catachrestic function for a perhaps almost completely unknown (previously unconceived and undescribed) subject.[61]

59 See Black, *Models and Metaphors*, 44ff.

60 In a related way, Pylyshyn understands metaphor as the way our mental world comes to terms with our experiences via the 'adaptive equilibrium' between two processes which Piaget calls 'assimilation' and 'accommodation'. '"Assimilation" refers to the process by which the environment is made cognitively accessible by incorporating some of its effects into relatively stable intellectual systems called "schemata". Accommodation, on the other hand, refers to the slower but no less systematic and persistent manner in which the schemata themselves change in response to the demand of the environment.' (Pylyshyn, 'Metaphorical Imprecision', 420–1.)

61 'The process of comprehension is identical to the process of selecting and verifying conceptual schemata to account for the situation (including its linguistic elements) to be understood' (where a schema is an 'abstract representation of a generalised concept or situation'). Therefore individual sentences are understood in terms of general schemata – that is, meaning is constructed from the 'top down' rather than

Uses of terms (including metaphorical uses) in naming or categorising seem plausibly related according to the principle of family resemblance. The way in which clustering of terms within a family resemblance set occurs according to nearness or similarity of use sorts metaphorical uses of language according to position on a conventional (close) – unconventional (distant) continuum and creates a 'fuzzy' outer boundary. It is nevertheless the process or language-game of metaphorising which, in the first place, effects the transfer of terms from one situation of use to another. Therefore, a family resemblance theory of metaphor (as, for instance, put forward by Hausman) has to take account of metaphorising as the construal of family resemblance. Merely to place metaphor within the category of family resemblance uses (as Hausman does[62]) is to subsume it within uses of general terms. This hardly allows it to be the unique entity it is. Again, this demonstrates the importance of a language-game ontology.

Perhaps the most valuable insight shared by both family resemblance and gestalt/cluster theories, best expressed by those theories which combine these models, is the realisation that reality is not comprehended in an atomistic 'building-block' way; instead the whole (gestalt or language-game) gives meaning to its parts.[63] Here, however, the language-game, being diachronic and partially independent of cognition offers a model which is not only more basic but also more comprehensive in explanatory power than the gestalt model. At this point, it is useful to remember that one of the implications of taking language-games to be epistemically

---

from the 'bottom up'. The parts are understood with reference to the whole. (Ibid. 85.)

62 Hausman, *Metaphor and Art*, 79–81. See also Douglas Berggren, 'The Use and Abuse of Metaphor', Parts I & II, *The Review of Metaphysics* 16, 237–58, 450–72.

63 This insight is consistent with Ricoeur's understanding of metaphor as pointing to a presently transcendent level of intelligibility– a 'higher code of pertinence'– a term coined by Jean Cohen in his *Structure du Langage Poetique* (Paris: Flammarion, 1966); Ricoeur, *The Rule of Metaphor*, 150f. See also Polanyi's similar concept of 'higher organising principle' in his *The Tacit Dimension*, Chapter 2: Emergence. I discuss these in my article, Sue Patterson, 'Gratuitous Truth: Metaphor and Revelation', *Colloquium* 23/3 (1991), 29–43. This present study picks up the issue again in Chapter 4 of Part Four.

basic is the exclusion of phenomenology from that position. Experience as received by an individual's sensory apparatus is not comprehensible in itself (hence self-authenticating) but depends on social consensual (rule-governed) practices. This perspective renders inadequate purely 'cognitive' (and hence individualistic) theories of metaphor which fail to see human perceiving and conceiving as constrained by activities in a social milieu. Thus a Wittgensteinian view must take 'environment' as talked about by cognitive psychologists to include the social milieu of forms of life.

While these gestalt, clustering and family resemblance models might seem to go some of the way toward explaining *how* transfer is effected, their explanations of *why* and *where* (aptness) appear limited to explanations of similarity and are therefore not explanations at all. It is not the elements that vehicle and topic have in *common* which add to knowledge, but the *combination of dissimilars*. If convention and similarity arguments are seen to fail, it is still not known why the metaphorical elements are combined in the way they are: it is still not possible to know if the combination expresses a true proposition. Is the metaphorical combination of dissimilars a filtering through of new practices and therefore the articulation of new language-world links? Or is it instead the initiator of an arbitrary new 'rule' which may or may not constrain us to adopt new understandings of language-world? According to Gillett, 'There is always the possibility of going wrong in a perceptual judgment or of introducing an item into one's conceptual structure in a tentative and perhaps even experimental way. Thus there are intentional objects which are vague, mistakenly identified, or which even turn out not to exist.'[64] These judgments are verifiable only by the language-games which are the language-world link for the form of life in question which enable us to 'call to mind' the criteria with which to judge a metaphorical utterance. The criteria may not be satisfied, in which case the would-be metaphor is deemed not to make sense. This judgment process is intuitive and incorrigible as it relies on normative practice rather than verbal prescriptions.

64 Gillett, *Representation, Meaning and Thought*, 21.

Thus the truth of a metaphor is a function of its fit with reality as mediated by the language-games practised in our forms of life. Again, it is the language-game which provides the verification of the (metaphorical) proposition. Yet the same language-game which verifies a new metaphor (as a new language-game move) may be itself a new language-game. How is this new language-game 'verified'? Whether our particular normative version of reality is in itself veridical is another question, the same question that was posed at the conclusion of Part One. The problem begins to smell of an infinite regress. 'What is' seems to persistently confound what the theories pronounce must or should be. But why should one expect to be able to formulate a complete, consistent and watertight theory of language, even by successive approximations? Must a sort of anti-realist relativism be settled for, or is there yet another alternative?

2.3.4. The Limits of Explanation

I have argued that metaphorising demonstrates that there is more to reality than we can conceive of at any given moment. Since our primary contact with reality is in our activities, where there is an interweaving and association of linguistic and nonlinguistic contact in language-world, it is there that new discoveries about the nature of reality are made and find their way to articulation. As the new lacks a terminology it is forced to borrow from the familiar, hence metaphors are born. As Jaakko Hintikka notes, 'In the last analysis we don't really understand a system of semantical relations between a language and the world before we understand the language-games in which these semantical relations consist and which link our language with our actual experience.'[65]

65 Jaakko Hintikka: 'Response to Robert Kraut', 'Replies and Comments', Radu J. Bogdan (ed.), *Profiles 8: Jaakko Hintikka* (Dortrecht: D Reidel, 1987): 341.

However, an explanation is also demanded of how this birth of metaphors might happen. While Gillett questions Kant's notion of 'blind imagination' or 'intuition' as an explanation, doubting whether this notion of 'productive imagination' can have any meaning,[66] on the other hand, Ricoeur endorses it. For Ricoeur, imagination is 'insight into likeness'.[67]

> The tension between sameness and difference characterises the logical structure of likeness. Imagination, accordingly, is this ability to produce new kinds by assimilation and to produce them not above the difference, as in the concept, but in spite of and through the differences. Imagination is this stage in the production of genres when generic kinship has not reached the level of conceptual peace and rest but remains caught in the war between distance and proximity ... In that sense we may speak with Gadamer of the fundamental metaphoricity of thought to the extent that the figure of speech that we call 'metaphor' allows us a glance at the general procedure by which we produce concepts. This is because in the metaphoric process the movement towards the genus is arrested by the resistance of the difference ...[68]

I concur with Hintikka that the human facility to convert new experience to speech simply cannot be explained. It is a given, and as such is consistent with a number of hypotheses of greater or lesser adequacy.[69] Metaphorising may be the mechanism of givenness but cannot itself explain it. The argument has come back to:

66 Gillett, *Representation, Meaning and Thought*, 181. '[T]he difficulty arising from the mind's role in generating experience is made acute when Kant contends "[S]ynthesis in general, as we shall hereafter see, is the mere result of the power of imagination, a blind but indispensible function of the soul, without which we should have no knowledge whatsoever but of which we are scarcely conscious" [Kant, B103] ... The imagination is the faculty which provides schemata by which our perception incorporates rules which determine perceptual types.' [Ibid. B179–80.]

67 Ricoeur, 'Metaphorical Process', 145.

68 Ibid. 146–7.

69 For instance, a 'Skinnerian' theory of metaphorical combination as entirely explained by learned associations through contiguity in the memory (the 'Premack Principle' – see D. Premack, 'Toward Empirical Behaviour Laws. I: Positive Reinforcement', *Psychological Review* 66 (1959), 219–33) for another option which may explain subjective aptness parsimoniously but still cannot explain or verify the incremental function of metaphor.

> [3] … *A purely extralinguistic reality (and the accompanying notion of absolute truth) is either a meaningless concept or inaccessible by definition unless 'given' within the epistemic foundation. Hence any conception of ontology is contingent on the epistemic foundation* …[70]

As I concluded in Part One, here philosophy ends and theology begins. This issue will accordingly be revisited in Part Four.

2.3.5. Summary and Conclusion to Part Two

I have suggested that metaphorising is a secondary language-game which involves the use of familiar terms unconventionally. As a process, it could be said to begin with the discovery or invention at tacit human activity level of a new language-world link. Yet, the basicality of language-games (with the priority of pragmatics over semantics) means that it is a change in the primary perceptive language-games such as 'seeing as' which effects a change in the use (and hence meaning) of terms. This change has been argued to be in the nature of a transfer and combination of trainings in the use of words to effect a gain in knowledge.

As this gain occurs through the novel re-patterning of conventional knowledge, metaphorising (which, it must be remembered, is more than the production of figures of speech and includes model formation and catachresis) initiates the development of new concepts from changes to the moves in language-games. This means that, at any given time, the totality of meaning is not subsumable by the currently existing conceptual framework.

If metaphors thus effect an increment in meaning, the question which remains is: whence comes this increment in meaning? I begin to address this issue in Part Three.

70 See Summary, Part One, Chapter 2, 47–8.

PART THREE

Metaphorising and Logic

CHAPTER ONE

Metaphorising, Actuality and Possibility

3.1.1. Introduction

In this chapter I review the previous discussion on language-games and metaphorising from a different perspective: the metaphysics of possibility and actuality. The aim is to expand the language-game ontology to take account of the dynamic, diachronic[1] nature of the metaphorising language-game.

In Parts One and Two I argued that language-games, are epistemically basic and that the language-game of metaphorising, in creating new moves in language-games, effects an increment to knowledge. 'Knowledge' was defined broadly as including 'knowing how' as well as 'knowing that' because, according to a Wittgensteinian perspective, propositions are inseparable from the rule-governed activities in which they are moves. While the process of metaphorising was found to be explained more or less well by various theories and the appropriateness and veridicality of metaphors were seen, from a Wittgensteinian viewpoint, to be relative to the language games which constitute given forms of life, no adequate explanation appears to have been advanced for the ultimate aptness and/or truth of these creations. For both Wittgenstein and Kant, such ultimate or absolute verification is inaccessible because human knowledge is subsumed by human forms of life – the local circularities or spirals of experience and concept, of 'knowing-how' and 'knowing-that'.

Yet it may be shown that these circles are not self-contained but depend on input from outside. Here 'knowledge' receives the added definition of

1 In the Saussurean sense of being (like *parole*) an event occurring over time.

cognisance of actuality. New knowledge as a product of such an expansion of actuality must come as a 'given' and as such it may be termed a revelation. If language-games are basic and yet the metaphorising language-game creates new moves in language-games, then the actuality of the complex of language-games at a given time cannot be basic. Metaphorising expands actuality.

3.1.2. Expanding the Actual

In his examination and critique of Aristotle's views on actuality and possibility, Jüngel considers that Aristotle inherited a 'metaphysical blunder' from Parmenides: namely that 'to think is to be'. This limits being to what is conceivable: the conceivable thus sets the boundary for actuality. The effect of this is to exclude from actuality the category of unconceived possibilities which includes possible novel metaphors.[2] Aristotle, working on this assumption, advances his 'metaphysical first principle': 'actuality is prior to potentiality'.[3] That is, 'the possible is defined as the possible by reference to the actual'. This sets up a paradox: while the possible exists only within the actual, the possible is not actual. Aristotle denies existence to the merely possible which does not 'exist in fulfilment' and considers that the ontological priority of the actual is not contradicted by the temporal priority of the possible (as the source of the actual).[4] The ontological presumption that the possible is contingent on the actual is thus deeply rooted in Aristotle. It will be seen that this presumption is built into some contemporary actualist theories of modality.

2 Jüngel, 'The World as Actuality and Possibility', *Theological Essays*, 95–123; 97.
3 Aristotle, *Metaphysics. The Complete Works of Aristotle*, 2 Vols: Book 1A, J. Barnes (ed.) (Princeton: Princeton University Press, 1984) 1049: 665; ibid. 98.
4 Ibid. 1047b 1f, 1049b 21; Jüngel, 'The World as Actuality and Possibility', 98–9.

3.1.3. Possible and Actual Worlds[5]

Plantinga's views on possible worlds are characteristic in this respect.[6] As the term has come to be conventionally used (for the most part), possible worlds are states of affairs which may or may not be actual. According to Plantinga, possible worlds must be 'maximal' or complete and may not be logically or naturally impossible.[7] Only one possible world obtains: the actual world. Objects and properties exist in possible worlds and objects have properties in possible worlds. While '[t]here are any number of merely possible worlds', 'each of them exists and exists moreover in the actual world, although none is actual'.[8]

This means that no merely possible world is in fact actual, but (confusingly) each possible world is actual at or in itself, How then can it be said that the actual world is the actual world? As Plantinga says, it just is. The actual world is actually actual and the other possible worlds are actually non-actual (the terminological convolutions are, I suggest, the main difficulty with possible worlds).[9] Every possible world, therefore, contains

5 The term 'world' used in this context is more or less synonymous with 'scenario'. References to 'possible worlds' or 'actual worlds' in this section and elsewhere are not to be taken to be references to physical (extralinguistic) worlds as separate from language.

6 Alvin Plantinga, *The Nature of Necessity* (New York: Oxford University Press, 1974). The idea of possible worlds originated with Leibniz.

7 These are challengeable assumptions (see below). Plantinga himself concedes this regarding the completeness requirement (personal communication, August 1991).

8 According to Plantinga, '[e]ach maximal possible set of propositions is the book on some world; the book on the actual world is the set of true propositions' [can we distinguish between states of affairs and propositions?] The set of 'world-books' remains the same for all possible worlds; 'what varies is the answer to the question which book contains only true propositions. But in the same way each world exists in each world ... Obtaining or actuality for states of affairs is like truth for propositions (they can be false but not nonexistent)'. (Plantinga, *The Nature of Necessity*, 47–8.)

9 Ibid. 46–9.

every other possible world in a dual sense. 'Each world W exists in each world W'' in that if W' had been actual, W would have existed.'[10]

According to Plantinga, while there are possible things that do not exist, there are no possible states of affairs or propositions that do not exist. Actuality must not be confused with existence, nor non-actuality or falsity with non-existence. A possible state of affairs or proposition does exist even though it happens not to be actual; that is, false propositions do exist 'but a possible object that does not exist is a horse of a different colour'[11] – one does not have to adopt an ontology of nonfactual objects to accept the possible worlds framework. Therefore one can simultaneously be a 'strict actualist' in identifying possible worlds only with actually existing objects and their properties[12] while allowing the existence of non-actuals apart from objects (these non-actuals here identified with constructions out of actually existing objects, that is, conceived possibilities actual or otherwise regarding these objects). It will be noted that, in order to accommodate this theory, 'actual' as a category has had to be expanded and a new category 'exemplification' put in the place of the usual application of the term 'actual'. Existence is able to be equated with possibility, but not *tout court*, because when it comes to objects, it is actuality that is equated with

10 Ibid. 55.

11 Ibid. 131–2. Elsewhere Plantinga quotes Russell: 'Being belongs ... to everything that can possibly occur in any proposition, true or false and to all such propositions themselves. Being belongs to whatever can be counted ... Thus being is a general attribute of everything, and to mention anything is to show that it is'. (Bertrand Russell, *Principles of Mathematics* (Michigan: University Press, 1903), 449; ibid. 134.) Plantinga adds: 'There is a critical difference between saying "there are things that do not exist" and saying "there are truths of the form 'A does not exist' – 'Pegasus does not exist, for example'" ... There are other areas where we make true assertions by using sentences that, taken strictly ... express what is false: "He's not himself today"'. [Alvin Plantinga, 'Self-Profile', *Profiles 5: Alvin Plantinga*, James E. Tomberlin and Peter van Inwagen (eds), (Dortrecht: D. Reidel, 1985) 31–2.]

12 Plantinga maintains that if something does not exist it cannot exemplify any properties – non-existence is not a property. This is the doctrine of serious actualism. (Ibid. 92.)

existence.[13] The existence of the unactual is, therefore, limited to states of affairs, some of which obtain (are actual), and some of which do not.

Plantinga's theory is in danger of being less than elegant in that he finds it necessary to make an exception of objects. This is required because for Plantinga objects (or 'substance') are primitive. Axiomatic to his theory is the idea that in essence actuality consists of actually existing objects. The non-actual can be only 'constructions out of' (can only exist within our conceptions of) these actual objects. I have already mentioned the shortcomings of such an ontology and will do so again. It is enough to note here that that adoption of a language-game ontology ousts objects from their privileged position as would-be monopolisers of reality and shows the problem of non-actual objects to be a spurious one.[14] For Wittgenstein, worlds, whether actual or merely possible, are always language-worlds.[15]

There is, however, another problem with Plantinga's understanding of possibility. Loux observes that Plantinga (and also Stalnaker[16]) are not only 'modal actualists', but, moreover, *de re* modal actualists. This means that they 'take as primitive modal entities and a modal property of those entities. That is, they take states of affairs or properties to be basic or irreducible, and hence unexplainable.'[17] Likewise, for Robert Adams[18] (who takes propositions to be basic), the system of possible worlds is a part of the actual world. While 'Soft Actualism' (which is Adams's position) holds that there are non-actual possible worlds, these are 'logically constructed out of the furniture of the actual world ... [therefore] the soft actualist is

13 See also Michael J. Loux, 'Introduction', in Michael J. Loux (ed.), *The Possible and the Actual: Readings in the Metaphysics of Modality* (Ithaca: Cornell University Press, 1979), 48. This situation gets more complicated when a Kantian conceptual realism or a Wittgensteinian language-game ontology is involved – how might these actual objects be separated from our conceptions of them?

14 In that an inextricable interweaving of language and world, objects and activities involving objects does not allow a separation of hypothetical object from hypothetical scenario.

15 But not, of course, in the sense of worlds constituted entirely by language.

16 Robert Stalnaker, 'Possible Worlds', in Loux, *The Possible and the Actual*, 225–34.

17 Loux, 'Introduction', ibid. 49.

18 Robert Adams, 'Theories of Actuality', in ibid. 190–209.

committed, as the hard actualist is not, to ascribe to the actual world furniture which is rich enough for the logical construction of a plurality of completely determinate [as per Plantinga] possible worlds'.[19]

I suggest that the main difficulty with modal actualism (apart from its terminology) lies in its tenure of a sort of conceptual positivism. If all possibilities exist in the actual world, is this actuality the actuality we conceive or an actuality which is transcendent of our conceiving? If the unactualised possibilities exist, can unconceived unactualised possibilities exist? (And if so, how?) Modal actualism cannot entertain such a notion because, under such a (conceptual) actualism, unconceived possibilities are taken to be impossibilities. Where logic (or modality) is held to be primitive, it is logic as presently conceived. If knowledge is limited to conceptual knowledge, it follows that unconceived possibilities are excluded from actuality.

While Wittgenstein's diachronic view of reality implicitly includes possibility within actuality (what is 'given', our 'forms of life',[20] being diachronic collections of activities or events in which possibility is continually yielding to actuality), such possibilities are not restricted to what concepts are able to suggest but are born of practice. If new possibilities arise out of new language-world linking activities, they are both (initially) transcendent of existing concepts and transcendent of the antecedent actuality of language-world. They are, as Jüngel says, a gain to actuality. This gain is eventually a gain to our conceptual framework of hitherto unconceived possibilities. The point has already been made that such a gain to actuality (as both practised and conceived) is made through metaphorising.

In the face of this argument, the Aristotelian conception of actuality (which may now be seen to be also Plantinga's) does not allow that the world may contain nothingness. It equates possibility with the 'not-yet of an actuality to come' therefore only distinguishes between the actual and the not-yet-actual. Any possibility beyond this has no substance.[21] Jüngel sees it as important that we 'dismantle the primacy of actuality' for theo-

19 Ibid. 200–3.

20 Wittgenstein, *Philosophical Investigations*, 226e.

21 Jüngel, 'The World as Possibility and Actuality', 104–10.

logical (Christological) reasons. It is also important that actuality be seen *logically* to be nonbasic. Yet the unseating of actuality from pride of place exposes a paradox, the metaphorical paradox. While possibility is shown by metaphorising to *subsume* actuality, possibility can only be asserted (and thereafter conceived) within actuality.

This assertion (or the judging of the truth of the assertion) requires that the possible be accurately distinguished from the impossible, a distinction which, as has been noted, is unverifiable from within actuality without resorting to a sort of conceptual positivism. Nevertheless the claim which this assertion constitutes is a claim of a possible (albeit unrecognised as such) state of affairs to be actual, the granting of which extends the borders of actuality. '[A] *space for freedom* is made in actuality in which that which is possible can arise.'[22] As possibility can only be asserted, the distinction between the possible and impossible cannot be humanly verified. Therefore, when in metaphorising a hitherto unconceived possibility is asserted as actual, what is asserted cannot at this point be understood as possible but must initially be seen as *impossible*. This point will be taken up again in Chapter 2 of Part Three.

3.1.4. Metaphorising and Possibility

In his essay, 'Metaphorical Truth,' Jüngel is concerned with the relationship between metaphor and possibility. Actuality (which contains possibility yet at the same time transcends actuality) is continually expanding as it incorporates unknown (humanly unconceived) possibilities by means of metaphorising. As noted, such possibilities cannot be humanly distinguished from impossibilities. Likewise, an absolute actuality which lies

22 Ibid. 119–20.

beyond human conceiving cannot be distinguished from non-actuality.[23] Traditionally, utterances which go beyond actuality (such as metaphor) have not been understood as having truth-conditions (as being propositional) because of the time-honoured correspondence of truth and actuality. 'The ancient world ... asserted the correspondence of being and concept' therefore nothing conceptual (meaningful) can be added to actuality; metaphor may only affect the effectiveness or persuasiveness of a statement.[24] Metaphorising, however, demonstrates empirically that what is actual at one time is not the same as what is actual at another (and, moreover, that not all knowledge is conceptual knowledge). If metaphors succeed, it is because they 'really bring to speech that which is'. Yet 'that which is' is more than actuality at time *t*, and thus expands actuality (expands the 'horizon of being'). The correspondence of the metaphorical statement to that which is the discovery of a wider actuality (or the comprehension of a wider actuality) constitutes 'a gain to being', therefore 'a gain to knowledge'.[25] Thus Jüngel acknowledges (although in not so many words) the pragmatical function of metaphorising as constituting its semantics.

It is now possible to attempt a description of how metaphorising effects a gain to actuality. A novel metaphor may be experienced as a kind of 'schizoid' entity which inhabits two possible language-worlds simultaneously: the current actuality within which it does not fit (but seems to be claiming to fit) and the seemingly impossible but dawningly possible actuality within which it may fit in a manner still to be determined. This dilemma must be resolved in favour of one world or the other: either the metaphorised product is accepted as expressing a true proposition (albeit as yet inconceivable) in the actual world, or it is rejected as expressing a false or nonsensical proposition. Its acceptance as true in the actual world thus

23 If language is universal medium, the totality of language exceeds our comprehension: our knowledge stops at the linguistic limits of our comprehension – it cannot be contained by our comprehension.

24 Jüngel, 'Metaphorical Truth', 24–5.

25 Ibid. 41.

means that the actual world has changed: it has expanded to incorporate a previous mere possibility (or even impossibility) as actual.[26]

In the light of this argument, it may be helpful to consider Levin's suggestion that it is not logically necessary to regard semantics as fixed.[27] According to Levin, there is the option of either construing the utterance so that it makes sense in the world, or construing the world so that it makes sense of the utterance. To preserve meaning as fixed (as Searle does[28]) is to require the world to change. There are, therefore, as Levin points out, two logics of metaphoric construal. There is the standard one in which the metaphoric utterance is seen as deviant, construed as another (literal) utterance, and then 'mapped onto' the actual world. And there is the converse approach in which the metaphoric utterance is taken literally and 'mapped onto' a possible world. The possible word is then construed in terms of the actual world. 'The result of the construal process, in both cases, is an interpretation – of the language in the first case, of a world in the second'. If the second logic is followed, 'the poet is a creator and the poem a world',[29] not that this logic is restricted to literary metaphorisings. Nor does it need to rule out metaphor's role in discovery. It can also be a discovery that the metaphorised possible world exists in the actual world.

However, Lakoff and Johnson's criticism of model-theoretic approaches to truth must be borne in mind. These approaches tend to suggest that 'world states' can be defined to fit any situation because such models do not take account of human understanding. Yet truth cannot be independent of this factor. Such semantics relies on an objectivity which simply is not there;

26 'If an author says that x is y, when we know in fact that x is not y, we must try to imagine a world in which x is y. This act of imagination is facilitated if, in the real world, x is like y in some respects, for then we can take their similarities as the author's grounds for saying that x is y. That is, 'the reader must imagine a world in which the metaphor, however incongruous it may seem, is true'. (Miller, 'Images and Models', 247.)

27 Levin's perspective is useful in spite of his isomorphic-tending (while critical) realism because it at least up-ends traditional entrenched ways of seeing the language-world relation.

28 Searle, 'Metaphor', 92–123.

29 Levin, 'Standard Approaches to Metaphor', 131–3.

meaning is a function of use by different people in different situations.[30] A pragmatical theory which explains the intersection of language-games and possible worlds could address these objections. In a way consistent with such an approach, Morgan, sees metaphor as requiring such a broader pragmatic context. For Morgan, metaphor

> is not a property of the sentence, but a matter of what one does in saying the sentence ... The hearer does not just carry out some operation on the semantics of the sentence; he must picture what the world would be like if the sentence were true, or he could never know that I do not mean to be taken literally. Then he must figure out what the world would be like to lead me to make such an outrageously false assertion. He constructs a picture of the world that is as close as relevantly and sensibly possible to the world that corresponds to the literal meaning of the sentence.[31]

I have already made a case for the inseparability of semantics from their pragmatic context. This is now underlined. To imagine a different world is to imagine different semantics – when the language-game changes, so do the meanings of words. Here individual sentences are understood in terms of their part in, or connection with, a particular whole scenario.[32] When a novel metaphor or model is encountered, schemata are assessed ('activated, evaluated and refined or discarded') in the search for coherence. Terms are employed in sets of alternatives. Here a schema as (according to Goodman) 'an implicit set of alternatives' is a possible scenario.[33] Goodman, in positing multiple actual worlds to account for true but conflicting statements,[34] makes the fundamental point that 'worlds seem to depend on conflict for their existence'.[35]

30 Lakoff and Johnston, *Metaphors We Live By*, 182–3.

31 Jerry L. Morgan, 'Observations on the Pragmatics of Metaphor', in Ortony, *Metaphor and Thought*, 136ff.; 140–1.

32 As has been noted in Part Two, this 'top-down' model of comprehension is the insight that language-game and gestalt theories have in common.

33 Goodman, *Languages of Art*, 73.

34 Nelson Goodman, *Ways of Worldmaking* (Sussex: Harvester Press, 1978), 110.

35 Ibid. 119.

The metaphorising language-game develops the schematic partial-fit into a new ('refined' or expanded and, to begin with, hypothetical) schema through establishing a new language-world link. That is, metaphorising creates new possible (language-) worlds. This is consistent with Richard Boyd's contention that 'general terms ... should typically be understood referentially, that general terms can refer even though they do not possess unrevisable conventional definitions, and ... that tokens of a term employed in different contexts ... within different paradigms, or in different 'possible worlds' may be co-referential, even though they are not associated with equivalent conventional definitions.[36]

In this way, new metaphors are signs of the entry of a hitherto unconceived possible world into actuality. Their violation of actuality is at the same time an extending of actuality – or the sign of the extending of actuality to incorporate more of actuality than can presently be comprehended. They are, in the language of scientific research (such as factor analysis or multidimensional scaling), the 'noise' in the system which is the sign of the existence of another, presently inaccessible, factor or dimension. At any one time, the signs of actuality's incompleteness are visible in the incongruence of new metaphorisings. This incongruence is experienced as a new language-game move which generates a new proposition which does not fit the size and shape of present actuality. From a Wittgensteinian viewpoint, it must be emphasised, such gains to actuality are not gains to *either* world *or* language, but to both: to language-world. Metaphorising is not simply a linguistic phenomenon but lets 'that-which-is' come to speech.[37]

36 Richard Boyd, 'Metaphor and Theory Change: What is "Metaphor" a Metaphor for?' Ortony, *Metaphor and Thought*, 356–408: 374–5.

37 Pylyshyn has the insight that metaphor can 'provide a way to introduce terminology for features of the world whose existence seems probable but many of whose fundamental properties have yet to be discovered'. Terms may or may not be precise but vary greatly in how tightly they are slotted into coherent systems – e.g. schemata and propositions are tightly constrained, whereas images, prototypes, analogues are not. Productive (more than superficial) metaphors do not provide a comfortable resting place, but point beyond themselves. (Pylyshyn, 'Metaphorical Imprecision', 429, 432.)

Hausman suggests that metaphorising 'articulates, "this is that which is not that and this which is new"'.[38] What is new may only be discovered within what is not – that is, through the interruptions to what is: namely, the present conceptual framework. Therefore, metaphorising advances intelligibility (as known actuality) beyond its level prior to the metaphor. Hausman sees that, accordingly, '[c]reative metaphors take a fundamental responsibility for language as a whole, making language responsible to something independent of itself, at least as it is construed at the moment of creation'.[39] This is consistent with Jüngel's insight that metaphors are articulated discoveries which as such relate to previous discoveries. What is discovered (or better, invented) are new language-worlds. A Jüngelian view of metaphorising as the agent of revelation means that a metaphor in proclaiming a new language-world requires the actual language-world as humanly conceivable to change. As Jüngel points out, Luther's insistence in taking 'is' literally could be said to:

> affirm the ontological relevance of metaphorical speech, in that through it a new context of being is disclosed grounded in a gain to language. The new metaphorical use of a word gives the word a new meaning and this new meaning brings new being to speech ... metaphor profits from the possible non-being of the world as we conceive of it [actuality as a conceptual entity (as conceived) is subsumed by actuality; new knowledge of actuality may refute parts of antecedently conceived actuality], in that it suspends it ... in order newly to bring to speech the being of the world. This is of course only possible since new being is only expressible in parables of the old.[40]

38 Hausman, *Metaphor and Art*, 72.

39 Ibid. 85.

40 Martin Luther, 'Confession Concerning Christ's Supper', *Luther's Works*, American Ed., 55 vols, Jaroslav Pelikan and Helmut T. Lehman (eds), (Philadelphia: Muehlenberg and Fortress, and St. Louis: Concordia, 1955–1986), vol. 37, 172ff., cited by Jüngel, 'Metaphorical Truth', *Theological Essays*, 51.

3.1.5. Summary and Conclusion

I have argued that gains to language must come from outside of language via a new language-world link which is a new move in a language-game. This gain is, therefore, ineffable. If, as Jüngel says, metaphorising confronts us with a reality which is not merely actuality as we can conceive it,[41] how do our conceptions of actuality change? They change through changes in language-games and the forms of life they constitute or represent. As has been seen, language-games themselves change through the transfer and addition of moves which may involve the combination or superimposition of other language-games, this transferring and combining activity itself being a language-game: the game which I have called metaphorising. As our concepts change with the addition of new 'metaphorised' entities, our conception of actuality changes and hence our access to actuality changes and grows, old concepts not so much being discarded as added to or recombined through metaphorising.

I have argued that if a metaphor 'profits from the possible non-being of the world as we conceive of it', it expresses not a conceived possibility as actuality but claims an unconceived possibility to be actual. Might metaphorising in addition bring into being not only a hitherto unconceived) world but also an inconceivably possible world: to human logic an 'impossible possible world'? If this were the case, metaphorising would demonstrate that logic and modality cannot be taken as primitive, and would suggest that a Wittgensteinian approach may be the only tenable way of developing a theory of possibility. This suggestion will be taken up in Chapter 2 of Part Three.

41 Ibid. 52.

CHAPTER TWO

Metaphorised Worlds

3.2.1. Impossible Small World-Pieces

I have argued that a Wittgensteinian theory of possible worlds (scenarios) may well be the most coherent option available. However, does a language-game ontology indeed permit the use of a possible worlds model set? Judith Genova explores this issue in her paper 'Philosophy and the Consideration of Other-Worldly Possibilities'.[1]

Genova notes that Wittgenstein himself (ironically considering his expressed doubt about the validity of such speculation) often asks us to 'imagine a form of life'. Wittgenstein is constantly imagining language-games, 'And to imagine a language-game means to imagine a form of life'.[2] Genova considers that Wittgenstein distrusts theoretical formulations because they shift the focus from what we do to what we might do, yet such formulations are a 'necessary evil' because without the consideration of alternatives it is hard to see what is actual or discover the limits of that actuality. Therefore Wittgenstein's intention in employing hypothetical examples is to contrast them with what obtains in actuality, to draw attention to perhaps unnoticed aspects of the way things really are. 'Instead of "imaginability" one can also say here: representability by a particular method of representation. And such a representation may indeed safely

1 Judith Genova, 'Philosophy and the Consideration of Other-Worldly Possibilities', Leinfellner et al., *Wittgenstein and his Impact*, 398ff.

2 Ibid. 399 (quoting Wittgenstein, *Philosophical Investigations*, #19).

point a way to further use of a sentence. On the other hand a picture may obtrude itself upon us and be of no use at all.'[3]

As Wittgenstein is dismissive of the possibility of formal semantic models, it is not surprising that he appears to neglect considerations of possibility and actuality with respect to language-games. However, while Wittgenstein's express concern is with actuality, a language-game ontology describes a diachronic actuality in which possibilities are continually becoming actualities. Wittgenstein's objection to semantic models may be countered on the grounds that such models need not pretend to be complete or other than heuristic, and, moreover, that such models need not require logic to take a transcendent position over language.[4]

Jaakko Hintikka notes that in the concept of a model set, the models 'are only partial descriptions of possible worlds. They need only be large enough to show that the possible world in question really is possible'.

> Many other important features of first-order languages can … be put into perspective from the vantage-point of the model set technique. For instance, the unsolvability of first-order logic means that you cannot (recursively) predict how far the attempted countermodal construction (what is not true in a possible world] has to be carried out in order to uncover any hidden inconsistencies that may lurk in the counter-assumption, or even find any recursive function which would give an upper bound to the length of the countermodal construction (as a function of the Gödel number of the given sentence) … [T]his fact of a logician's professional life provides an answer to Wittgenstein, who disparaged such metalogical results as the undecidability of first-order logic as being merely formal theorems in another calculus. What Wittgenstein failed to see is that undecidability is a very real feature of those calculatory practices whose importance he was emphasising.[5]

The partial nature of semantic worlds (or scenarios, as Jaakko Hintikka prefers to call them) is caught up with their multiplicity: 'meaning concepts

3 Ibid. Wittgenstein, *Philosophical Investigations*, #397.

4 And, noting that so-called semantic models do not (in spite of their pretensions) manage to explain the language-world link at all, are such models, even when expanded to include pragmatic functions of language, any more capable of explaining the language-world connection than language-games?

5 Hintikka, '"Self-Profile" Jaakko Hintikka', 12–14.

involve essentially and deeply a multiplicity of possible worlds'.[6] Multiplicity precludes comprehensiveness or large-scale-ness. Possible worlds can accordingly 'be quite short histories of quite a small part of the universe'.[7] Travis, in commenting that Wittgenstein 'has the intuition that, in some way, the present semantics of an item leaves its "future application" – so at least some of its evaluative semantic properties – open',[8] is in effect pointing out the compatibility of a Wittgensteinian understanding of language with a particular type of possible worlds model, the open-ended 'small' world. The intimate relation of meaning to use in possible worlds which necessitates their multiplicity and partialness is also noted by Saarinen: '[W]hen discussing sentences ... the reference of [a] singular term ... in the actual world is not all that counts. The reference of this singular term in other possible worlds also has to be taken into account ... [T]he idea is that in intensional contexts a singular term as it were has a multiple reference, for in the different possible worlds it may refer to different objects.'[9]

It is not that a Wittgensteinian perspective rules out the possibility of possible world model sets, but that it serves to reform conventional thinking in this area. From a Wittgensteinian viewpoint, if we regard forms of life as 'small worlds' (or scenarios) we may logically regard possible forms of life thus as possible 'small worlds'.[10] Jaakko Hintikka, unlike Plantinga, does not require a possible world to be maximal: he does not even require it to be conventionally possible. The term 'world' must not be taken at its face value. 'A possible world need not be possible in the traditional sense ...

6 Jaakko Hintikka, 'Degrees and Dimensions of Intentionality', in Leinfellner et al., *Wittgenstein and his Impact*, 69ff: 70.

7 Hintikka, 'Semantics: a Revolt against Frege', 63–4.

8 'The application of a word is not everywhere bounded by rules', 'the extension of the concept is not closed by a frontier'. (Wittgenstein, *Philosophical Investigations*, ##84, 68.) 'We think that the meaning of "chair" is fixed somehow by its past use. But why should we be biased in favour of that particular time and direction?' Therefore we cannot determine the semantics of "chair" now; it is not determined yet for its determination depends also on future uses'. (Travis, *The Uses of Sense*, 15–16.)

9 Esa Saarinen, 'Quantifying in and on Trans-World Identity', Bogdan, *Profiles 8: Jaakko Hintikka*, 91ff: 92–3.

10 Ibid.

Even more conspicuously, a possible world … need not be a world, that is, an entire universe or world history. It can be an alternative state of affairs of a small fragment of "the world" or an alternative sequence of events during a relatively short span of time in some small nook or corner of the universe. ('Scenarios' might have been a better term) …'[11] According to Hintikka, '[p]ossible worlds are best thought of as being determined by the associated possible totalities of experience'.[12] This suggests that one certainly might take the language-game complexes which constitute forms of life as the basic components of possible worlds. Wittgensteinian complexes of 'forms of life' arguably fit this description in appearing to define a totality of existence for certain people in a certain time and place – actual activities plus their multifarious accompaniments and consequences. Possible worlds in the shape of forms of life may be viewed as complexes of language-games. As such they are diachronic rather than synchronic entities.[13] Language-games and scenarios may, however, also be viewed as orthogonal. The activities create the scenarios (states of affairs or forms of life) and thus bring them into existence ('Imagine/enact a form of life in which …'). Possible scenarios are on this account particular conceivable contextually-conditioned instances of activities or complexes of activities. 'Impossible' possible scenarios are, by the same token, previously inconceivable possible forms of life, inconceivable (naturally or logically) because they have no exemplars, because they lie outside the present (or past) patterns of language-world.

Where Plantinga as a modal realist takes modality as primitive and thus subsuming of all possible worlds, Hintikka does not. If language-games are basic, practice is prior to logical constructions. If forms of life are taken as constituting a model set of worlds, this model set must subsume the

11 Hintikka, 'Self-Profile', 24–5. Hintikka, like Wittgenstein, is deeply suspicious of any claims to completeness (of particular worlds or a set of worlds as a whole). 'Model sets are, intuitively speaking, partial descriptions of possible worlds which utilize potentially unlimited resources of description'. (Ibid. 14.)

12 Hintikka, 'Degrees and Dimensions of Intentionality', 77.

13 Again, these terms are used in the Saussurean sense of temporal/dynamic and atemporal/static networks respectively.

logical categories of possibility and necessity.[14] Genova also sees that, on a Wittgensteinian view, the creation of a new possible world may involve the creation of a new logic.

> [W]hen we imagine something, we must also imagine the method of representation in which it could make sense [the poet, scientist or theologian considers possible candidates for metaphor or model, accepts some and rejects others] … that aspect of thinking which we call imagining and which is essential for language is still linked to the possibility of projecting our thought in a method [model] of representation. This seems to be a necessary condition, if not a sufficient one, for thinking to make sense.[15]

Therefore, 'even logic can be otherwise … provided one varies the form of life sufficiently to accommodate them. Thus Wittgenstein's belief that only a matter of degree separates an empirical truth from a logical one enables him to establish a hierarchy of other-worldly possibilities ranging from the conception of other logics to the mere contradiction of contingent facts'.[16]

This view of logic is made possible by a language-game ontology which (as chapter one concluded) views relations as prior to individuals. Such a view would be inconceivable for a world-model which took objects

14 '[T]he farther away from the actual world we have to venture in order to spell out the semantics of a concept, the more intentional the concept is … This distance we can interpret as the dissimilarity of the worlds in question, the actual world and its alternatives. The most radical way in which a possible world can differ from the actual world is in the failure of some logical laws.' (Hintikka, 'Degrees and Dimensions of Intentionality', 72–3.)

15 Genova, 'Philosophy and the Consideration of Other-Worldly Possibilities', 399. '"So does it depend wholly on our grammar what will be called (logically) possible and what not – i.e. what the grammar permits?" – But surely that is arbitrary! – Is it arbitrary? It is not every sentence-like formation that we know how to do something with, not every technique has a use in our life: and when we are temped in philosophy to count some quite useless thing as a proposition, that is often because we have not considered its use sufficiently'. (See Wittgenstein, *Philosophical Investigations*, #520.)

16 Ibid., 399–401. 'The rules of grammar are arbitrary in the sense that the rules of a game are arbitrary. We can make them differently. But then it's a different game'. (*Wittgenstein's Lectures, Cambridge, 1930–32*, from the notes of John King and Desmond Lee, ed. Desmond Lee (Oxford: Blackwell, 1980), 57; quoted in ibid. 235–6.)

as primitive. Accordingly, Lycan considers that the great virtue of using propositions as constituents of possible worlds (as does Adams) is that 'it makes room for impossible worlds as well as possible ones'. Lycan makes the point that things have to exist before they can be false, therefore false propositions include contradictory or impossible propositions.[17] However, proposition-worlds will lack the diachronic nature of forms-of-life worlds unless one takes a Wittgensteinian view of propositions as incorporating the language-games which are their verification.

These writers lend support to Jüngel's argument that there is more to possibility than what is conceived as potential actuality. As has been noted, in the first instance, possibility is to be distinguished from impossibility.[18] It is here that being is distinguished from nothingness. Thus both actuality and possibility can be seen to be 'factors in being'. Possibility is the coming of being out of nonexistence: it 'lets being become ... The world's possibility is not within actuality but external to its actuality and external to its futurity [always transcendent]'. It is 'actuality's ultimate concern'. Therefore, possibility as limited to human conceivability does not capture the fullness of possibility.

How, then, does a Jüngelian and Wittgensteinian understanding of possible worlds take account of metaphorising? When one makes a model or metaphor or interprets an utterance as metaphorical, one appears to

17 William Lycan, 'The Trouble with Possible Worlds', in Loux, *The Possible and the Actual*, 274–316; 313–15.

18 Jüngel, 'The World as Possibility and Actuality', 116–17. Jüngel takes up the subject of actuality and possibility again in 'Metaphorical Truth'. Actuality as conceived or experienced at a given time is incomplete because it is only actual at that time: present actuality is transcended by possibility. 'Intrinsic to our notion of actuality, it seems, is the fact that [what presently obtains] accepts itself as only a limited measure of that which is. Actuality is not the sum total of being; it represents being only in time ... [T]he possibility of an actual state of affairs is more than its actuality. In the dimension of possibility, the being of an actual state of affairs encounters possibilities which, although they are not themselves actualised, still belong to the being of that actual state of affairs. Part of the process of understanding actuality is discovering what would and would not count as such possibilities'. (Ibid. 16–17.)

choose from a number of possible worlds.[19] Yet this choice of possibilities is more apparent than real because these worlds are inconceivable possible (or impossible) worlds. That is, there are possible states of affairs and propositions which are conceivable as possible, but metaphors do not come into this category – metaphorising brings the inconceivable possible into actuality.[20] Without a notion of possible world in which logic is allowed to vary with worlds, metaphorical propositions which involve logical contradictions would be false in all possible worlds. In this way, as the previous chapter concluded, metaphorising may be seen to call into question the universality of actual human conceptions of logic as well as actual facts.[21]

Thus metaphorising makes it difficult to dismiss the idea that possible worlds may, by conventional logic, be impossible worlds. The limits of model-set theory are reached in the questioning of its holding of presently

19 This selection is to begin with a provisional one. Where metaphorising is the inventor of 'impossible possible worlds', metaphorical propositions and their entailments are possible (but inconceivable as such) worlds until such time as they are accepted as true and thus actual. However, this acceptance is provisional pending acceptance by the metaphor's judges, the community of hearers and potential users.

20 To see metaphor as (merely) a hitherto inconceivable part of actuality is to see the metaphorical proposition as separate from the language-game move which it incorporates. Granted, metaphor's entry into actuality is in the first instance into a hitherto unconceived actuality of the language-game basis of our knowledge. However, this is not a temporal first instance because the move in the language-game and the metaphorical proposition which it includes, being inseparable, are born simultaneously. Once the language-game move is actual, the proposition expressed by the metaphor is true. A statement which expresses a false proposition cannot be a metaphor. In metaphorising, it is our conception of what can be true, not the reality of what is true, which changes.

21 It would be conventional but incorrect to call this position non-Leibnizian. It would be conventional in that so-called Leibnizian world-models take modality as primitive. However, Leibniz himself located the origin of this modality in the mind of God (I would prefer to locate it in the relating activity of God – see Part Four Chapters 3 and 4). Therefore, as Jüngel maintains, the decision as to what is possible or impossible is not a human one and, accordingly, logic as absolute is not humanly accessible. What is available to us are relative logics which will vary with human uses of language in various forms of life.

conceivable necessary truths to be universally necessary truths. Jüngel takes a classically Leibnizian position in holding that God alone can distinguish between the possible and the impossible. Such a judgment is not a human prerogative. To say that some state of affairs or proposition obtains or is true at an 'impossible possible world' is to admit that in the final analysis we are unable to determine what is possible and impossible – that these matters transcend our understanding. Is there, then, a particular type of 'world' model which would take account of the peculiar characteristics of metaphorising as seen from a Jüngelian and language-game perspective?[22]

3.2.2. An (Almost) Classically Leibnizian and Combinatorialist World

The model which first springs to mind is some form of combinatorialism. Metaphorising recombines what is actual to create a new actuality. Combinatorialism takes a set of entities of some sort to be the basic building blocks which are rearranged to constitute various possible worlds. At second glance this option may seem problematic. In a recent exposition of a form of modal combinatorialism, D. M. Armstrong describes non-modal combinatorialists as 'actual-world chauvinists' because of their insistence that 'the possible is determined by the actual, and so, saving recombination, cannot outrun the actual.'[23] Certainly 'traditional' non-modal combinatorialism (as exemplified by Cresswell[24]) takes the hardline actualist view that 'possible worlds other than the actual world may be construed only as

22 When talking about model sets in this context, it is interesting to remember that (as I maintained in Part Two) models are conceptual developments of metaphors.

23 D. M. Armstrong, *A Combinatorial Theory of Possibility* (Cambridge: Cambridge University Press, 1989), 56.

24 M. J. Cresswell, 'The World Is Everything That Is the Case', in Loux, *The Possible and the Actual*, 129–45.

alternative combinations of entities populating the actual world'.[25] As all possibilities are limited to recombinations of what already exists, it seems no new entities can come into being.[26] However, I suggest that recombination changes the nature of what is combined and brings about an addition to actuality. This would appear to indicate a sort of modal combinatorialism.

This indeed is what Armstrong suggests. Armstrong wants to retain the virtues of combinatorialism while rejecting its actualist positivism. Why, he asks, can we not allow inconceivable or alien possibilities? 'Confusion between what is really possible, and what is merely conceived to be possible (i.e. what is doxastically possible), a confusion still rife in our philosophical thinking, may then be appealed to as explaining, in part at least, the strength of the intuition in favour of the possibility of alien universals.'[27] It is worth noting that Armstrong is here in effect conceding that the decision as to what is really possible cannot be humanly made.

A more fundamental drawback of combinatorialism for the present argument is its atomism. How are we to separate a language-world which is an inextricable interweaving of activities, words and objects into discrete entities? Conversely, how essential to combinatorialism is the premise of atomism? If such a premise were not essential (and I suggest that this is arguable), a theory such as Armstrong's which accommodates impossible (humanly inconceivable) worlds could be compatible with a Wittgensteinian view of metaphorising. Metaphorising demonstrates that the combination and recombination of non-atomic entities is possible. It is possible for basic combinatory building blocks to be understood as non-atomic without such an understanding being a contradiction in terms. According to Wittgenstein, the nature of reality is an inextricably

25 Lycan also sees the problem inherent in non-modal combinatorialism of accounting for an increase in actuality, but apart from this thinks that the adequacy of combinatorialist theories depends on the choice of atoms. The choice of atoms constrains possible states of affairs – there may be more basic 'stuff'. (Lycan, 'The Trouble with Possible Worlds', 305.)

26 Michael J. Loux, 'Introduction: Modality and Metaphysics', in Loux, *The Possible and the Actual*, 15–64; 60.

27 Armstrong, *A Combinatorial Theory of Possibility*, 56–7.

interwoven complex of objects, activities and signs; any pulling away of a part to a new arrangement would be the pulling away of a piece of complex entity. As such, it does not 'come clean' as a discrete piece, but leaves trailing 'threads' (like soft toffee) which keep it attached to its previous context while attaching itself onto its new surroundings and becoming inseparable there also. This 'dragging' and recombining epitomises the activity of metaphorising. Thus, if we take language-games as building blocks, these, in their inextricable overlapping and interwoven-ness, would be non-atomic entities, and in their various hypothesised alternative relations or combinations would constitute possible forms-of-life worlds.

While metaphorising, as an apperceptive production of the unfamiliar within the rearrangement of the familiar, would certainly seem to suggest some species of combinatorialism, at the same time, metaphorising's incompatibility with a view of reality which takes logical necessity as foundational suggests that a modified Leibnizian theory (preserving the Leibnizian divine role in bringing to actuality humanly inconceivable *possibilia* without the Leibnizian absolutising of actual logic) might be not merely consistent with but necessary to a Wittgensteinian account of metaphorising. This suggestion is essentially programmatic and requires further development. I agree with Loux that much hard work is still needed in this area.[28]

3.2.3. Metaphorising, Possibility and Truth

It may be seen that metaphorising provides evidence for a reality beyond human conceiving, which, while unverifiable, is not meaningless unless meaning is taken to be the monopoly of human conceptualising. Our intuitions regarding the truth of the products of our metaphorising indicate that truth as such must indeed encompass possibility, but a possibility which is

28 Loux, 'Introduction: Modality and Metaphysics', 64.

not subsumable within human conceptions of actuality, and hence also not subsumable within human conceptions of possibility. Truth transcends our conception of actuality. The sort of possibility to which metaphor gives actuality is, by our conception, impossibility. Metaphorical truth makes conceivable the inconceivable and thus gives birth to new concepts. Hence, 'Metaphors in language preserve the movement of being into language by continuing this movement within language and expanding both our language and our relation to being. They participate in truth by leading the actual beyond its (presently conceived) actuality without asserting anything false about it ... So metaphor does say more than is actual, and yet precisely in so doing it is true'.[29]

However, are intuitions to be trusted? How is it to be known that the more-than-actuality of metaphor is the truth? Says Jüngel, 'All sophistry trades on this ambivalence'.[30] While, as has been seen, metaphorising may be said, in bringing a new language-game into being, to fix a new reference or reveal a new referent, on the surface metaphors appear instead to involve false propositions.[31] As has been noted, a metaphor may in the first instance, before its acceptance as containing a true proposition in the actual world, constitute or create a possible world in that it presents us with a literally false proposition which will remain false if it cannot be construed metaphorically. Therefore it seems reasonable to see the products of metaphorising as expressing hypothetical propositions which are true at a possible (non-actual) world.

Yet, as has been emphasised, it is of the nature of metaphor to claim an ('impossible') equation of dissimilars. At the same time, a metaphor is an at least implicit, if not explicit, predication that has no qualification suggesting hypotheticality. Something is predicated of a state of affairs which is claimed by the metaphorical assertion to obtain in the actual world. In this sense the metaphorical process 'selects' a proposition from the (infinite)

29 Jüngel, 'Metaphorical Truth', 56–7.

30 Ibid.

31 As Davidson points out. (See Donald Davidson, 'What Metaphors Mean', in Sacks, *On Metaphor*, 29–45: 31, 39.)

set of possible proposition-worlds (or forms-of-life worlds) which are not actual, even conceivable. The metaphor takes from this possible proposition its linguistic expression (the sentence or utterance expressing it) in order to express a novel true proposition in the actual world. This proposition would otherwise be inarticulable through the lack, because of its novelty, of its own linguistic 'hardware'. Here then is a borrowed linguistic articulation – seemingly, because borrowed, of a false proposition – being employed to express a new truth about a new reality. If the metaphor's claim to being the truth about actuality is accepted by the hearer, the metaphor is accepted as metaphor, as the statement of a true metaphorical proposition rather than as merely a statement of a false proposition.

In other words, if a metaphor is accepted as actually (as opposed to hypothetically) veridical, its possible world is accepted as actual. Therefore its predication becomes the predication of a no longer merely hypothetical but actual property. Such is the human desire for coherence and comprehensibility that both metaphorical subject and predicate undergo modification of meaning under pressure of the claim to actuality. While the incongruity of the claim to actuality continues, paradoxically, to suggest the falseness of this claim, giving the metaphor its characteristic tension, eventually all traces of hypotheticality – that is, existence at a merely possible world – may be lost and the metaphor become fully 'resident' in the actual world. Then the metaphor may be said to have 'died' as a metaphor. As has been seen, before its acceptance as a metaphor a metaphorical statement (taken literally at its linguistic face-value) may not be true in any conceivable (naturally or logically) possible world: it may be necessarily, not just contingently, false. If its claim to express a true proposition (that is, to exist in the actual world) is not upheld by its hearers' finding it meaningful, it may simply be false or meaningless in all conceivable possible worlds. As some true propositions representing actual states of affairs are not articulable as sentences expressing literal uses of terms, insofar as a metaphor is accepted as expressing a true proposition it belongs to the actual world. A case can thus be made for including non-literal expressions within the actual world. Metaphors, once accepted as such, do not depict merely possible (or impossible) worlds. Upon recognition or endorsement of their aptness (expression of a true proposition) metaphors cease to be hypotheses and become novel facts.[32]

While the complex of language-games is self-authenticating, metaphorising has been seen to show its incompleteness. For all this, the question is still posed: what verifies the additions to actuality which are at odds with actuality? Even when metaphors become accepted as concepts, these are arguably only an aspect-view of reality which has become conventional. This view necessarily excludes other, incompatible or inconsistent, aspects. Thus the success of a metaphor or model which leads to its own death (acceptance as 'literal' truth) is no guarantee of the truth – or at any rate of more than the local or partial truth – of what it claims. As the metaphor is a move in a language-game, it is part of an irreducible self-authenticating unit within a form of life.

It must be concluded that a Jüngelian theory of modality requires an absolute truth which is transcendent of human forms of life and thus only tenable theistically: 'the language of faith does not allow [our conception of] actuality to dictate what it has to say to us about actuality ... This does not mean that actuality is passed over or missed. Rather, it is enhanced. But this has consequences for actuality ...' Possibility, and hence a wider than presently conceivable actuality, enters our known actuality, our world, and confronts it with 'the possibility of its non-being, from which alone new being can arise'.[33]

32 A metaphorical sentence may express a true proposition with a predication (actual or implied) borrowed from the expression of another proposition. This cannot make its own unique proposition partially true or false; instead it upholds the truth of this proposition while simultaneously implying or alluding to (bringing to our minds) the other (borrowed from) proposition.

33 Jüngel, 'Metaphorical Truth', 66–7.

3.2.4. The Consequences of Diachronic Worlds

It is in keeping with a diachronic Wittgensteinian (as opposed to a semantic synchronic) view that the reality beyond known actuality be seen to be more than actuality at a given moment. The language-game of metaphorising operates diachronically to bring what is diachronic (the model or metaphor) into a present actuality conceived as synchronic. As the reality beyond presently conceived actuality comprises both conceivable and inconceivable possibilities, metaphorising is a bringing of the inconceivable within the conceivable and also a bringing of the possible within the actual. The wider reality beyond known actuality may thus (in being both metaphor and language-game) be seen to be both linguistic and nonlinguistic: there is no warrant for a scheme-content dualism in which conceptual (hence linguistic) organisation of experiential input is added on arrival.[34] The given includes the proposition or concept which organises the experience as well as the experience itself. If our complexes of language-games (forms of life) are given, truth and reality are integrated in this givenness. The language-game of metaphorising in which the metaphorical proposition is a move combines in its revealing function other propositions and their language-games.

Wittgenstein's diachronic view of reality means that his given 'forms of life' are diachronic complexes of language-games in which possibility is continually yielding to actuality. Furthermore, a language-game ontology means that such diachronicity entails that 'knowing-how' (or skill-type knowledge) is epistemically basic. In bringing new moves in language-games into being, metaphorising demonstrates empirically that new knowledge is the incorporation within actuality (through recombination) of previously inconceivable possibilities. This may be seen as a double or two-stage gain to actuality: to actuality first as practised, second as conceived. A language-game ontology entails that, first, possibility subsumes human

34 See Donald Davidson, 'On the Very Idea of a Conceptual Scheme', *Inquiries into Truth and Interpretation* (London: Oxford University Press, 1984).

conceptions of what is possible (in being beyond both human experience and human conceptions of that experience); second, inconceivable possibility becomes actual through metaphorising (where knowledge of that actuality is both 'knowing-how' experience of actuality and 'knowing-that' conception of actuality).

Moreover, if language-games are basic, relation (as language-world linking which includes language-language linking) is basic. As I suggested in Part Two, if the metaphorical new relation in effect creates or reveals a new reality, then being is constituted in relation rather than in 'substance'. Therefore it is not the individual which is primordial but relation. However, if the diachronic nature of a language-game based ontology is sustained by metaphorising, then it is not so much relation itself as the becoming of relation (the coming into being of new relation) which is basic. It may be seen that this entailment leads straight to theological considerations.

3.2.5. Summary and Conclusion to Part Three

I have argued for metaphorising's role as the creation of a new (hitherto unconceived, or even inconceivable, hence 'impossible') possible world. The discovery of this possibility to obtain in the actual world is a further stage which entails the acceptance of the possible world of the metaphorical proposition as actual, on the basis of fittingness to a form of life which has been modified by the addition of new language-game moves (as opposed to the direct-realist criterion of fittingness to an extra-conceptual reality). Metaphorising accordingly changes and extends actuality by hypothesising possible partial scenarios ('small' forms-of-life worlds), which are then (if the metaphor or model is accepted as apt or true) accepted as actual. This constitutes a repatterning which is revelatory of a new actuality beyond the actuality antecedently known. When language-games change so do forms of life. Language-world links change through a change in the pattern of language-world interaction, showing that relation, *a fortiori* the coming into being of relation, is prior to the substance or content of that relation, of reality. But whence comes the new pattern?

After all this it appears that the regress has merely been pushed a stage further. Granted that metaphorising is both the sign of the incompleteness of known actuality and the agent of known actuality's increase and is therefore itself transcendent of known actuality, whence comes the relation-creating transcendence of which metaphorising is both agent and part? If metaphorising shows that givenness does not rest with language-games and forms of life but with a further 'given' which is constitutive of these, is an infinite regress inevitable? I suggest that the only way to avoid such a regress lies in theology. Therefore this debate concludes not here but with Part Four.

The argument so far may be stated as follows:

1. If language-games are basic yet metaphorising is a primordial language-game, then the actuality of the complex of language-games as conceivable at any given time is not basic and the actual (facts or states of affairs known to obtain at any given time and place) may be seen to be less than reality. Therefore the language-game subsumes actuality through metaphorising.

2. If metaphorising is the language-game which creates or reveals new moves in language-games (hence brings into being new knowledge in a broad sense of the term), then metaphorising extends actuality and effects a continuing gain to language-world. In metaphorising the unconceived or even inconceivable possible reveals itself as actual in a new relation within actuality. As hitherto inconceivable possibility, the metaphor claims to be actual but appears to be impossible, forcing old logic and categories to give way to a new coherence and relation. The impossible, in utilising the raw material of antecedent actuality, claims a new, wider actuality at the expense of the old.

It follows that:

3. A Wittgensteinian perspective on metaphorising and possible worlds, requiring as it does the construal of possible worlds as forms-of-life to be small, partial and transient, is consistent with a Jüngelian view of metaphorising. Such a perspective allows that the impossible – that is, inconceivable – properties or states of affairs predicated by metaphors may be veridical or actual.

4. The interwoven nature of language-games and their moves does not permit the recombination effected by metaphorising to be atomistic. Combinatorial models succeed in capturing the nature of the metaphorical process only when their atomism is abandoned. The relata are not discrete entities. This captures Gestalt Psychology's 'top-down' insight, identified in Part Two, that the whole determines the meaning of the parts. The relata are inseparable from the relation (it was noted in Part One that Peirce shares this insight with Wittgenstein.

5. Metaphorising provides evidence that a reality beyond human conceiving, while unverifiable, is not meaningless. While the complex of language-games is self-authenticating, metaphorising shows its incompleteness. This is a 'bootstraps' situation where acceptance confers acceptability. What verifies the additions to actuality which are at odds with actuality?

6. If the metaphorised new relation in effect creates or reveals a new aspect of reality, it follows that it is not substance that is primary but relation. Moreover, if the diachronic nature of a language-game based ontology is sustained by metaphorising, then it is not relation itself so much as the becoming of relation which is basic.

PART FOUR

Language-Games, Metaphorising and God

CHAPTER ONE

Metaphorising and Revelation

4.1.1. Shifting the Paradigm

So far, the argument has been presented in terms of a linguistic-philosophical paradigm. However, it could be argued that its conclusion is a theological one by any other name – that this argument cannot be complete without a theological conclusion and that the purportedly 'plain-wraps' metaphysical conclusion is an implicitly theological one.[1] My purpose in this chapter is to make this implicit theological conclusion explicit. The argument will, therefore, make a paradigm shift: it will now be stated in theological (as well as philosophical) terms and its theological implications examined.

First, as has been seen, the basicality of language-games means that metaphors are moves in language-games and cannot therefore be considered apart from those games. As the language-game is inseparable from its (linguistic or other) moves, metaphor cannot be simply a linguistic entity (nor a model entirely nonlinguistic). What applies to language in general must apply to theological language. Theological language cannot be separated from its language-games. Moreover, what applies to metaphorical language in particular also applies to theological language.

1 Dummett also considers that the coherence of realism requires a theistic conclusion: 'The realist is challenged to explain how an assertion is capable of being true or false when the evidence for or against it is, in principle, unavailable – at least by tacit implication, to *us* ... for the realist view to prevail, the existence of a supra-temporal perspective on the world is covertly admitted.' (Dummett, *Truth and Other Enigmas*, 'Introduction' xxxix; see also the discussion in Kerr, *Theology After Wittgenstein*, 128.)

4.1.2. Fitting the Shape of God

> *It is in practice impossible to separate that which is to be represented from previous representations: the model, map or metaphor is a representation of a reality which is an inextricable mix of new extra-conceptual information with antecedent representations and concepts.* [2.1.4.]

Soskice and Gunton have both made a case for the rationality of theology's obvious dependence on metaphor.[2] Both these theologians see metaphor's ability to convey the truth (firstly about the world, secondly about God) as crucial to the credibility of theology. In her book, *Metaphor and Religious Language*, Soskice is accordingly concerned to demonstrate that religious metaphors, like scientific ones, are able to effect an increment to knowledge, to provide access to a transcendent reality. In establishing her working definition of metaphor Soskice is careful to cover three main points: metaphor's anchoring in language, its public nature, and its paradoxicality and open-endedness (in going beyond the words present).[3]

Soskice, like Jüngel, is concerned to show how an understanding of metaphor as more than mere ornament, substitute, comparison or vague emotive agent has been blocked by the traditional insistence on a distinction between literal and non-literal uses in which only the literal uses correspond to a truth fixed antecedently to the object which the words describe. Soskice begins with scientific metaphors. There have been two main misconceptions of the function of metaphor in science: metaphor has been seen, first, as a helpful but superfluous illustration; second, purely as

2 As has Sallie McFague in her *Metaphorical Theology: Models of God in Religious Language* (London: S.C.M. Press, 1983).

3 For Soskice, metaphor is 'that figure of speech whereby we speak of one thing in terms which are seen to be suggestive of another'. (Soskice, *Metaphor and Religious Language*, 15.) Metaphor is inherently linguistic, but while its definition is primarily a matter of form rather than of function, this form is a logical, not a syntactical one because as a unit it is defined semantically rather than syntactically. See Part Two Chapter 1.

a device for plugging gaps in terminology (catachresis). While metaphors may serve this latter function, an incremental theory of metaphor is, contends Soskice, the only coherent option for science. However, a scientific theory, in suggesting a new hypothesis about the world, is using familiar terms to talk about unknown (or partially known) things or relationships. As a 'speaking of one thing in terms suggestive of another', theories are by definition metaphorical.[4] Therefore, metaphors and models in science, as well as everywhere else, are extenders of knowledge, the agents of discovery.

From Soskice's critical realist perspective, the provisional access provided by metaphors makes further questions possible. Models and metaphors can generate 'existential hypotheses' which suggest the existence of other things and show us where to look for them. Knowledge is continually revised by 'successive approximations'; exactness is not possible because reality cannot correspond exactly to our concepts. In seeking to establish metaphor's veracity or credibility, therefore, Soskice is concerned with the (revisable) correspondence of the content of metaphorical terms to 'the world that is the case'. For Soskice, metaphors are not only 'reality depicting' and hence indispensable to both science and a traditional (that is, realist) theology; they are also the only way we can speak of God because (like theoretical terms in science) metaphor makes a provisional reference revisable by human experience, individual and communal. Metaphor thus becomes the only possible form of religious language.

Soskice tends to limit her investigation of metaphor to semantical considerations. As was discussed in Part One, she adopts Wittgenstein's understanding of propositions as pictures and defines metaphorical propositions thus as depictions of reality. Yet she does not appear to acknowledge these 'depictions' (as the later Wittgenstein does) as moves or rules in language-games.[5] Language for the later Wittgenstein is not a self-contained system

4 Likewise, as showings of one thing in terms suggestive of another, demonstrations of scientific principles cannot fail to be models. A theory which is entirely abstract, stateable entirely in mathematical terms, can say nothing new about the world.

5 In the absence of such a spelling out of the inseparability of language and truth-conditions from rule-governed, language-involving activities, there is the suggestion

separate from physical reality; it is a component in the reality with which we engage by means of our activities.

While this unqualified 'depiction' or representation model may appear to work quite well in science when dealing with things whose properties are partially known, the construal of an isomorphism between language and the nonlinguistic world it assumes and entails cannot provide the direct reference it promises. The concept of such an isomorphism is itself the product of a language-game. As Kerr notes, we are up too close to our language-games to notice the connecting role they play between the words and objects in our lives.[6] This failure to notice may be troublesome in theology. Critical realism's removal of the stipulation of exactness does not in turn remove the requirement of verification, but without a recognition of the referring function of language-games, where else is there to go but to fall back on the idea of a direct correspondence? As I have sought to demonstrate, Wittgenstein's main contribution to the literal-metaphorical debate is to demonstrate that no reference is direct: all of our knowledge of reality depends upon language-games.

That is the first difficulty. The second is that some sort of verification is required of the aptness of words to the reality in question. If this 'verification' is very vague, so to speak; if it amounts to such statements as: 'whatever it is that is out there, or, whatever is the cause of this experience, is God', can this vagueness about the properties of the divine referent be construed as epistemic imprecision? Does it count as knowledge (however imprecise) to know our referent simply as the causer of what is epistemically accessible to us: that is, human experience? This line of argument begs the question: what then is the relation of religious experience to the source of that experience?

---

that Soskice is inhabiting a *Tractarian* world which in effect severs linguistic from nonlinguistic reality. (See Wittgenstein, *Tractatus.*)

6 'The aspects of things that are most important for us are hidden because of their simplicity and familiarity. (One is unable to notice something – because it is always before one's eyes.) The real foundations of his enquiry do not strike a man at all'. (Wittgenstein, *Philosophical Investigations* #129; Kerr, *Theology After Wittgenstein*, 118–19.)

Soskice's case for theological metaphorical truth, carefully constructed though it is, disappoints in its apparent conclusion that the veracity of theological metaphors depends upon analogy. Implicitly at least, Soskice's entire argument depends upon analogy. This is why she constructs her case for scientific metaphorical truth and metaphorical reference before she considers theological metaphors. However, analogy cannot perform the task she requires of it, even with the help of a critical, as opposed to a direct, realism (nor even with a theory of reference based on language-games). If an *analogia entis* were employed, our theological metaphorisings would amount to anthropomorphic projections. However, an *analogia proportionalis* turns out to be equally unsatisfactory in this role; an analogy of relation, as a construal of an isomorphism between the divine and the human, requires the basis of some knowledge of both the divine and the human. If the divine being transcendent is unknowable, no such analogy is possible unless it is either stipulated or given.[7] And whence comes the verification of a mere stipulation?

In his book, *The Actuality of the Atonement*, Gunton supplies a synthesis of the work of Soskice and Jüngel on metaphor and theology. For Gunton, the central issue is that 'metaphor involves the transfer of a word or words from one context to another. It is something done to and with language'. That is, it is a process within language. 'This is what makes metaphor a metaphor'.[8] According to Gunton, metaphor becomes a misuse (as opposed to a use) of language only because it 'offends against rationalist canons of meaning' which require truth to be 'utterly clear and distinct'. By this definition anything less than precise, such as metaphor, simply cannot be truth.[9] This, of course, begs the question of the catachrestical use of

7 I argue below that an 'analogy of proportion' or 'analogy of relation', when applied in theology, must either fail to be an analogy at all or become a Barthian 'analogy of faith.'

8 Colin E. Gunton, *The Actuality of the Atonement: A study of Metaphor, Rationality and the Christian Tradition* (Edinburgh: T. & T. Clark, 1988), 28–9.

9 Ibid. 28–30. Metaphor has been viewed as an abuse of language since Aristotle, although this understanding reached its 'hardline' climax in the Age of Reason.

metaphor, as Jüngel demonstrates.[10] What if there is no 'literal' equivalent to the metaphorical expression? According to this understanding, such uses (so important in science) are meaningless, yet surely this is how new uses of language are born.

Gunton considers that there have been two main approaches to the topic of metaphor in recent philosophy.[11] These two approaches may be distinguished according to their view of the metaphorising process. The first approach (represented by Ingolf Dalferth), holds that the making of the metaphor is necessarily prior to the discovery of new knowledge about the world. We must expand our 'linguistic equipment' to place ourselves in a position to reach a better understanding of the world.[12] At the very least the problem with this approach, as Gunton points out, is that by requiring changes in language to be prior it separates language and discovery. In contrast, the second approach interrelates language and discovery. Boyd argues that metaphors enable us to have 'epistemic access' to the world. The understanding of new facts about the world and new uses of language go hand in hand. Metaphor is therefore part of the process of discovery. Gunton regards this second insight as of extreme importance: 'Language, to speak about the world must become, so to speak, "world-shaped"'. It is language which must change in order to fit the (prior) shape of the world. The implications of this are, first, that imagination is important in science in the selection and transfer of images from one sphere of human experience to another. Imagination is thus integral to our discovery of the truth. Second, this means that our relationship with nature 'consists of an

---

On this view, if a metaphor was not capable of translation into an equivalent literal expression, it could not be considered to be true.

10 Jüngel, 'Metaphorical Truth', 37.

11 'Both hold, in distinction from the old view, that no advance in knowledge of the world is possible without changes in the meaning of words, that is to say, by means of the development of metaphors or other figures of speech'. (Gunton, *Actuality of Atonement*, 30.)

12 Ingolf Dalferth, *Religiose Rede von Gott* (Munchen: Christian Kaiser, 1981), 230–5; in ibid. 30–1.

interaction, a dynamic process, in which language is moulded to reality as different features of the world are revealed with its assistance'.[13]

Gunton goes on to examine more closely this interrelationship of words and things. A linguistic idealism has been inferred by some[14] from Wittgenstein's purported abandonment of his earlier picture theory of language in favour of meaning as use (here referred to out of its language-game context). On this view, all that is humanly available are networks of words and so-called 'discoveries' about the world 'are no more than the imposing of mental constructs upon an essentially unknown world'.[15] However, Gunton suggests that realism is not to be abandoned simply because of the incoherence of naïve realism's view of language as an exact mirror image of world (which itself quickly becomes idealism in the matching of concepts and physical world). We do not have to dispense with the relation of words to things on the basis of the inadequacy of one realist theory. It is possible, Gunton maintains, still to say that there is a correspondence between language and the physical world, albeit a 'partial and provisional' one.[16]

The issue of reference now arises explicitly. As Gunton observes, 'the two enquiries about words and things are so closely intertwined that they cannot be completely abstracted from each other'. At one level words are arbitrary – the particular noise or cipher which happens to denote a thing is usually quite arbitrary in the first instance,[17] but once past this stage there is the question of how, and how successfully, language tells us things about the world. Gunton advances the Wittgenstein-like argument that 'words function ... as part of human interaction with nature. They are ...

13 Boyd, *Metaphor and Theory Change*, 356–408: 358; Gunton, *Actuality of Atonement*, 31–2.

14 Notably Don Cupitt – see, for instance his, *The Sea of Faith* (London: BBC, 1984).

15 Gunton, *Actuality of Atonement*, 33 (see Soskice, *Metaphor and Religious Language*, 103f). While this may appear a feasible alternative to realism given the seeming inaccessibility of the world beyond language, the ultimate endpoint of this argument, as Gunton notes, is Nietzsche's view that the 'irreducibly metaphorical structure' of language means that there can be no truth. (See also Jüngel, 'Metaphorical Truth', 26ff.)

16 Ibid. 33–4.

17 Ibid. On a Jüngelian interpretation, these would be 'absolute metaphors'.

the articulate level of our many-faceted relationship with the world about us, perhaps the highest level of our indwelling of our environment.' Yet Gunton does not go on to describe metaphor's role in this interaction, except to say that it is metaphor's indirectness which makes it 'the most appropriate form that a duly humble and listening language should take'.[18] While he adopts Jüngel's understanding of metaphor as the 'taking place of truth'[19] (concluding with him that 'because the world is, so to speak, our shape and we are world-shaped, there is a readiness of the world for our language, a community of world and person which enables the world to come to speech'[20]), Gunton is silent on the subject of how metaphor enables the 'taking place of truth' to happen.

Having established that 'metaphor is one of the ways, perhaps *the* way in which the world as it exists outside the mind of the observer is discovered and understood', Gunton moves to theology. Disappointingly, it is more to a consideration of metaphor *in* theology than to an exposition of the role of metaphor in bringing the reality of God (as well as the reality of language-world) to speech. Gunton has implied that metaphor is an agent of revelation not only within language as religious imagery but also as the bridge between the explicit language of our concepts and the immanence of God within language-world, but (here at least) he fails to develop this argument. After making a case for the compatibility of realism and metaphor, the topic changes from world-talk to God-talk without any attempt to bridge (at this stage at least) this epistemological gap.[21]

For Gunton, theological (as well as scientific) metaphor is conceived of as a 'dual process of discovery and the development of our language better to speak about its object ... [which is] the very core of reference'.[22]

18 Ibid. 36–7.

19 Jüngel, 'Metaphorical Truth', 56.

20 Gunton, *Actuality of Atonement*, 38.

21 While a study concerned only with language (as distinct from language-world links) has no need to do other than consider types of language, I maintain that the starting point of theology is not within language, but at the meeting-point of language with the reality beyond it – that is, with the coming of God to speech.

22 Gunton, *Actuality of Atonement*, 45; Boyd, *Metaphor and Theory Change*, 398f.

According to Gunton (and Soskice), reference may be made by 'baptism' (Kripke's term[23]) in the first instance, but discovery depends upon some filling in of our knowledge of the entity so baptised. How is this done with respect to God? It is not enough to stipulate as Gunton does that we must have the right metaphor. This merely begs the question: how is the right metaphor to be identified if the properties of the entity to which reference is being made are unknown?

4.1.3. Theological Language-Games

While Soskice and Gunton are concerned to establish a referential function for metaphor in order to justify the use of theological metaphors, for a 'language-game theology' the 'problem of metaphorical reference' is a red herring. If metaphorical utterances are moves in language-games, they cannot be considered apart from those games. What applies to uses of language in general applies to particular, including theological, uses. Yet what is maintained here is that, more fundamentally, ultimately most if not all knowledge, conceptual or otherwise (hence all language and uses of language) owes its existence to the activity of metaphorising understood in a broad sense. Metaphorising reveals reality within the basicality of language-games. In the consideration of theological as well as scientific and literary metaphors, there is no way of avoiding the basicality for human experience (and thus knowledge) of the language-games which constitute

23 Kripke sees reference as stipulative – as 'picking something out of the world'. That is, we need only identify an entity; it is not usually necessary to determine reference via something unique about the referent. Because the reference we make is thereby excused from the need to be cast-iron in its accuracy, it becomes easier to establish the credibility of God-talk. However, once the 'something out there' has been picked out, one is then faced with the task of describing its properties as a bare 'something' (except that the very language used in saying 'something' has already implied certain properties) (Kripke, 'Naming and Necessity', 44).

human forms of life. A consequence, therefore, of a 'language-game theology' is that instances of theological language cannot be separated from the practices involving the use of theological language in which they are moves. New theological metaphors are moves in new theological language-games formed by metaphorising through the transfer and combination of other theological and no theological language-games. Therefore, specifically 'religious' and 'non-religious' practices are involved in this transfer and recombination of games and their moves.

If a metaphor, as a gain to knowledge, constitutes a gain to knowledge-involving activities or practices (knowing how), as well as to concepts (knowing that), then new theological metaphors and models are not simply a gain to theological conceptual knowledge but also a gain to the practice of theology and religion. However, the reality for which theological concepts are vehicles transcends humanly conceivable possibilities because, as the appearance of new metaphors indicates, it includes humanly inconceivable possibilities. A gain to knowledge is a gain to actuality, both conceived and practised, yet reality itself transcends actuality as presently practised and conceived because it includes both practised and unpractised, conceivable and inconceivable possibilities.[24] If metaphorising disrupts existing conceptual patterns, a new theological metaphor or model disrupts existing theological formulations. Metaphorising reshapes doctrines. This is a sign that the reality which theology attempts to be a part of (or more accurately, a participation in which is given), while accessible within language-world, cannot be subsumed within theological formulations. The subject of theology necessarily is greater than theology itself and may not be reduced to it.

Gunton appears to be expressing the same insight when he suggests that, if it is possible that metaphor is created at 'the initiative of that to which the language refers (at least partly)', then this would also apply to theological metaphors. This may be expanded on. God comes to us both

24 Therefore, idealist-tending kinds of theology which rely on conceived possibilities alone are inadequate and cannot explain the appearance of new theological metaphors. Such theologies may purport to take experience as basic, but this is in fact a conception of experience.

as Truth in the language-world connection (as God known tacitly) and as Truth about God in the theological language which arises from the first-order activities and words of the intertwining of language-world. If this initiative does take place, says Gunton, then metaphor 'can have a revelatory function'.[25]

4.1.4. Summary and Conclusion

The foregoing has been an application of my argument concerning the nature of language and language-games in general, and metaphorical language and language-games in particular (theological or otherwise), to specifically theological language and specifically religious practices.

If metaphors are moves in language-games, they cannot be considered apart from those games. What applies to uses of language in general applies to particular, including theological, uses. A consequence, therefore, of a 'language-game theology' is that instances of theological language cannot be separated from the practices involving the use of theological language in which they are moves. If metaphor is a disruption of existing conceptual patterns, a new theological metaphor disrupts existing theological formulations.

However, the application of a 'language-game theology' has far more fundamental consequences than the issue of theological language. If metaphor as a gain to knowledge constitutes a gain to knowledge-involving activities or practices (knowing how) as well as to concepts (knowing that), then new theological metaphors are not simply a gain to theological

25 Gunton, *Actuality of Atonement*, 50–1. As Roger White suggests, we may in fact discover the 'real and primary meaning' of words 'when we understand their use in theology'. (Roger White, 'Notes on Analogical Predication and Speaking about God', B. Hepplethwaite & S. R. Sutherland (eds), *The Philosophical Frontiers of Christian Theology: Essays Presented to D. M. McKinnon* (Cambridge UK: Cambridge University Press, 1982), 197–226.)

conceptual knowledge but also a gain to the practice of theology and religion. The gain to actuality through metaphorising's incorporation within actuality of that which is transcendent of actuality (through that which itself subsumes actuality: the language-game) may be interpreted theologically as revelation.

CHAPTER TWO

Language-Games and Grace

4.2.1. The Metaphysics of a Wittgenstein World

> *'What has to be accepted, the given, is – so one could say – forms of life.'* [1.1.2][1]

As I concluded in the previous chapter, the application of a language-game ontology has far more fundamental consequences for theology than the issue of theological language as such. In this chapter I will argue that a Wittgensteinian ontology is consistent with a theology of grace. Theologians have not generally understood Wittgenstein's work as implying any such thing; linguistic philosophy of a Wittgensteinian brand has been thought not to address metaphysical issues at all. On a Wittgensteinian view, all ontological theories arise out of language-games and forms of life and theological reflections can be said to be dependent on forms of life (Wittgenstein himself refers to theology as 'grammar' – rule-like formulations which conceptualise the language-games constituting a form of life). However, no perspective is exempt from an implied metaphysics. To run with Wittgenstein's own avowed dismissal of metaphysics is possibly to overlook his most important contribution to theology.

As I have suggested, religious experience is prior to religious reflection and is beyond description; it cannot be 'contained' conceptually. Kerr comments that, as might be expected, a Wittgensteinian metaphysic rules out any direct knowledge of God. 'We have no access to the divine independently of our life and language ... we have nothing else to turn to

1 Wittgenstein, *Philosophical Investigations*, 226e.

but the whole complex system of signs which is our human world ... "Our actions/gestures are our meaning, believing, feeling – there is no need to insist that these are states of mind".[2] Therefore, to ask 'what would it be like if there were such a thing as God' is like asking 'what would it be like if colours were to exist?'[3] The experience and concept of God are so intertwined with each other and bound up with forms of life that the question is meaningless.

While this may be the case, by and large theologians and philosophers of religion who have sought to adopt a Wittgensteinian perspective have taken the further step of assuming that such an ontology rules out a metaphysical approach to religion. D. Z. Phillipps, for instance, considers that the impossibility of separating knowledge of God from language about God necessitates the rejection of the possibility or existence of a God beyond language.[4] In his book, *Religion, Truth and Language-Games*, Sherry remarks that to date the application of Wittgenstein's thought to religious issues (especially by the so-called 'Wittgenstein Fideists', Phillipps and Winch) has featured a wrong or an over-simplistic use of the concepts of 'language-game' and 'form of life' as categories within language alone rather than practices which interweave language and the physical world.[5] Then an attempt to identify these entities with categories, such as 'religion' or 'theology' has encouraged a tendency to overestimate their size and underestimate their particularity.[6]

2 Ibid. #589, Kerr, *Theology After Wittgenstein*, 147–9.

3 Ludwig Wittgenstein, *Culture and Value*, G. H. von Wright with Heikki Nyman (eds), Peter Winch (tr.), (Oxford: Blackwell, 1980), 82ff; ibid. 154–5.

4 D. Z. Phillipps, *Belief, Change and Forms of Life* (London: MacMillan, 1986).

5 Patrick Sherry, *Religion, Truth and Language Games* (London: MacMillan, 1977), 193.

6 See Nicholas Lash, 'How Large is a "Language Game"?' *Theology* 87 (1984) 19–28. Varieties of religious practice and language defy a general definition and cannot therefore be a single form of life and language-game respectively. Instead they comprise a number of forms and games related by 'family resemblance'. (See also Sherry, *Religion, Truth and Language-Games*, 60, 480, and W. Donald Hudson, *Wittgenstein and Religious Belief* (London: MacMillan, 1975) 181–2.)

In the hands of the 'Wittgenstein Fideists' this sort of redefinition of the small-scale concepts <form of life> and <language-game> as broad categories like 'religions'[7] has been used to argue that as the meaning of terms within a language-game is confined to that language-game, those terms cannot be understood in terms of their meaning within that language-game from a position exterior to it. This has been labelled the *sui generis* thesis.[8] Accordingly, religious truth as internal to the 'religious language-game' is held to come in a self-contained form or forms which are immune from any external critique.[9] However, in the face of allegations of 'fideist' overestimation of the size of language-games, Phillipps maintains that '[i]t is a misunderstanding to speak of a religion as a form of life. What can be said is that it is impossible to imagine a religion without imagining it *in* a form of life'.[10] Phillipps rejects the label of 'fideist', denying subscription to the thesis of *sui generis* and maintaining that language-games are distinctive but not autonomous. Belief and understanding are not inseparable – one does not have to inhabit a form of life to understand it. In line with Wittgenstein's stated view on the relationship between language-games, there is 'no common thread' running through all, but a family resemblance between games which precludes autonomy of meaning of terms and activities.[11]

It appears that Phillipps is seen as 'fideist' by others in spite of his protestations. Hudson, for instance, aims his main criticism of Phillipps at his

7 Of course language-games are not categories: categories are things which language-games may incorporate as moves.

8 By Phillipps – see below.

9 See Kai Neilson, 'Wittgensteinian Fideism', *Philosophy* 42 (1967), 191–209. Sherry cites Winch as offering a similar view: 'Criteria of logic are not a direct gift of God, but arise out of and are only intelligible in the context of ways of living or modes of social life. Peter Winch, *The Idea of a Social Science* (London: Routledge, 1958); (Sherry, *Religion, Truth and Language-Games*, 35). Winch believes that there are various modes of logic with their own criteria of intelligibility corresponding to our various forms of life and universes of discourse (for example, science). The *Tractatus* Wittgenstein thought that God was answerable to the laws of logic. (Phillipps, *Belief, Change and Forms of Life*, 69.)

10 Phillipps, *Belief, Change and Forms of Life*, 79.

11 Ibid. 11.

'no-justification view' of religious belief as a 'given' form of life. Along with Sherry, Hudson maintains that religious language-games cannot be entirely self-contained because only a few of their terms have esoteric meaning.[12] Therefore they cannot be immune to critique from without. But whether or not Phillipps is guilty as charged, refutation of the *sui generis* view of religious language-games does not attack what is arguably the main problem with Phillipps's reading of Wittgenstein. It may indeed be possible to evaluate one form of life from the perspective of another because, as is obvious, there is overlap of concepts and activities between forms of life. Yet in so doing it is only possible to point out similarities and differences; we come no closer to being able to assess any language-game's or form of life's overall value. If there is no viewpoint which transcends all forms of life, there is no basis for their overall evaluation. If, as Wittgenstein argues, what is given are forms of life – if human life is lived encased in these – how can human thought take a God's-eye view? While Sherry and Hudson are attracted by Wittgenstein's insights, this is their sticking point.[13] The option of taking the notion of givenness to its ultimate (theological) conclusion does not seem to occur to either of them.

A consequence of the Phillippsian 'no-justification' thesis is that all talk about truth reduces to talk about meaning. 'Correct' can only mean correct usage, or meaningful application of terms, within a particular community.

12 Hudson, *Wittgenstein and Religious Belief*, 156–7. While Sherry considers that Phillipps is correct in maintaining that 'true religion' is more than just a body of true theological propositions, his argument with Phillipps takes the line that 'although such propositions are an integral part of religion', religious truth must be more than a peacefully co-existing collection of culturally or socially determined meanings. It is obvious that when individual beliefs within a belief system contradict each other, then at least one must be false. Even within one religion not all beliefs can be accommodated as different reflections of the same truth. (Sherry, *Religion, Truth and Language-Games*, 43.)

13 Against the autonomist position: 'There is no point in claiming that God has his own kind of reality or religion its own kind of truth unless there is at least some similarity between these and other kinds of reality or truth; otherwise, Like Humpty Dumpty, we are merely using words to mean whatever we choose to mean by them'. This is what Winch calls a 'Protagorean Relativism'. (Ibid. 40.)

For Phillipps, as for Wittgenstein, philosophy cannot arbitrate which is right, but can only describe. Nor can theology adjudicate, for 'in theology questions of meaning and truth are often inextricably mixed'.[14] Theology after all is just another language-game. The theologian as a member of a faith community (form of life) is in no position to offer a God's-eye view, but can only present what is rational in that context.

While for Phillipps the anti-metaphysician there is no God's-eye view, in making givenness axiomatic Phillipps proves to be closer to the present thesis.[15] Sherry points out the parallels between Barth's rejection of natural theology and Phillipps's rejection of rational justification of religious beliefs. Sherry, however, is critical of Barth's dismissal of *analogia entis*[16] while relying himself on a theory of analogy[17] to explain human knowledge of a transcendent God. For Sherry, religious concepts 'latch on to' the world through, first, metaphor or analogy (he does not distinguish between these), second, through our relating them to 'personal transforming experience'.[18] The attributes of a transcendent God may be inferred analogously from the same imperfectly expressed attributes in ourselves. The difference is simply one of degree.[19]

14 Phillipps, *Belief, Change and Forms of Life*, 39–40.

15 Phillipps is correct to maintain that we cannot establish the true-to-fact-ness of language-games by measuring them against some sort of exterior 'reality'. (Ibid. 67.) To even think this way is to misunderstand the nature of language-games. For Wittgenstein no statement can be a statement of absolute value. We run up against the walls of our cage (of language-world) when we attempt an absolute ethic or religious statement. (Ibid. 82, 85.)

16 Sherry, *Religion, Truth and Language-Games*, 59.

17 Sherry bases this on Hick's application of the Wittgensteinian model of 'duck-rabbit' to religious belief. We see certain experiences and events as of God, or as religious (John Hicks, *Faith and Knowledge*, 2nd edn (London: Macmillan, 1967), 142ff; *Christianity at the Centre* (London: Macmillan, 1968), 53; (ibid. 101). Hick, however, maintains that we cannot know whether or not we have got it right – at least not in this life.

18 Ibid. 110–12.

19 Likewise, Hudson attempts to escape the dilemma of a transcendent God by defining transcendence as surpassingly more of characteristics humanly possessed, such as goodness, wisdom, power: that is, a difference in degree rather than in kind. Hudson

I maintain that such a line of argument does not solve the problem at all. The nature of these characteristics must still be defined by God and given to us, otherwise we remain in the realm of anthropomorphic projection.[20] The Phillippsian notion of givenness, lacking though it does the notion of a Giver, at least avoids this error.

Sherry concedes to Phillipps that the *Sui Generis* 'only insiders can understand' thesis is Wittgensteinian insofar as one needs to grasp the grammar (rules for the use of terms) to have insight. Grammatical propositions are in the nature of revelations that cannot be doubted.[21] However, their locally axiomatic character dooms any attempt by Sherry to accommodate Wittgenstein's grammatical propositions within his theory of analogy. While on a Phillippsian 'no-justification' thesis (lacking a God's-eye view), one grammatical proposition may have just as much validity as any other, for Sherry analogy must reveal that 'some are more equal than others'.

Putting aside the 'fideism' question as not central (whether or not Phillipps is guilty as judged), I maintain that Phillipps is correct in seeing our understanding of and language about God as inextricably intertwined with our activities in the world. Any suggestion that human beings can arrive (single-handedly) at knowledge of a transcendent God within their language-world framework (analogy or no analogy) is, as Kant points out, contrary to logic,[22] as is any watering down of the concept <transcendent>

---

maintains that transcendence does not have to be equated with otherness, total alienness. 'Beyond' admits two senses. (Hudson, *Wittgenstein and Religious Belief*, 140.)

20 According to Sherry, the paradox of claims to knowledge of (or talk of) the transcendent makes it tempting to reduce the transcendent to categories of human experience (as per Hudson). For Sherry, our God-pictures must at least be seen to be reliable by analogy. But whence comes the analogy?

21 S. C. Brown, *Do Religious Claims make Sense?* (London: S.C.M., 1969), 140ff.

22 Therefore 'Kant queries the use of the term "grace" … [H]e insists that we cannot distinguish between the effects of grace and nature, because we cannot recognise a supra-sensible object within our experience'. Sherry, *Religion, Truth and Language-Games*, 139. (Immanuel Kant, *Religion within the Bounds of Reason Alone*, 2nd edn, T. M. Greene and H. H. Hudson, J. R. Silber (trs.) (Illinois: La Salle 1960), Bk IV es Pt 2#2.) This is where a specifically Christian (Christological) understanding of grace is required.

to make such knowledge humanly accessible.[23] Phillipps's argument is thus helpful in clearing away any illusions about direct or truly analogous human knowledge of a transcendent God. Where Phillipps is unhelpful to theology is in his positivistic insistence on dispensing with transcendence altogether. This leads inevitably to theology's demise at the hands of socio-linguistics, for a God who is subsumed by or equatable with such may be reduced to such. Accordingly, <God> becomes a redundant concept. While at times he is tempted by the notion of grace, a reading of Phillipps forces the conclusion that on a Wittgensteinian reading of reality, God must be entirely immanent in human religious forms of life. That is, all understanding, whether of God or anything else must on a Wittgensteinian view be (on a grand whole-of-world scale at least), *sui generis*.

However, the acceptance of a language-game ontology need not automatically entail a reduction of theology to socio-linguistics. As I have noted, a logical conclusion to the thesis of radical givenness is that the totality of forms of life and their language-games may owe its existence to a transcendent Giver. On a theological viewpoint, religious language-games, as indeed all language-games, may be ultimately not human in origin, however much they are humanly shaped and focused. Granted the impossibility of avoiding the demise of theology through reductionism by the other option, a radical *sola gratia* arguably becomes the only form of theology capable of surviving in a Wittgensteinian world.[24]

It should be apparent from the above that any assertion, however anti-metaphysical, about the nature of reality is itself a metaphysical statement. Although Wittgenstein himself appears to dismiss metaphysics as

23 As per Hudson, *Wittgenstein and Religious Belief*.

24 It is not my intention to claim that a Wittgensteinian language-game perspective makes a theology of grace mandatory. This would be tantamount to claiming that the demonstration of the coherence of such an ontology provides evidence for the existence of God. What I do argue instead is that any theological reading of any ontology, Wittgensteinian or not, requires a 'leap of faith' – a Barthian '*analogia fidei*' (some theologies are more easily leapt to from a Wittgensteinian position than others). My intention is to demonstrate the consistency of such a theology with such a metaphysic.

a worthwhile pursuit, it does not follow that his work does not express a metaphysical stance.[25] As has been noted, the later Wittgensteinian metaphysic is both simple and devastating: all that there is and all that is known is 'the given'. Yet such a metaphysic may be seen to be consistent with a theology of grace.

4.2.2. Justification by Faith

> *According to Plantinga, what we have instead of objective self-evidence is commitment to the reliability of what we have learned …* [1.1.4]
>
> *It seems reasonable to ascribe a Plantingan kind of foundationalism to Wittgenstein in that he treats language-games and forms of life as primitive and these entities arguably comprise a form of knowing.* [1.1.4.1]

Having reached this point, it is a worthwhile digression to revisit the earlier digression in Part One on foundationalism and reformed epistemology.

25 For Wittgenstein, '"the Beyond" occurs not in language but through language … In Philosophical Investigations the "Beyond" does not appear … But the notion of how language "shows" what is already there to be seen is developed in terms of "grammatical" utterances.' (Anthony C. Thiselton, *The Two Horizons: New Testament Hermeneutics and Philosophical Description with Special Reference to Heidegger, Bultmann, Gadamer and Wittgenstein* (Grand Rapids, Michigan: Eerdmans, 1980), 370). Again, Sherry: '[I]t is tempting to argue that Wittgenstein dissolved the branch of philosophy known as "ontology" when he showed that we learn the nature of reality through language-games, e.g. when we learn what physical objects, pains and intentions are, and that we learn how to use the term "God" in a similar way …' However this cannot be so. The dilemma is that we learn to use 'God' as applying to a transcendent being. This being so, how can we learn what or who God is? Anyone who claims some Christian orthodoxy must come to terms with this problem. (Sherry, *Religion, Truth and Language-Games*, 191–2.) See also Hudson (*Wittgenstein and Religious Belief*, 64–5) on this point.

To some extent the rest of this chapter will recap on Part One, but with a different focus.

In his critique of foundationalism, Phillipps summarises Wittgenstein's position:

> our world-picture cannot be thought of as the foundation of our thinking. It is what shows itself by being taking for granted in our thinking. Similarly, we cannot think of our world-picture as the presupposition of the ways in which we think, as though those ways of thinking could be derived from it. We cannot first identify our world-picture and then go on to describe the ways in which we think, because it is only in terms of how we think that we can speak of our world-picture. We are not talking of any priority over the ways we think, logical or temporal, when we speak of our world-picture.[26]

A language-game ontology in which activities are basic rejects the axiom shared by both classical foundationalists and reformed epistemologists that knowing is an entirely conceptual phenomenon. This aspect of Cartesian thought 'misrepresents the phenomenon of following the rule to suppose that some act of reflection has to be present, however tacitly and fleetingly, on every occasion ... Wittgenstein uncovers and neutralises the attractions of the doctrine that understanding is always interpretation.'[27]

While a form of life includes certain indubitable propositions, foundationalists 'treat religious beliefs (unlike Wittgenstein's basic propositions) as alternatives within a class of propositions whose truth or falsity can be assessed by common neutral criteria.'[28] Yet it is not a matter of which propositions are basic, but a matter of questioning whether propositions as such can be basic at all. For Wittgenstein, it is an inversion of the real state of affairs to suppose that beliefs and ideas (including theological beliefs and ideas) are at the bottom of the way people live. Basic axioms

26 D. Z. Phillipps, *Faith After Foundationalism* (London: Routledge, 1988), 41.

27 Kerr, *Theology After Wittgenstein*, 111. 'Our action, on the whole, is an unreflective and instinctive reaction to the manifold pressures and appeals of the common order to which one belongs' (115). '[I]t is the language games that give rise to the possibility of rational thought in the first place'. (118.)

28 Ibid. 117.

and beliefs arise from a way of being in the world; they are lived before they are articulated or explicitly subscribed to. While such a position is partially expressed by Kant's dictum that ontology is contingent on epistemology, the Wittgensteinian view of knowledge (including as it does 'knowing how' as well as 'knowing that') is broader than Kant's conceptual framework. What is given is what is accessible to human experience through activities (including the interaction with objects and the having of emotions, volitions and sensations) which include, and are conceived of through, language.

Kerr maintains that the activities of our lives are our only access to knowledge. 'Our human forms of knowing [transcendent] matters seem hopelessly inadequate and indirect ... we dream of the direct route to the centre of the mystery but we are never allowed to take it.'[29] The knowledge that is divinely accessible is offered to mere human beings only in the 'materiality of signs'.[30] This knowledge transcends human ability to conceive it: our forms of life are foundational to our concepts. 'The background which is ... the swarming carpet of human activity cannot be captured in any representation. The ineffable is the whole burly-burly; the whole hurly-burly is the ineffable ... What constitutes us as human beings is the regular and patterned reactions that we have to one another. It is in our dealings with each other – in how we act – that human life is founded.'[31]

To think of a conceptual framework is to think of a language, but for Wittgenstein, to think of a language is to think of some activity.[32] In the first instance human beings have activities in common and share a mutual understanding of these activities. For Wittgenstein, 'what we share lies at the level, not of views ... and belief, but of reactions and forms of life'.[33] As I have also suggested, this Wittgensteinian primacy of activities underlies, controversially, even our logic: 'it is not a question of opinion. They [the

29 Wittgenstein, *Philosophical Investigations*, #426.

30 Kerr, *Theology After Wittgenstein*, 45.

31 Ibid. 65.

32 Wittgenstein, *Philosophical Investigations*, #19.

33 Kerr, *Theology After Wittgenstein*, 108–9.

truths of logic] are determined by a consensus of action: a consensus of doing the same thing, reacting in the same way.'[34]

In his criticism of classical and Reformed varieties of foundationalism, Phillipps does not seem to consider the possibility of a Wittgensteinian type of foundationalism. I have suggested that if the traditional foundationalist language-world dichotomy is abandoned in favour of a language-game ontology in which practices are epistemically basic, a type of foundationalism may survive, for it is arguable that what is fundamental to foundationalism is not propositional knowledge as such, but the self-evidence of this knowledge. Where the classical foundationalist believes that this self-evidence is accessible through logic and the 'evidence of our senses', a Wittgensteinian foundationalist maintains that such self-evidence is a given built into a form of life.[35]

I suggested in Part One that there could be some affinity between this sort of 'Wittgensteinian foundationalism'[36] and that of Reformed epistemology. For Reformed epistemology's chief exponent, Alvin Plantinga, the assignation of self-evidence to a proposition is an act of faith. Yet 'It is not the relatively high-level and general proposition God exists that is properly basic, argues Plantinga, but instead propositions detailing some of these attributes and actions'.[37] As has been demonstrated, for Wittgenstein,

34 Ibid. 183–4. Cora Diamond (ed.), *Wittgenstein's Lectures on the Foundations of Mathematics, Cambridge, 1939, from the notes of R. G. Bosanquet, Norman Malcolm, Rush Rhees and Yorick Smythies* (Ithaca, New York: Cornell University Press, 1976).

35 On such a view, therefore, there can be no universally self-evident beliefs, merely local ones. What constitutes self-evidence is built into the language-game, is a given. Truth comes culturally and locally mediated and faceted.

36 As I concluded in the discussion in Part One, it depends on our definition of foundationalism, or perhaps on how far we are prepared to stretch this concept, whether we see Wittgenstein as anti-foundationalist, or as espousing a new variety of foundationalism.

37 '[B]elief in God, although not dependent on evidence for being known, is also grounded in and justified by the conditions in which it is held. These conditions are experiences in which the believer is aware of God in his creation, aware of God's anger at his sins, aware of God's presence and of the need to thank and praise him, and so on. If we were to speak strictly, Plantinga says, belief in God is not properly basic.

propositions are moves in language-games and therefore cannot be basic. Instead, it is the language-games which comprise our forms of life that are epistemically basic. Our 'bedrock' forms of life hold our basic propositions fast. 'All testing, all confirmation and disconfirmation of a hypothesis takes place within a system. And this system is not a more or less arbitrary and doubtful point of departure tor all our arguments: no, it belongs to the essence of what we call an argument. The system is not so much the point of departure as the element in which arguments have their life.'[38]

While Plantinga seems at times to employ Wittgenstein-like arguments, '[t]his emphasis on the practice is something on which ... Plantinga himself relies in order to meet the objection that, in the absence of a criterion of basicality, anything ... could be a basic proposition. He emphasises, quite rightly, that in certain circumstances, it is obvious that something is properly basic'.[39] Therefore the similarity is more apparent than real. Propositions, rather than the activities within which propositions are embedded, remain basic for Plantinga (although some are more basic than others); for the Reformed epistemologist knowledge and belief must be propositional in nature.

Accordingly, Plantinga's quarrel with the classical foundationalists does not concern the propositional nature of foundationality so much as the basis upon which a belief is justified. 'Plantinga attacks the foundationalist for thinking that all propositions depend tor their rationality on standing in appropriate relations to other propositions which cannot be doubted such as self-evident or incorrigible propositions.'[40] Upon what criterion is it possible to base these judgments of self-evidence and incorrigibility?

What is properly basic are such beliefs as "God is speaking to me", "God has created all this", "God is to be thanked and praised."' Phillips, *Faith After Foundationalism*, 20–1; Alvin Plantinga, 'Reason and Belief in God', in Alvin Plantinga and Nicholas Wolterstorff (eds), *Faith and Rationality* (Indiana: University of Notre Dame Press, 1983), 81.

38 Ludwig Wittgenstein, *On Certainty*, G. E. M. Anscombe and G. H. von Wright (eds) (Oxford: Blackwell, 1969), #105.

39 Phillipps, *Faith After Foundationalism*, 28.

40 Ibid. 32–3.

While both Wittgenstein and Plantinga maintain that the justification of our beliefs and practices lies beyond our reach – that we have no criteria for so judging – Wittgenstein would say that the whole notion of external justification of epistemic practices is confused. Phillipps, following Wittgenstein, comments: '[w]hat we have seen is that the intelligibility of our practices await no such verdict, neither do they need it. They are simply there as part of our lives'.[41]

As suggested, the possibility that Wittgenstein and Phillipps do not address is that the notion of a transcendent justifier may be compatible with the notion of the radical givenness of our epistemic practices by way of the theological concept of grace. Phillipps criticises Plantinga for not developing his argument against classical foundationalism into a positive alternative, pointing out that Plantinga has shown the invalidity of the classical foundationalists' epistemology rather than established the validity of his own: 'the essence of his attack consists in berating the foundationalist for claiming to have a criterion, which in fact he does not possess ... The foundationalists' failure then enables Plantinga to play the same foundationalist game and place belief in 'God in the foundations of his noetic structure in the absence of any epistemic criterion which would forbid him from doing so'.[42]

Yet what other option has he? 'Since the criterion has not yet been arrived at, our practices can be deemed innocent until proved guilty'. As the justification (for Plantinga, the Eternal Justifier) of our propositional framework must be transcendent of that framework itself, all that we deem self-evident or incorrigible is necessarily taken to be so purely on faith.[43] On a human level self-evidence must indeed be a given. For Plantinga this presupposes a Giver, a requirement that, as I have suggested, Wittgenstein and Phillipps do not address.

41 Ibid. 33.

42 Ibid. 32–3.

43 Ibid. 33. If the classical epistemologists (being truly children of the Enlightenment) claim to be able to discern the truth by means of reason, the Reformed epistemologist not only denies this, but 'claims to show that the foundationalist too, although he does not realise it, lives by faith'. (Ibid. 55.)

However, while Plantinga does allow this givenness, his adherence to a propositional foundation for knowledge prevents him from taking a language-game epistemology on board. Again Phillipps contrasts this with Wittgenstein's perspective: 'foundationalists and Reformed epistemologists regard epistemic practices as though they were descriptions of a reality which lies beyond them. Wittgenstein, far more radically, insists that distinctions between the real and the unreal get their sense within epistemic practices'.[44] For Plantinga, as has been seen, beliefs are propositions about the world or about God. They are separate from the external reality to which they correspond, the world they describe or evaluate,[45] whereas for Wittgenstein they are embedded in language-games and forms of life.

Phillipps, observing that for the Reformed epistemologist '[a]ll justification, in this context, is justification by faith', asks: 'But what is it that we are justified in believing?' It seems the Reformed answer is that what we are justified in believing is that 'our epistemic practices do, in fact, show us how things are'.[46] Remove this built-in assumption of correspondence between a set of propositions and an external separate 'reality' and the structure of Reformed epistemology threatens to collapse. For in the end it is the very idea of grounding or foundingof beliefs or opinions in an extralinguistic reality that cannot be sustained from a Wittgensteinian viewpoint. As Phillipps points out, 'one of the ways in which epistemology overreaches itself is in thinking that the grammars of the various forms of discourse we engage in are themselves descriptions of, or hypotheses about, a reality which is independent of them all. Sceptical worries then take the form of worries about whether the language within which claims of truth and falsity are made itself makes any contact with reality'.[47] For a subscriber to this ontology, before belief in the God-givenness of our belief enters the picture one must first have faith that one's propositions (basic beliefs) are

44 Ibid. xiv.

45 Likewise, Phillipps seems to be able to embrace language-games and forms of life seemingly without a full recognition of the incompatibility of such an ontology with traditional language-world separating ontologies and epistemologies.

46 Ibid. 56.

47 Ibid. 135.

true of, or correspond to and are faithful to one's experiences of the world. Then one must also have faith that this truth is able to mediate the truth about the even more 'external reality' of God. The God-givenness of all that is, for such an ontology, must be a two-stage correspondence process.[48]

While an abandonment of the notion of correspondence between propositions and 'reality' could suggest that our ways of thinking are ultimately arbitrary or groundless, within a form of life itself the notion of grounds or lack of them makes no sense. Justification is indeed by faith in the validity of a whole way of life (not in a series of foundational propositions, although the way of life will include assent to certain propositions). Wittgenstein observes: 'But I did not get my picture of the world by satisfying myself of its correctness; nor do I have it because I am satisfied of its correctness. No: it is the inherited background against which I distinguish between true and false.'[49] Wittgenstein's 'foundation' lies beyond Plantinga's foundation of properly basic beliefs, not because its propositions are 'more properly basic', but because its axioms are, in the first instance, lived rather than conceived. As I suggested in Part One, a language-game foundation is not a solid floor one's beliefs rest on, but more like a high-rise apartment complex which contains everything one does and thinks.

Thus, according to a language-game ontology, faith is not subscription to a series or system of beliefs about an external world and an even more external deity, but a lived-out commitment to God-given and God-inhabited forms of life which include various practices involving the use of words. We do not consciously act on faith. It is rather that doubts (as to the validity of a form of life as a whole) simply do not arise. Although changes to a form of life occur through the testing of various aspects (metaphorising) and in the end a form of life may simply disappear, doubts do not arise through our not knowing the constitution of some Ultimate Reality beyond the reality we live and the correspondence of our beliefs to that

48 See both Chapter 2 of Part One and Chapter 4 of Part Four for a critique of this sort of realism.

49 Wittgenstein, *On Certainty*, #947.

reality, but because we are simply acting in faith within what we are given. We know what the state of affairs is: we know how to go on.

Phillipps shows some sympathy with this line of reasoning:

> It may be said that Wittgenstein is a philosopher who makes us see the wonderfulness of the ordinary, the wonderfulness of what is given! If this wonder takes a religious form, it is not difficult to see how these gifts of nature can be seen as gifts of grace – a grace of nature, one might say. But, someone might object, aren't religious possibilities given too; doesn't it follow from what has been said that the existence of religious modes of thought too are not guaranteed by any kind of necessity? That is correct. But, then, why should we assume that there is any necessity in our coming to God? Is not that possibility, too, a gift of grace?[50]

Phillippsian 'no-justification' thus shows its potential to become *sola gratia* – a short-lived development, alas, as Phillipps, committed to an anti-metaphysical stance, concludes that because we are held captive by our forms of life and cannot measure them against an independent ultimate reality, religion can do without an ontology of transcendence.[51] Perhaps in this case (though not in Plantinga's) the philosopher of religion cannot also be the theologian,[52] although the reverse may hold true.

I have suggested that the weakness of Reformed epistemology and its real incompatibility with a Wittgensteinian sort of foundationalism lies

50 Phillipps, *Faith after Foundationalism*, 127.

51 Thus in critiquing George Lindbeck's, *The Nature of Doctrine* (Philadelphia: Westminster, 1983), he asserts: 'No use of capitals in talking of the "Most Important" and the "Ultimately Real" can hide the fact that he is trying to place these concepts, whatever they are, in a logical space which transcends the language-games and forms of life in which concepts have their life'. (Ibid. 206.)

52 Phillipps notes that there is a fundamental problem with approaching revelation from a philosophy of religion angle: from the point of view I have expressed in this work, philosophers (as opposed to theologians) are by the very nature of their discipline unable to posit grace: 'we can say no more from within philosophy than, "Human life is like that". Our task is a descriptive one'. (*Belief, Change and Forms of Life*, 33.) However, Phillipps's stance is merely indicative of how a world-view (in Phillipps's case, anti-metaphysical positivism) can hold one captive and prevent one's reaching certain conclusions.

not in its dictum of justification by faith which can be read as taking on faith the givenness of what we do (Plantinga here supplying what is missing in Wittgenstein in positing a Giver), but in its denial of basicality to human practices. Reformed epistemology, on the contrary, requires 'what we do' to be supported by a foundation of 'given' propositional beliefs which form the basis of our knowing about the world. Thus Plantinga also sees the need for a perspective that includes grace but is operating with quite a different view of reality. 'Wittgensteinian foundationalism' must, therefore, be seen as an alternative to Reformed epistemology rather than merely as a different paradigm for the same thing.

4.2.3. Summary and Conclusions

While his use of Wittgenstein has been criticised, I consider Phillipps to be correct in seeing our understanding of and language about God as inextricably intertwined with our activities in the world. Moreover, Phillipps's arguments are useful in dispelling any illusions about direct or truly analogous human knowledge of a transcendent God. However, a Phillippsian anti-metaphysical positivism, in dispensing with transcendence altogether, leads inevitably to a reduction of theology to socio-linguistics. While at times he leans toward grace, Phillipps is bound by his belief that, on a Wittgensteinian reading of reality, God must be entirely immanent in human religious forms of life. That is, all understanding (whether of God or anything else) must on a Wittgensteinian view be *sui generis* on a human-world scale, if not on a local form-of-life level. A Phillippsian God, therefore, ultimately must be no more than a creature of human social traditions.

Yet the adoption of Wittgenstein's ontology need not automatically entail a reduction of theology to socio-linguistics. Although Wittgenstein himself appears to dismiss metaphysics as a worthwhile pursuit, any assertion about the nature of reality is automatically a metaphysical statement.

The metaphysic his work reveals is both simple and devastating: all that there is and all that is known is 'the given'. The notion of givenness suggests a Giver: radical givenness suggests that the totality of forms of life and their language-games arguably may owe its existence to a God who is giver of all. Perhaps *sola gratia* is the only theology capable of surviving in a Wittgensteinian world. Theologically, such a position is consistent with Barth's 'analogy of faith' in stipulating a givenness not only to language, but of language itself, and not only of words and things, but of their inseparable interweaving in language-games. This argument will be pursued in the next chapter.

I suggested in Part One that the basicality of language-games might be construed as a sort of 'Wittgensteinian foundationalism'. Similar emphases on givenness also suggested an affinity between this 'Wittgensteinian foundationalism' and Reformed epistemology. However, although Reformed epistemology's 'justification by faith' position on self-evidence is consistent with a *sola gratia* thesis, in its denial of basicality to human practices it is ultimately incompatible with a Wittgensteinian sort of 'foundationalism'. As Reformed epistemology insists in maintaining that propositions form the basis of our knowledge of the world, it thus operates with quite a different view of reality.

CHAPTER THREE

The Case for a 'Language-Game Theology' (1)

4.3.1. Wittgenstein and Barth

> *If the metaphorising language-game (being the source of new moves in language-games) is basic with respect to other language-games, then the metaphorising process itself will not be subject or accessible to verification.* [2.2.2.]

I have suggested that a language-game ontology, in stipulating a givenness not only *to* language but also *of* language itself (and not only of words and things but of their interweaving in language-games), may be consistent with Barth's 'analogy of faith'. In this and the next chapter I will argue for a 'language-game theology' on the basis of this consistency. These ideas are developed further in chapters 5 and 6 of my book, *Christian Realist Theology in a Postmodern Age*.[1]

When Barth talks about the capability of language as world-bound, humanly shaped and conditioned, he asks: how is it possible for such language to 'grasp' revelation? How is it possible for God's revelation to be expressed in human language? – and concludes that language does not so much grasp revelation as is grasped by it. As Jüngel states it, for Barth language is 'commandeered' by revelation. 'Where such "commandeering" of the language becomes event, there is a gain to language. It consists in the fact that God as God comes to speech.'[2] This is not to be confused with a

1 Patterson, *Christian Realist Theology in a Postmodern Age*.

2 Eberhard Jüngel, *The Doctrine of the Trinity: God's Being is in Becoming*, Horton Harris (tr.) (Edinburgh: Scottish Academic Press, 1976), 7–11. Karl Barth, *Church*

commandeering of language by revelation on the basis of an *analogia entis*. In that instance God comes to speech as name, or idea: concept rather than person.[3] Accordingly, this means a loss of revelation (a reduction of God's being) rather than a gain to language. On such a view theological language is illustrative rather than interpretative. However, talk about God is possible not simply because the idea of God enters language, but because God's very self enters language. This means that God's being becomes expressible in language in an act of divine self-interpretation. Thus the language we use to speak of God is the language of God's self-interpretation given to us by God. Where such language predicates of God human or creaturely characteristics, this constitutes an analogy which we believe on faith is given to us by God, hence it is an 'analogy of faith'. Conversely, for God to enter (and hence 'commandeer') language is for God's being to be entered by language.[4] Language itself becomes a part of God. 'When language itself aims to be revelation it loses itself as language. But where revelation commandeers language, the word of God takes place. The word of God brings language to its true essence'.[5] That is, language becomes truly language, has its true being, in the word of God. It is primarily as God's self-interpretation that it is given to be human language.

Accordingly, for Barth, revelation is the incorporating of language from its very beginning in the being of God. This incorporation is a pragmatical event, an act of divine speaking, not a divine semantical self-depositing into text: 'The revelation of God thus "commandeers" language not as a dumb aggressor but enters into language as a movement of speech. The

---

Dogmatics, Vol. I, Part 1, G. W. Bromiley and T. F. Torrance (eds and trs.), 2nd rev. edn (Edinburgh: T. & T. Clark, 1975 & 1977), 11.

3 Alan Torrance demonstrates that Barth does not see these two analogies as opposed, provided that 'knowledge of the being of God [is] … subordinated to the knowledge of the activity of God'. Alan J. Torrance, *Persons in Communion: Trinitarian Participation and Human Description* (Edinburgh: T. & T. Clark, 1996), 162. I maintain that what is being 'conquered' is not language as such but a certain second-order sort of language: our existing categories and conceptions of reality.

4 Jüngel, *Doctrine of the Trinity*, 11–12.

5 Ibid. 14. (See also Gunton, *Becoming and Being*, 136.)

revelation of God is no silent demand for language but by its speaking makes demands on the language. Thus the revelation of God itself is the enabling of the interpretation of revelation. It is so … "because revelation is the self-interpretation of this God"'.[6]

Jüngel suggests that this is what Barth means when he says that 'Revelation is the Person of God speaking'. 'And since in revelation "the fullness of the original self-existent being of God's word" reposes and lives, then revelation is that event in which the being of God itself comes to word.'[7] In 'The Becoming of God in Barth's Theology', Gunton notes that 'For Barth the problem of theological language cannot be discussed prior to the question of the being of God.'[8] The event of revelation includes God's self-interpretation. As Gunton puts it, language about God 'must conform to its object and not the reverse … Theology begins from the circle drawn around the theologian by God's subjecting himself to human thought and reasoning'.[9] There is a suggestion in Gunton's way of putting Barth's position that Gunton (if not Barth) construes an isomorphic relation between language and world in which ordinary human language about the physical world is the vehicle for an extralinguistic divine content. Gunton takes Barth's question, 'whether this possibility (of theological language is to be understood as that of the language and consequently of the world or man, or whether it is to be regarded as a venture which is, as it were, ascribed to the language, and consequently to the world, or man, but the possibility of revelation'[10] and appears to read it as posing a dichotomous choice. Are the

6 Ibid. 15. Barth, *CD* I/1, 311. See also Patterson, *Realist Christian Theology*, 132–5.

7 Barth, *CD* I/1, 304–5. The truth of God thus comes to our language as gift, but not simply to language per se (language as text or statement), because it comes as a speaking to us by God: through the action of address (Wittgensteinly-speaking, through the language-games in which God relates to us within the activity of human living). (See also Jüngel, *Doctrine of the Trinity*, 15–16, and 'Metaphorical Truth', 63–7.)

8 Gunton, *Becoming and Being*, 121.

9 Ibid. 126. According to Jüngel, however, Barth understands God as the object of human knowledge, God to be revealed as event (Barth, *CD* II/1, 5). God can only be known and expressed as event. God as event is God as Word (ibid. 4). This event is the act of God which makes God expressible. (Jüngel, *Doctrine of the Trinity*, 45.)

10 Barth, *CD* I/1, 339.

words revelatory in themselves, or are they merely vehicles for something which lies beyond them?

While Gunton's construal of Barth appears to be based on the premise that language and the physical world are separate from each other and from God (which is related to the apparent identification of knowledge, and implicitly language, with concepts), Jüngel maintains that the being of God does not come to human speech as mere content.[11] If revelation is the self-interpretation of God, such a self-interpretation is absolute reality. It is not a content subject to a form which lies outside of that interpretation. God's self-revelation as self-interpretation (as a gain to language-world) is as both *event and content*. Jüngel adds that revelation as God's self-interpretation is God's 'reiteration'. Barth insists that what God is in self-revelation, God must be in God-self.[12]

It follows from Barth's interpretation of revelation as incorporating verbal as well as nonverbal reality, and also his understanding of the pragmatical nature of this incorporation as an act of divine 'speaking', that a language-game perspective which takes language and world as together comprising reality would be consistent with this position. On this view, it is consistent with Jüngel's reading of Barth to argue that Ultimate Reality does not come to speech as a nonlinguistic reality from outside of speech but comes to language-world as divine language-games in which theological thoughts and utterances are moves.[13] It could be said that revelation itself

11 Jüngel, *Doctrine of the Trinity*, 16.

12 Barth, *CD* I/1, 316; Gunton, *Becoming and Being*, 299. God alone interprets (is capable of interpreting) God. This means that all predications, including humanly accessible historical ones, depend upon God's self-reiteration. 'The ability to possess predicates … is the event of the word which is there before all predications and which makes all predications possible. In this sense it will have to be true that God's being, which has been formulated from the event of revelation, is in himself verbal (*wortlich*) and precisely in this same measure also historical.' (Jüngel, *Doctrine of the Trinity*, 95–6.)

13 That this has more than simply logical warrant is suggested by its consistency with biblical understandings of God (for example, as engaged in language-games of judging, saving, guiding, teaching). An examination of these is beyond the scope of the present work, but examples will come readily to mind.

is a self-disclosure language-game played by God.[14] Such a 'language-game theology', like Barth's own theology, begins with God's bringing the possibility of interpretation within the human sphere. Language and reason, divine possessions in the first instance, become human in the second instance as 'givens'. In Gunton's terminology, God may be a 'concrete word in the present' (the 'given') as well as the source of that concrete word in being the becoming of language-world: of language-games.

On this account, God as Word comes to language-world first in the inarticulate or unreflected pre-conceptual communicative activities of human life and only secondly in the conceptual orderings of these activities.[15] The Word is a new move, or new entire language-game in the first instance. Thus, the language-world linking activity of metaphorising may be seen to perform the double function of bringing transcendent being to actuality, and bringing that actuality to concept. In such a theology, God's self-revelation is understood in terms of (although not exhausted by) the totality of human world-and-language-involving activities. The coming into being of language-world may be seen as integral to the revelation of God's being, yet not in itself a summing up of God's being. God is agent and agency as well as content.

Daniel Hardy appears to be operating from a comparable ontology when he suggests that the interweaving of our human contextuality is an interweaving of the Trinitarian God with the field of our contextuality.[16] Where Wittgenstein talks of language-games and forms of life, Hardy also recognises the structuring of human institutions by rule-governed activities. For Hardy these are 'the codes through which societies structure themselves'. In revelation God enters and 'commandeers' our interweavings, repatterning our beliefs and practices. In this repatterning of codes, 'perturbations' (disruptions to the patterns) keep the 'edges' of these social complexes

14 Patterson, *Realist Christian Theology*, 132–5.

15 While the relation of language-game to conceptual 'rule' is circular (feeds back), the former cannot be reduced to the latter: as Dietrich Bonhoeffer warns, God cannot be reduced to human ideas of God. [Dietrich Bonhoeffer, *Christ The Centre*, Edward H. Robinson (tr.) (New York: HarperCollins, 1960), 27–39.]

16 Daniel Hardy, 'The Spirit of God in Creation and Reconciliation', 252.

flexible and ensure a sort of dynamic quasi-equilibrium within which change is constant yet constrained by the previous structures.[17] A language-game ontology is able to explain the place of the linguistic components in this interweaving and the particular and fundamental contribution of the metaphorising language game in the disruption and repatterning of codes. Here God the source and agent of metaphorising language-games restructures reality and provides the models and metaphors which participate in the language-world interweaving of reality: the immanence of God upon and within which the 'dynamic self-structuring' of the human complex of language-games is contingent. The person of God revealed through metaphorising as relating activity is seen to operate through the 'given' of the metaphoric perturbations to and repatterning of language-games.

I have sought to demonstrate that the ontology on which a theological account is based cannot but assume a certain relation of language to world. Here Barth and Wittgenstein may be seen to share a language-world integrating metaphysic. Yet the relation within revelation of God's being to God-talk requires not merely assumptions but explanations of how language and world are connected. This is where Wittgenstein's work is valuable to theology. When an ontology which integrates language and world is specifically adopted in a 'language-game theology', theological language may be seen as integral to revelation.[18] God-talk can no longer be thought of as a picturing, modeling or mapping isomorphically (even if fuzzily and partially as per the critical realists) of a separate reality, but one in which the words and models we are given by God in worship, prayer and reflection enable religious practices and theological language to participate in the very life of God.

17 Ibid. 249. Hardy observes that '[b]oundaries, which are relative and not absolute, are a natural counter-part of the self-structuring by which this self-maintenance occurs'.

18 As Downey observes (with quite a different theology in mind), 'There is no Wittgensteinian theology, but theology can be done from a Wittgensteinian perspective.' (Downey, *Beginning at the Beginning*, 143.)

4.3.2. Words are Real Too

> *In later Wittgenstein there are no longer one-to-one language-world relations. One language-game links several different words with the world. Linguistic 'pictures', insofar as they can still be said to be pictures, are pictures of reality as represented by language-games. At the same time, these language-games, as the 'projective links with reality', also have to be incorporated in the 'picture' if the picture is to serve its purpose of depiction. The verbal picture or proposition has become sentence plus use of sentence. Accordingly, language-games must be seen as components of propositions and conversely, the terms which express propositions receive their meaning from the language-games.* [1.2.3.]
>
> *Language-games, as language-world links (activities or practices) which interweave language-world, 'slice reality up vertically', as it were, into a multitude of language-world 'pieces'.* [1.2.3.]

It will by now be apparent that a language-game *theology*, in employing a language-game ontology which views language as a part of the physical world, will not only cut across traditional realist and idealist categories but accordingly view the traditional distinction between reality and truth as problematic. This discussion will recap on chapter two of Part One, employing a different focus.

In his examination of Wittgenstein's position in the idealist-realist debate, Kerr comments: '[w]e cannot get outside our skin to compare our relationship to the world with some alternative. But the model of meaningful activity as essentially based upon designating objects blinds both sides in the idealist/realist debate to our embodied condition. Realists just as much as idealists fail to acknowledge that *das leben* is "the given"'.[19] The myth of objectivity 'encourages us to treat languages as representation of

19 Kerr, *Theology After Wittgenstein*, 133. 'The realist is challenged to explain how an assertion is capable of being true or false when the evidence for or against it is, in principle, unavailable – at least by tacit implication, to us ... The anti-realist suspects

reality, and thought as mirror-images of the world',[20] but, Wittgenstein asks, '[w]ould it be correct to say that our concepts reflect our life? They stand in the middle of it'.[21]

As I have maintained, the assumption that words (or more accurately, concepts) can be simply matched up with things is troublesome and misleading. Such an assumption entails one or other of two views concerning the structure of reality. The structure of the world may be seen as vested either in a reality which lies beyond human understanding or, as Hardy notes, in a human construction from events which in themselves have no order.[22] On such a view, either we receive our categories *en naturelle* (as it were) as a 'semantical deposit' from a world beyond our thoughts, or we think these categories and impose them as an arbitrary semantics upon the world; that is, we 'think' our world. However as Hardy points out, the process of knowing requires a two-way flow of information.

> [W]hat is required is a noetic qualification whereby the 'knower' is capacitated by the reality to be known, and therein achieves a 'selectivity' whereby he can discern what are the basic conditions which define what is actually the case ... Such a selectivity does not abstract from the physico-chemical, biological, mental, and socio-cultural structures of the world, but finds the basic constraints which define what is actual and relevant – which are intrinsic to the real, not external to it.[23]

This selectivity appears to operate like a skill (and could thus be said to be subject to training). 'As such it is very nearly indescribable and unprescribable.' Accordingly, Hardy sees the need to be rid of the traditional distinction between 'knowing-how' and 'knowing-that': 'it is also incapable

---

that we cannot find meaning in assertions ... unless it is related to the means of verifying them that we human beings actually possess'. (128–9.)

20 Wittgenstein, *Philosophical Investigations*, #96.

21 Ludwig Wittgenstein, *Remarks on Colour*, G. E. M. Anscombe (ed. and tr.), (Oxford: Blackwell, 1977), III, #302 – see also Wittgenstein, *Philosophical Investigations*, ##428, 435, 7.

22 Daniel Hardy, 'Christ and Creation', in T. F. Torrance (ed.), *The Incarnation* (Edinburgh: Handsel, 1981), 93.

23 Ibid. 97.

of being separated into an antecedent methodology which can be considered in isolation from the actual process in which one is qualified by the reality to be known or lived with; there is no forecourt to the temple, in which we can discover knowledge without knowing (as Hegel used to say)'. The selectivity is also one of mutual constraint. Not only must there 'be a constant correction by the object … the thinking never claims to achieve a final definiteness … a thinking of the object is a complexity of definiteness and openness … toward the object to emerge more fully' – the information is also constrained by the human processes of perceiving and knowing and their reliance on antecedent experience and knowledge. As such it is always less than the reality. Knowing is restricted by capacity to know and be known.[24]

How might Hardy's 'post-critical' realism be related to a language game perspective? While a language-game ontology (and hence epistemology) in being non-dualistic with regard to words and things cannot be typed as either traditionally realist or idealist, to accept the existence of a divine reality transcendent of human concepts is to be a realist of a sort – a 'theistic realist'.[25] For a 'language-game theology', this means accepting a Wittgensteinian ontology and epistemology without (ultimately) accepting its relativism. This is not as contradictory as it sounds. Ultimate reality and truth are not humanly available except as signs of transcendence, disruptions within what we take to be basic (our local patterns and categories) that point to a more general and comprehensive pattern and coherence. Kerr believes that 'Under imaginative enough anti-realist pressure … a non-dualistic realism may become available'.[26]

24 Ibid. 98.

25 I argue that this is the only sort of theism which survives reductionism – see Part Four, Chapter 2.

26 Kerr, *Theology After Wittgenstein*, 128, 136–7. Kerr endorses Dummett's view that 'While anti-realism is ultimately incoherent, realism is tenable only on a theistic basis … The realist is challenged to explain how an assertion is capable of being true or false when the evidence for or against it is, in principle, unavailable – at least, by tacit implication, to us'. (Ibid. 128. See also Dummett, *Truth and Other Enigmas*.)

There are, however, difficulties in calling this 'both-and' type of epistemology 'realist'. Kerr recognises that a Wittgensteinian 'realism' must recognise the role of training in a consensual interpretation of the 'blooming buzzing confusion' of sensory experience. Such a consensus and training is part of the givenness of forms of life. However, as Kerr has pointed out, commonly 'Realists, just as much as idealists, fail to acknowledge that *das leben* is "the given"' and, 'Words have meaning only in the stream of life'.[27] The categorisations which arise through metaphorising are not, therefore, 'natural kinds' or human constructions in a dichotomous sense, but represent a diachronic reality which, as Hardy observes (and Wittgenstein would endorse), is the product of an on-going dialogue between the object and our concept of the object, a dialogue whose participants are inseparable.

Kerr (like the Hintikkas) maintains that the later Wittgenstein was concerned to demonstrate the epistemological basicality of language-games, arguing that without their ordering of shared practices no understanding of reality would be possible. However our practices involving first-order uses of language are up too close for us to notice. 'Our signs are so natural that we come to imagine we could communicate without them: meaning becomes a purely mental activity. Our reliance on language is so complete that we become oblivious of it ... thus the metaphysical paradigm of the self is generated ... The meaning is on the surface – emotions are personified'.[28] Yet it is this very basicality of language-games and the ensuing ineffability of the language-world link which 'forces' realism, if it is to be maintained in the face of this ontology, to become theological.[29] If truth and reality cannot be separated, then together they transcend our conceptions of them;

27 Wittgenstein, *Remarks on the Philosophy of Psychology*, Vol. II, #687; Kerr, *Theology After Wittgenstein*, 131–4.

28 Wittgenstein, *Philosophical Investigations*, #693; ibid. 137.

29 I contend that realism itself, as with any metaphysical stance, is a position tenable only on faith. What is here being argued is that to follow realism to its logical conclusion is to follow it into theology. That is, to plump for a coherent realism is to plump for a theological metaphysic. This does not mean that God is a matter of logical inference, merely that one metaphysic held in faith leads to another, and that a given metaphysic may have hidden implications!

therefore both must come as gift. As Hausman observes: 'the question in the final analysis is not how to label one's position as idealist or realist; the question concerns the locus of the constraints of interpretation. If anyone willing to agree that some fundamental condition must account for constraints that surpass antecedent organisations of our ways of interpreting experience and wants to call this condition mind dependent, that person must have a preconception of some more fundamental source'.[30]

Another theological implication of an abandonment of the realist-idealist distinction is the loss of the traditional subjective-objective dichotomy. If, in a language-game theology, the realist anti-realist dichotomy is not observed, the reality of God cannot be simply either objective or subjective because this reality, in encompassing all other realities, is mediated and understood in terms of language-games. As Hausman notes, to be transcendent, God does not have to be either ultimate object or ultimate mind. This is not to deny the existence of transcendent realities beyond the scope of human forms of life, but it is to see that the reality (divine and created) which comes to us must come to us within our forms of life. To rephrase Max Black, natural kinds are 'natural kinds under a certain description'. As Barth puts it, the description is given as part of the revelation: God's self-revelation includes self-interpretation. Thus theism does not depend for its rationality or success upon a primitive or naïve realism entailing a subject-object (hence language-world) demarcation. What such a demarcation ultimately ensures is the demise of realism in favour of idealism and the annihilation thus of a realist theology.[31]

30 Hausman, *Metaphor and Art*, 189–90.

31 As both Soskice (*Metaphor and Religious Language*) and Gunton (*Actuality of Atonement*) point out. See also my article, Sue Patterson, 'Janet Martin Soskice, Metaphor and a Theology of Grace', *Scottish Journal of Theology*, 46/1 (1993), 1–26.

4.3.3. God Comes in Perturbation

> *[Ricoeur]: As we must operate within an existing language order, metaphor's creation or discovery of a new order must be by way of creating rifts in the old order which was itself created in the very same way.* [2.3.1.]

For a language-game theology, an ontology of givenness means that metaphorising, in creating new moves in language-games, is evidence of the essential incompleteness of the creaturely language-world. Metaphorising's disruption of existing conceptual patterns transcends conceived facts and possibilities. As has been noted, the gain to actuality through metaphorising's incorporation within actuality of that which is transcendent of actuality may be interpreted theologically as revelation. As has also been suggested, this revelation is manifested in a disruption to and repatterning of conventional practices involving use of language within (a thereby extended) actuality. Hardy sees the need to replace the assumption that reality is a fixed state of affairs by a view of reality including 'dynamics of different kinds within a harmony of being'.[32] Within the interweavings of human forms of life there are 'undetermined interactions – perturbations – which "trigger" changes for both'. For a 'language-game theology', metaphorising is a means of these 'perturbations' (the linguistic expressions of which are metaphors), a way in which disruption and repatterning of the complex of language-games occurs and a new pattern or logic is achieved. In metaphorising's bringing of perturbation, the metaphor's incongruence with presently conceived actuality challenges the reality and truth of that actuality. As Jüngel expresses this:

> Theological metaphor enters into actuality in such a way that it encounters not only a horizon of meaning other than its own, not only another 'world' … Rather, it enters the actuality of the world (insofar as the world assumes the metaphorical

32 Hardy, 'The Spirit of God in Creation and Reconciliation', 13. This is not to dispose of 'fixities' but to make them nonbasic. An individual or sentence is like a 'still' taken from the moving picture of a language-game.

> quality of being predicated of God) in such a way that the world is confronted with the possibility of its own non-being, from which alone new being can arise. One who speaks about God speaks to the hearer of the fact that the nonbeing of both the hearer and the world is a possibility overcome by God alone. This is the essence of all religious language.[33]

As I argued in chapter 2 of Part Three, the basicality of language-games entails that practice is prior to logical constructions. The creation of a new possible world or scenario may involve the creation of a new logic.[34] This view of logic is made possible by a language-game ontology, which, as I concluded in Part One, views relations as prior to individuals.[35] Wittgenstein's forms of life may be regarded as proposition-worlds which incorporate the language-games which provide their verification and which may include contradictory or impossible propositions or perturbations.[36] According to a language-game theology, metaphorising, as the breaking through of a new and wider logic, is responsible for these seeming contradictions or impossibilities. As I suggested in Chapter 2 of Part Three, in interpreting an utterance as metaphorical, one appears to choose from a number of states of affairs and propositions which are conceivably possible, but where the new metaphor is a challenge to logic, metaphorising may turn an inconceivable possibility into actuality and in so doing, call into question the universality of human conceptions of logic as well as contingent facts. Thus a consequence of metaphorising's bringing of perturbation is

33 Jüngel, 'Metaphorical Truth', 67. The Biblical root-metaphor which pre-eminently expresses this challenge to the being of the world 'is the identification of the risen one with the crucified man Jesus'. This is the metaphor upon which all other Christian metaphors are built.

34 Genova, 'Philosophy and the Consideration of Other-Worldly Possibilities', 399–401. (See also Winch, *Ethics and Action*, cited by Sherry, *Religion, Truth and Language-Games*, 35.)

35 See also Chapter 4 of Part Four below. Such a view would be inconceivable for a world–model which took objects as primitive as things have to exist before they can be false, and a false object is a contradiction in terms (see Part Three).

36 Lycan, 'The Trouble with Possible Worlds', 313–15. This, as I note in Part Three chapter 2, is why Lycan prefers to take propositions as constituents of possible worlds: '[doing so] makes room for impossible worlds as well as possible ones'.

that theological language as metaphor asserts that certain 'impossible' possibilities (re-patternings which cut across the existing patterns) are integral to actuality. Such possibilities, being inaccessible to our conceptual logic, must be understood as givens.[37]

Jüngel has shown how metaphorising may be seen as a sign of transcendence within that which it transcends. However, while its product the metaphor is visible and ultimately comprehensible, the process of metaphorising is itself incomprehensible because that which effects a gain to conceptual knowledge transcends that knowledge. In other words, to know that metaphor *is* is not to know *how* it is. In this way, metaphorising, while itself a language-game, necessarily reveals that which lies beyond the limits of human conceptual knowledge: the complex of language-games and forms of life. Metaphorising thus requires an input from unknown actuality expressed in terms of a rearrangement (new relation) of known actuality in order for that actuality to be. As has been noted, the transcendent input is not merely transcendent of our conceptual grasp of language-world; it must also be transcendent of the practical knowledge we have of the business of living because metaphorising not only creates new metaphors, but creates the new moves these metaphors constitute in the language-games in which they occur.

When it comes to logic, Jüngel and Barth take a classically Leibnizian position. As Gunton notes, Barth sees human ability to exercise reason as divinely given. Comprehension of God cannot be by way of reason or logic because that would entail a priority of reason over God. God must therefore be the Author of logic.[38] In 'The World as Possibility and Actuality', Jüngel argues that the distinction between what is possible and what is impossible is prior to ('incomparably more fundamental than') the distinction

37 'Christianity is quite specific in that it understands such possibilities as a *donum* (something given) to which actuality is not of itself entitled, i.e. as a *potentia aliena* (outside power) which, however, still belongs to the being of actuality. Possibility is a gift. And in the judgment of faith, actuality lives by such gifts of possibility, however much this escapes our attention as our minds fasten onto actuality. The language of faith presupposes revelation'. (Jüngel, 'Metaphorical Truth', 16–17.)

38 Gunton, *Becoming and Being*, 126.

between the actual and the not-yet-actual. There is more to possibility than what is conceived as potential actuality: possibility as limited to human conceivability does not capture the fullness of possibility.[39] A distinction between the possible and the impossible is in effect a distinction between truth and falsehood in that only the possible is capable of being true and only the true is possible: what is impossible cannot be true (although the reverse does not apply).[40] Therefore truth is prior to actuality.

However, as has been noted, this conclusion is theological in its implications. If truth is prior to actuality and we reside in actuality, the determining of truth is beyond the reach of human judgment. The determining of the aptness of a model or metaphor cannot rely on what is presently known to be true or real in actuality. Any human judgment of possibility or impossibility can be provisional only: the ultimate judgment is a divine matter and must come to us as gift from beyond the bounds of our actuality. Therefore Jüngel concurs with Barth that if God makes these distinctions, then God is the source and revelation not only of fact but also of logic.[41]

39 Jüngel, 'The World as Possibility and Actuality', 116–17; 'Metaphorical Truth', 16–17.

40 As I noted in Part Three, Jüngel appears to equate truth with possibility. The corollary is that falsity is to be equated with impossibility. This is to be contrasted with Plantlnga's 'serious actualist' view that the impossible is not simply false; it is non-existent, the distinction between true and false being the distinction between the actual and the merely possible. On a 'serious actualist' view such as Plantinga's, God's creation of actuality is in the first instance a separation of being from non-being, and in the second instance a separation of the true from the not-yet-true, whereas for Jüngel there are no first and second instances: the two are the same. On this account falsehood is not merely non-actuality: it is non-being. However, both positions are consistent with the statement that God, in creating what is actual (the actual world), distinguishes possibility from impossibility and truth from falsehood.

41 Jüngel, 'The World as Possibility and Actuality', 110–11. As I pointed out in Part Three, while so-called Leibnizian world-models take modality as primitive, Leibniz himself located the origin of this modality in the mind of God (I would prefer to follow Barth, Jüngel, and Alan Torrance, and locate it in the relating activity of God. Therefore, as Jüngel maintains, the decision as to what is possible or impossible is not a human one and, accordingly, logic as absolute is not humanly accessible. What are available to us are relative logics which will vary with human uses of language in various forms of life.

Accordingly, metaphorising may be construed as a sign of the finitude of human logic. If logic is prior to actuality yet is only accessible to us relative to actuality because it is limited to human ability to judge, absolute logic is not a given. Instead, what is given is the human plurality of judgments. In Wittgenstein's language, what is given is 'forms of life'. Our determining of what is possible or impossible (itself a language-game) must be discerned within and through our forms of life. This conclusion is consistent with the later Wittgenstein's understanding of the role of logic as the rules (or 'grammar') regulating language-involving activities. However, a language-game theology requires Barth's and Jüngel's Leibnizian perspective to save Wittgensteinian logic, like Wittgensteinian truth, from drowning in a sea of relativism. God as the source, the bringer into being of logic, is prior to logic and as such may not be explained by logic. The human inaccessibility of absolute logic does not need to usher in a verdict of relativism (as Winch and Phillipps would maintain[42]). As Jüngel emphasises, God is not identifiable with the possible or the true. Instead it is God who distinguishes the possible and the true from the impossible and the false. In so distinguishing, God brings into being what is actual (the possible which is also true). 'If distinguishing between the possible and the impossible is a matter for God, then God's divinity must be actualised in such a way that the act of distinguishing determines what is possible and what is impossible. This means that only this act constitutes that which is possible as possible and that which is impossible as impossible ... As the one who does this ... God distinguishes himself from the world, God lets the world be actual.'[43] God is distinguished from world as the One who distinguishes as opposed to that which is distinguished. As such, God's being is revealed in the making possible of possibility, the bringing of the actual into existence.

Thus, in a 'language-game theology', as has been noted, metaphorising's bringing of perturbation produces a metaphoric incongruence with presently conceived actuality which challenges the reality and truth of that actuality.

42 This ultimately divine source of an absolute logic is what the 'Wittgenstein Fideists' find themselves unable to posit (see Part Four Chapter 2).

43 Jüngel, 'The World as Actuality and Possibility', 111–12.

> Theological metaphor enters into actuality in such a way that it encounters not only a horizon of meaning other than its own, not only another 'world' ... Rather, it enters the actuality of the world (insofar as the world assumes the metaphorical quality of being predicated of God) in such a way that the world is confronted with the possibility of its own non-being, from which alone new being can arise. One who speaks about God speaks to the hearer of the fact that the nonbeing of both the hearer and the world is a possibility overcome by God alone. This is the essence of all religious language.[44]

In connecting Hardy's concept of perturbation with metaphorising, I have made the case for a language-game theology's being seen to complement the Trinitarian theologies of Barth and Jüngel in which reason is a 'given' in relation to which the person of God is primitive. If, on a Wittgensteinian perspective, logic is inherently bound up with language and thought processes as the rules or 'grammar' of language-games, it follows that logic is necessarily given along with language-games. Moreover, metaphorising, as the agency of God in the forging of new logic, demonstrates that logic is integral to God's being. The giving of logic is part of God's self-disclosure language-game. Metaphorising as perturbation is, therefore, a divine giving of a new logic presently beyond our comprehension,[45] which disrupts our present logic in order to 'expand' it into a new pattern.

4.3.4. Giver as Given

The question posed at the end of Part Three was this: if metaphorising provides evidence that a reality beyond human conceiving (while unverifiable) is not meaningless in that while the complex of language-games is self-authenticating metaphorising shows its incompleteness, what verifies

44 Jüngel, 'Metaphorical Truth', 67.

45 As noted in Part Two, Ricoeur calls this a 'higher code of pertinence' (see his *Rule of Metaphor*). As also noted, there is an affinity here with Polanyi's, 'higher organising principle' (see his *Tacit Dimension*, Chapter 2: 'Emergence').

the additions to actuality which are at odds with actuality? How are we able to discern the truth? Such an absolute truth or reality must be either inaccessible or accessible only as a 'given'. As has been seen, paradoxically, this 'given' (as the only access to the absolute) must be given within the local and transient actuality of language-games. However, metaphorising in effecting a gain to an actuality composed of the totality of language-games obtaining at a given time poses the question: instead of a 'given', do we have an infinite regression of 'actualities' or 'realities'? If language-games are basic to human actuality and the totality of language-games continually expands, such a regression could be said to obtain. That which produces the 'given' is transcendent of it but might it not itself, in its product, in turn be a given in a new expanded actuality?

I suggest that the only answer to this conundrum (while not logically required) is theological. The act of giving necessarily transcends what is given. God as absolute Agent is unique in being revealed not only within what is give but also in the act of giving: the creation of language-games. God as absolute foundation is revealed in what is humanly foundational. Here is the sense in which Wittgenstein's 'given' forms of life and language-games are indeed given. As such, this is a givenness which contains the beyond in the disruptions to the coherence of human categories. In language-game theology, God, as giver and player of language-games, produces and enters the foundation of language-games within and upon which we build our lives. That which God has made foundational God now shows to be truly foundational only when rooted in God.

Metaphorising, then, in its perturbation of existing patterns and logic, provides evidence that our epistemic foundation is rooted beyond our forms of life. It appears that the patterns of language-world are contingent not simply on human practices but on an ordering activity which transcends the language-world complex of human activity. It is counter-intuitive (as well as illogical) that this transcendence should be capable of explanation in terms of the natural linguistically unconditioned universe. Such explanations can only end in a vicious regress. Transcendence (here taken to be divine) is here seen to be necessary to a coherent epistemology.[46] Yet, as Hardy puts it, 'if God (as the Transcendent) is to be knowable, we must be able 'to find the impact of the presence of God (Revelation or Grace) on the forms of our contextuality (Nature)'.[47] Metaphorising's continuing disruption and repatterning of this contextuality is one such impact. Thus, for a 'language-game theology', Hardy's question, how is God both transcendent and yet present in our contextuality?[48] – is seen not only to have a Trinitarian answer *simpliciter*, but a Trinitarian answer which gives a specific 'how' in terms of language-games.

The issue thereafter becomes that of acceptance of the givenness of theological metaphors. In *The Actuality of Atonement*, Gunton appears near to this insight (although maintaining a traditional language-world separation) when he speaks of language as the recipient of the gift of meaning given to us by the world as it gives itself to be known and, spoken by us as metaphor, shapes our language to fit the 'causal' structures of reality.[49] As Gunton says, it is the first-order language of scripture describing the events surrounding Jesus of Nazareth which becomes the reference for our speaking about God. In 'language-game theology', the language-games which show us Jesus Christ in the world and in Scripture differentiate God from not-God within our forms of life and shape our language-world to fit the reality of God.

It is through an inextricable interweaving of divine activity with divine content that, as Hardy remarks, we experience the 'pressure of God' upon us to differentiate God from world within world.[50] Therefore, while it may appear that I am making a distinction between what is absolutely basic and what is humanly (relatively) basic, language-game theology upholds Barth's

46 In any case, as was pointed out in Part Four Chapter 2: <God> reduces to <not-God> if subject to or contingent on any other.

47 See Part Four, Chapter 4 for further discussion on this point.

48 Hardy, 'The Spirit of God in Creation and Reconciliation', 237ff.

49 Gunton, *Actuality of Atonement*, 48. As I have argued, along with Barth and Jüngel, if language-world gives itself to be known, this gift is a gift of God. As such, it is part of God's gift of self. Our world is given to us as a vehicle of God's own self-revelation.

50 Hardy, 'Christ and Creation', 106.

insistence that what God is in God-self, God is for us. God is revealed within the human basicality of language-world in Jesus Christ. As Gunton observes,

> What is distinctive about Barth's formulation is that the three-foldness is a three-foldness of event, of something that really happens and can properly be described as God … Because this revelation [of God in Jesus Christ] is where God happens among men, it is impossible to distinguish between God's world and himself, between what God does and what he is … if Jesus Christ is God, then God is really given in him and does not have to be sought behind or apart from him.[51]

What is revealed as God within what is humanly basic is what God is in reality. No other conclusion, argues 'language-game theology', can do justice to the Christian doctrine of God.

Hardy offers this interpretation: for God to be the source and ultimate comprehensiveness of meaning is for God to be a comprehensiveness upon which all of reality is contingent. As such, this comprehensiveness is necessarily transcendent. It is impossible for the creatures contingent on this higher organisation to grasp its entirety from within it. This entirety is only graspable if it is translated into 'the inner logic of the world'.[52] For God to be knowable, God must be immanent. Human knowledge of the actuality which lies beyond human conceiving demands not only that the meaning and justification of all that is both world and human lie beyond our human context, but also that this justification and judgment enter language-world as a given which is self-gift.

However, for a 'language-game theology' such knowledge is broadly based. Conceptual or propositional truth is inseparable from the particular and local reality of human practices carried out by human persons. It comes

51 Gunton, *Becoming and Being*, 128–9. This is consistent with the Trinitarian doctrine which is the starting point of Barth's theology ('God reveals Himself. He reveals Himself through Himself. He reveals Himself.' *CD* I/1 296). Gunton sees that 'Barth is claiming that there is a threefoldness about the way in which the God of the Bible authenticates his reality, and that he does it in such a way that we are led to think of him as threefold in himself'. (Ibid. 128.)

52 Hardy, 'Christ and Creation', 108.

clothed in the new relation of the familiar and the concrete: as language-games.[53] As has already been observed, a Wittgensteinian perspective provides the insight that this entry of God's reality into world is inseparable from the entry of God 's truth into language. To come within world is to come within words: within language-world.[54] Given that the basis of all human communication lies in language-games, divine self-communication would require to be couched in language-game terms.[55]

Bonhoeffer's Christological concept of 'counterlogos'[56] is another alternative interpretation which expresses some of the above insights. God comes to language-world as the Other who is beyond conception, who enters the categories of human language use, disrupting and reforming them so that they may truly speak of God. As has already been mentioned, Bonhoeffer makes the point that the reality of God cannot be contained within a conceptual formulation: the Word of God is not idea but personal address. In thus seeing God in terms of personal activity inseparable from language, Bonhoeffer is implicitly employing an ontology not dissimilar to Wittgenstein's in which the pragmatic function of language is primary and linguistic activity is seen to be a part of reality.[57] For language-game theology, God's entering of creation is God's entry into language-world; God comes in the first instance as activity involving words (as personal address). As such, the person of God is beyond conception but an experience which provides the possibility of comprehension.

53 I maintain (with Hardy) that for God to be knowable as more than a pervasive and fragmented immanence, it is necessary for God to be incarnated. However, further Christological exposition is beyond the scope of the present work.

54 Again, the reminder needs to be given that this is not a (linguistic-idealistic) world within language but the inextricable interweaving of words and things that comprise the complex of language-games and forms of life.

55 The material in this and the following paragraph first appeared in my article, Patterson, 'Gratuitous Truth: Metaphor and Revelation'.

56 Bonhoeffer, *Christ the Centre*, 29f.

57 Ibid. 27–39. Jüngel's pragmatical understanding of metaphor (metaphorising) as essentially address – the coming of truth – which challenges and revises prior ideas of truth – appears to be a development of Bonhoeffer's thinking.

4.3.5. Summary and Conclusion

Theologically, Wittgenstein's metaphysic of givenness is consistent with Barth's 'analogy of faith' in stipulating a givenness not only to language, but of language itself, and not only of words and things, but of their inseparable interweaving in language-games. Revelation is thus the incorporating of language from its very beginning in the being of God. God's self-revelation is understood in terms of (although not exhausted by) the totality of human world-and-language-involving activities. The coming into being of language-world may thus be seen as integral to the revelation of God's being, yet not in itself an exhaustion of God's being. If a language-game theology, in being non-dualistic with regard to words and things, cannot be typed as either traditionally realist or idealist, it entails the further consequence of a blurring of the traditional distinctions between reality and truth, objective and subjective. While to accept the existence of a reality transcendent of human concepts is to be a theistic 'realist', it is the foundationality of language-games and the ensuing ineffability of the language-world link which 'forces' realism to become theological.

Where metaphorising as perturbation challenges and reshapes the reality and truth of actuality, metaphor is evidence of the essential incompleteness of a human milieu whose roots lie beyond. For a language-game theology, what is ultimately basic is the activity of bringing into relation (through metaphorising) in which the beyond is both exemplified and brought to human living and thinking. This shows that language-world is contingent on an ordering activity which transcends the language-world complex of human activity. This transcendent agency may be identified with the being of God. Metaphorising reveals God as absolute Agent, revealed not only within what is given: the complex of language-games, but also in the act of giving. While the relating agency of metaphorising as transcendent of the actuality of language-world is incapable of explanation (such explanations can only end in a vicious regress), such a transcendent agent is necessary to a coherent epistemology. For language-game theology, metaphorising's continuing disruption and repatterning of this contextuality provides evidence and knowledge of a 'higher organising principle' (Polanyi's term) through its impact on human forms of life.

Finally, I have argued that explanation of how God is both transcendent and immanent in our forms of life requires *both* a Trinitarian *and* a language-game theology as the language-games which reveal Jesus Christ in life and in Scripture differentiate God from not-God within our forms of life and shape our language-world to fit the reality of God.

CHAPTER FOUR

The Case for a 'Language-Game Theology' (2)

4.4.1. Metaphorised Relations

> *[A] language-game ontology entails that both properties and individuals are defined by the various language-games in which they play a part. Viewed in this light, semantic* relata *(language and objects) cannot be distinct items or entities, but by nature are interwoven in activities, in roles and language-games.* [1.2.2.]

I have argued that the way in which metaphorising achieves a gain to knowledge is by means of transfer and combination of our prior training in playing language-games – that the extent of our knowledge is increased by a new relation of previous knowledge.[1] It follows that the new noetic relation is prior to the newly combined content of knowledge. A language-game ontology views reality as irreducibly relational, therefore a theology which takes language-games as basic must also take relationality as primitive.[2] According to Jüngel,

1 As has been argued, metaphorising demonstrates the existence of new relations which may be inconceivable possibilities within actuality. Metaphorising brings to conception a hitherto unconceived or even inconceivable possibility, which is then recognised to be not merely possible but actual. This gain to actuality is achieved (via the metaphorising language-game) through a new relation of aspects of known actuality in a transfer and combination of language-games and their moves. As I argued in Part Three, world-scenarios construed as Wittgensteinian forms of life cannot be reduced to individual 'atoms'; their interwoven language-games, like a mass of sticky toffee, leave trailing threads when an attempt is made to separate them.

2 As was argued in Part Three Chapter 2: if the diachronic nature of a language-game based ontology is sustained by metaphorising, then it is not so much relation itself

> [T]heology cannot formulate the purity of the relationship without an origin of relationship, which as the origin of the relationship is, in that it sets itself in relation. Such setting-itself-in-relation is, understood theologically, pure relationship. And in the sense of such a setting-itself-in-relation God's being is essentially relational; God's being is 'pure relationship' … God sets himself in relation to himself, in order so to be he who he is. In this sense, God's being is in becoming.[3]

It is the activity of initiating (and then sustaining) relation which, according to Jüngel, characterises God's being, yet the activity of initiating (and then sustaining) relation is the same activity that I have described as the metaphorising language-game. A doctrine of God which takes the initiation of relation as basic to God's being should thus be able to accommodate a language-game ontology. Two of these doctrinal approaches will be examined here.

First, to continue with Jüngel's interpretation of Barth: God's being-as-relational is evidenced by the fact of revelation. Primary to God's being is God's decision to become – to be in relation. 'Decision sets relationship; for it is as such a setting-oneself-in-relationship.'[4] Non-being is excluded as 'that which is not willed by God'.[5] Being is thus prior to – that is, precedes – non-being. For God to be in relation and yet non-contingent requires a double understanding of God's relationality. In the first instance, argues Jüngel, God's being is related to itself in the Trinitarian relation;[6] in the second instance God's being is related to that which is

---

as the becoming of relation (the coming into being of new relation) which is basic. It may be seen that theologically this entails that God's being is constituted in relation. However, as Jüngel points out, 'it is not enough to formulate God's being simply as a being in relationship. A conscious or unconscious natural theology certainly does not become Protestant by making the relation the basic category of its statements. And the relation as "pure relationship" is still not formulated adequately enough so long as its purity is not formulated theologically'. (Jüngel, *The Doctrine of the Trinity*, 101–2.)

3 Ibid. 102.

4 Ibid. 68.

5 Ibid. 79.

6 If revelation is God's self-interpretation as Trinity, and God's being is thus self-related, God's being is constituted in relation (ibid. 63). However, 'the modes of God's being

other than God. This second relation is a 'becoming' which is 'peculiar to his own being, a becoming which allows us to comprehend God's being as a "being-in-act"'.[7] This being-as-activity is language-involving in being constituted in the Trinitarian relation in which, as Jüngel puts it, 'God says [or (Wittgenstein-ly) plays the language-game of saying] "yes" to Himself'. At the same time this self-communication and affirmation constitutes God's historicity. Through the Trinitarian relation, God 'makes space' within God-self for time. 'This making-space-for-time within God is a continuing event'.[8] In this way, revelation as God's entering into time ('eternity in a single moment') makes history.[9]

It is in the space within God occupied by time that God's being-for-us takes place. In a language-game theological paradigm, time-space may be understood as the diachronicity in which the life-forms of language-world (the totality of language-games) continually come into being. Therefore the event of revelation as both a 'moment of eternity in time' and a 'gain to language' is a language-game event (metaphorising) which, as a gain to language, is a gain to the totality of language-games.

In a similar way, using a different paradigm, Hardy sees the immanent Godhead as 'a dynamic structured relationality in whom there is an infinite possibility of life'. The contextual activity of God is simply identified neither with Christ (as congruence) nor with the Holy Spirit (as energy). Both of these depend on 'the initial conditions which we conventionally identify as the "Father"'. The signs of this divine activity are the initiation and sustaining of contextuality through perturbation and repatterning.[10] God is not prior to the 'diversity of all things' but is an immanent and

---

which are differentiated from each other are so related to each other that each mode of God's being becomes what it is only together with the two other modes of being. The relational structuring in God's being … is thus a being in becoming' (ibid.). Barth's concept of being thus 'holds together being and act and does not tear them apart like the concept of "essence"'. (Barth, *CD* II/1 262; ibid. 64.)

7 Ibid. 99–100.

8 Ibid. 96.

9 Ibid. 97.

10 Hardy, 'The Spirit of God in Creation and Reconcilation', 246–7.

active unity 'which arises in their diversity, rather than preceding it'. God as interweaver (agent of unity in diversity) of contextuality is as such transcendent (subsuming) of contextuality while being immanent in it as creator and sustainer. Contextual diversity as particularity, involving '"relativities" with their own integrities', is thus created and sustained by the interweaving activity of the Godhead.[11]

Thinking all this together with a 'language-game theology', metaphorising may, therefore, be seen as an action of God which shows God's being to inhere, first, in the bringing into relation of the unrelated (the act of metaphorising), a process described by Hardy as 'perturbation' and 'repatterning'; second, in the relation or new pattern itself (the language-game); and third, in the new coherence or congruence which is given by the relation (the proposition, rule, or criterion) inferable from and embedded in the language-game. This process results in the appearance within this complex of language-world (Hardy's 'contextuality') of particular new secondary links which provide a new coherence. These links might be termed theological language-games. As such they are lived as much as articulated. Novel metaphors are thus new expressions of congruence, of the divine-human relation, within the context of the human person as player of language-games and inhabiter of forms of life.[12]

While Jüngel and Hardy have developed their Trinitarian theologies of relation intensively within their different paradigms, the possibilities of relating such a theology to a language-game ontology are only touched on here. I continue this line of inquiry in my later work.[13]

11 Hardy comments, 'By the way, this changes the character of universality, and avoids the monistic tendencies ... against which the postmodernists rightly protest'. (Ibid. 252.)

12 From a Trinitarian viewpoint, the God-human relating activity expressed in the person and work of Jesus Christ is the criterion for this relation, Jesus Christ's being God-with-us as the proposition embedded in and inferable from the divine self-revelatory language-game.

13 See Patterson, *Realist Christian Theology*, Chapter 6.

4.4.2. Things and Persons

> *[T]o question the idea of an individual as a distinct entity is also to call into question the classical notion of 'substance' as basic, for the very idea of an individual has, on this account, become the product of language-games and will vary between language-games; 'The notion of individual simpliciter makes no sense. The reality can be conceptualised structured into individuals in more than one way, none of which reduces to the others.'* [1.2.2.]

Given that the process of new relation is prior to its content, a theology of relation must hold that substance, as the content of relation, is nonbasic. Regarding what he refers to as 'the classical view' of God as absolute substance, Gunton comments that if 'the "substantial" analogy describes what God really is in himself ... the events in which he becomes man cannot be described as God because they are the actions of something timeless and unmoving'. Moreover, to say that nothing can become without being is to be 'the prisoner of the past and of language of the past'. While God's being has traditionally been understood as substance, it does not follow that this is the only possible conclusion.[14]

For Jüngel also, Creator-as-Agent is to be distinguished from creation-as-substance. 'God is to be thought of out of the event of justification as the one who, in the very act of distinguishing himself from the world, relates himself to it.'[15] As Jüngel points out in his critique of Gollwitzer, to comprehend (even implicitly) the divine being in terms of the clas-

14 Gunton, *Becoming and Being*, 170. See also Torrance, *Persons in Communion*, chapter 4 for an extended discussion on this.

15 Jüngel, 'The World as Possibility and Actuality', 113. Of course, the term 'substance' will not describe a creation comprising language-games any more than it will describe its creator. Moreover, a language-game theology, in maintaining a universal nonbasicality of substance, would not allow that the Creator-creature distinguishing factor could be agency-substance – not that it is suggested that Jüngel's doctrine of God ultimately relies on such simplistic categorising!

sical notion of substance[16] is to pose problems for the notion of God's relationality. A God construed as 'first substance' must be unrelated to any other because relation extends being to include the relatee: relation means reciprocity.[17] From the standpoint of a substance foundation, this would make the God-human relation necessary to the being of God: God would not be God without humanity.[18] However, asks Jüngel, how can personal being not be constituted in relationship? Gollwitzer supposes he has solved the problem by seeing God's being-for-us as flowing from 'the freedom of his being-for-himself', but how can these two things be different? On a Barthian view they cannot be. 'Whoever, like Gollwitzer, wants to maintain and think of God's independence cannot avoid the task of conceiving God's independence ... out of God's own subsistence.' Such a subsistence (as essential substance), therefore, necessarily excludes revelation. Instead, 'God's independent being must ... be understood from the event of revelation as an event granting this event of revelation'. God's being as subsistence is self-movement: agency not substance. Whereas God's being-as-substance precluded revelation, 'As self-movement God's independent being makes revelation possible.'[19]

As I have argued, a 'language-game theology' also takes substance as nonbasic. Drawing Jüngel's argument now into a language-game theological paradigm: it is the divine language-games of relation and affirmation played within the Trinitarian relationship which constitute God's being and enable, through God's language-game of self-communication, God's being-for-us.

Connecting all this now with the conclusion to Part One: if substance is nonbasic, it follows that so too is the individual.[20] An 'atomic' world-view is ruled out by the basicality of relation. It was argued in Chapter 2 of Part One that a language-game ontology precludes a phenomenalistic

16 Jüngel, *Doctrine of the Trinity*, 89.

17 Ibid.

18 Ibid. 90.

19 Ibid. 91–3. See also Patterson, *Realist Christian Theology*, chapter 6.

20 See Patterson, *Realist Christian Theology*, chapter 6.

foundationalism based on sense-data. The point was also made that such foundationalism, explicit or implicit, has unhelpful theological implications. As these implications underline the requirement for a relational doctrine of God, some of them will be explored here.

Theological approaches which rest on a phenomenalistic foundation will hold as axiomatic the primacy of the individual. As Hardy observes, such theologies deal with 'the-world-as-it-is-for-me', assuming that the world is inaccessible as it is 'in itself' and can only be known 'from the "inside"', as it were, 'as for me and [as] made important by me'. In these cases, the nature of reality, or of historical truth and meaning, is held to be dependent on the experience of the knower. The premise is that all understanding of reality or historical truth depends upon the 'experience of a knower and his method'.[21]

Even allowing that God might create order through our co-agency in the imposing of a conceptual order upon an external chaos, an individualist theology must inevitably give the human mind a monopoly on God's revelation as well as imply that God is also a human conceptual creation (as if the source of all order lies within our minds). However, asks Hardy, is not the reverse the truth? Are not our concepts informed by the patterning inherent in the things and their relations to each other themselves? A 'language-game theology' adds the rider that God does not form our

21 This gives rise to a (Saussurean-style 'structuralist') view that human language places a conceptual structure on events which in themselves have no order. On such an interpretation concepts order experience. As would be expected, such an ontology itself makes conceptual demarcations between types of events. While this sort of demarcation frequently uses spatio-temporal terms, it 'is methodologically established and bears little relation to what is actually known of these spatio-temporal conceptions today'. (Hardy, 'Christ and Creation', 90–3.) Hardy comments further: 'Some of the insights afforded by these positions are helpful, especially those which undertake a thorough elucidation of epistemology (e.g. Popper and Lonergan) or historical reasoning (e.g. Pannenberg), though this is not the case where the epistemological analysis simply establishes the comparability of religious with other interpretations of the world such as those employed in science (e.g. Hick and Barbour). Still less is it the case where epistemology is introjected into the inaccessible subjectivity of the believer, as in most existentialism'. (Ibid. 92.)

concepts via a 'direct-line' to our minds; the whole of creation is involved in the revelatory process through the interweavings of language-world in language-games.

Theological deconstructionism utilises a variant of such an individual-as-basic ontology. Deconstructionism claims to have done away with the separation of language and world but has done so by reducing world to language. According to Wesley J. Robbins, 'the fundamental deconstructionist discovery about language (is] that its purported reference to an extra-linguistic world is a ruse'. The deconstructionists claim that this deception began with the written word and is responsible for our 'illusions' regarding a transcendent God and a transcendent self. Prior to literacy, oral discourse was inseparable from experience of the world and could not therefore be transcended by nonlinguistic world. Any ideas of the reference function of language have therefore been occasioned by the written language's implicit false separation of the verbal and the nonverbal.[22]

While one must have some appreciation for what the deconstructionists are trying to do in their attempt to rid us of a troublesome dichotomy, there are certain difficulties with their position which reveal themselves in implications for theology and philosophy. The implication for theology is: if God is to exist, God must exist within the 'ceaseless flux' of language. As, however, reality is linguistic reality only, God cannot transcend language but must be immanent in it.[23] God in effect becomes the 'ceaseless flux' of language itself (as opposed to certain religious formulations in language). Divinity becomes 'meaning as boundless, inexhaustible flow ... the vital force resident in language' rather than the 'permanent, transcendent referential framework of language'.[24] The divine being and gift is the whole force of language. Writers are the priests of this divine force and its prophets, the recipients of the revelation: 'It is these *literati* who, in and

22 Wesley J. Robbins, 'Pragmatism and the Deconstruction of Theology', *Religious Studies* 24 (1988), 377ff: 375.

23 Ibid. 377. This is reminiscent of Phillipps's position (see Part Four, chapter 2 above).

24 Ibid.

through writing, are closest to, and thereby in a position to keep the rest of culture close to, the divine reality'.[25]

Yet how can these *literati* 'set up shop' when there is no position inside of language from which they can mediate the 'divine reality' of language as a whole, and in any case no reality outside of language? This reveals the philosophical implications of this ideology. In effect, Theological Deconstructionism shares the Wittgensteinian view of language as universal medium without accepting its entailment of inaccessibility to explanation of that which is taken to be primitive and without understanding that use of language is prior to its linguistic 'moves'. It therefore fails to be coherent on this count. It also fails on another count. As its reality is entirely linguistic (no metaphysic, however Nietzschean, can do away with reality – reality is merely redefined), there is no way of establishing the truth of language.

However, this obstacle does not prevent the Deconstructionists from undertaking to make judgments about the truth and reality of language as a whole. Their fundamental dictum, 'the world is Text' is just such a judgment. Accordingly, for the Theological Deconstructionists, it is not in the end the reality of the flow and flux of textuality which occupies the position of God, but the individuals who decide what is or is not true to that reality.[26]

As has been noted, theologies which rely on the premise of the primacy of the individual are problematic for several reasons. These reasons will now be summarised. First, as Hardy notes, an individual-mind-centred theory of knowledge leads inevitably to an idealist or nominalist world-view:

> When the transcendent ground is thus separated from the ordinarily-knowable, it lapses into the position of a 'brute fact' knowable only as the 'sheer transcendence' of an other ... [T]he transcendent other can only be connected with ordinary nature and history by an extrinsic relation made in human experience, never by an inner

25 Ibid. 379.

26 The irony is that in so deciding they do the thing they decree to be impossible: they transcend the flow of language. Thus Theological Deconstructionism is ultimately self-referentially incoherent.

> relation which presents itself to human knowing ... So strong is this demarcation usually assumed to be that the claim for a relation between the ordinarily-knowable and its ground, or between the conditions of the world and man and their ground in a logos of creation, is considered to be arbitrary and unjustifiable.[27]

Second, such an ontology may lead to yet another misconception about the nature of knowledge: that it 'consists in a direct act, much like the act of perception, in which there seems to be a relation between the knower and the known'. In the case of religious knowledge, this can lead to the attempt to know God directly, mediated, if at all, only by 'the activity of knowing and its methodological constraints', or by one's capacity to make that knowing of God cohere with a particular religious tradition. However, knowledge of God through a 'direct act' of knowing is precluded by the logical impossibility of knowing the transcendent. If this impossibility is overlooked and such access is thought to be available, the 'spatio-temporal, conscious and social structures' of a mediated revelation (and the particularity of their instances) will be bypassed or relegated to the status of circumstantial or qualifying conditions for the direct revelation. 'The effect of this stress on direct knowledge is thereby to reach through creation and Christ without taking them fully seriously as mediations of God' presence.' They are not seen as bringers of the knowledge of God 'for that capacity is taken to be natural to human beings.'[28]

Third, as a consequence of the second danger, there is also the danger of confusing the absolute truth about reality with particular human perceptions of it. Indeed, according to this ontology, there is no distinction to be made here. All is subjective: 'what is true is what is true for me'. Therefore, such a system has 'no stringent method of establishing knowledge, and a greater willingness to equate it with belief and disposition'.[29] Theology in general (and the idea of a transcendent deity in particular) is thus either

27 Hardy, 'Christ and Creation', 94. Gunton considers that this is the main weakness of McFague's theology (see her *Metaphorical Theology*), noting that the utilisation of such a theory of knowledge entails that 'a collapse into idealism is inevitable'. (Gunton, *Actuality of the Atonement*, 41.)

28 Hardy, 'Christ and Creation', 94–6.

29 Ibid. 95.

in danger of (on an individualistic level) being swallowed by solipsism or (on a social level) captured by contextual relativism.

I contend that such pitfalls are to be avoided only by the adoption of a theology which employs a language-world-integrating ontology. Such an ontology is both required by and entails the fact that an transcendent God is unknowable by any 'direct act' and only accessible through the mediating moves (activities, propositions and utterances) of human language-games. It also entails that God cannot be either the creation of human subjectivity or subsumed within (or equated with) the totality of language-world, but is the source of that totality as the creator of moves in language-games through the agency of metaphorising.[30]

In *Theology after Wittgenstein*, Kerr sets out to destroy the grip of this foundationalism (as Cartesian mind-world dualism) on Christian thought.

> Much theological knowledge, not to mention everyday Christian piety and discourse, is permeated by the conception of the knowledge-seeking self which [Wittgenstein's] later work is out to deconstruct … this picture of the cognitive subject has roots, far beyond modern philosophy, in religious ideas about the soul … [in] the vitality of the myth of the soul as a ghost inside the body … human beings as angels fallen into flesh.[31]

Kerr applies Wittgenstein's thought as a healthy corrective to this view:

> To say that one's sensations are private is like saying that one plays patience on one's own (*PI* 248): it is perfectly obvious to everyone else what is going on … a whole

30 A phenomenalistic foundation is so built into our Western world-view that it is usually assumed unwittingly by default in the absence of the choice of any other. Therefore it has been important to make a case for the foundationality of language-games as a viable and superior alternative. As I emphasised in Part One, one can accept that knowledge of the physical world is caused by the having of sensations without having to be a phenomenological foundationalist and claim that this sensory mediation is epistemic.

31 Kerr, *Theology After Wittgenstein*, 168. Kerr considers that 'The only real problem for theologians in reading Wittgenstein lies in reluctance to acknowledge that the myth of the soul … has as strong a grip on our imagination as it ever had …' (Ibid. 169.)

> cultural-linguistic network has to be in place before pretending becomes a possibility ... [Wittgenstein] retrieve[s] the natural expressiveness of the human body and reaffirm[s] the indispensability of belonging to a community ...[32]

It is disappointing that when it comes to applications of Wittgensteinian insights to theology, Kerr does not address the theological implications of the ontology and epistemology implied by the acceptance of the basicality of language-games and forms of life in Wittgenstein's later work. If mind-world separation has been exposed as a dangerous myth, what, for Kerr, is to take its place?[33]

A 'language-game theology' holds that consciousness is a product of relation to surroundings. To recap on Part One, if language-games are basic, language-world linking activity is prior to individual perceptions of world, therefore sense-data are epistemically nonbasic. Humans are truly a 'blank slate' to begin with. Training in the language-games of our forms of life provides both the perception and the articulation of the perception which is empirical knowledge. We are trained by our social milieu in the moves of matching sense-impressions to physical-object-language. Without the meaning conferred by use in a language-game, the objects of sensations can have no meaning. Therefore the sensations in themselves are devoid of content and communicate no information. 'To equate the self with the world of experience is a radical way of bringing it out into the open, so to speak, without eliminating it. The "I" is not hidden in the head; it is the world viewed.'[34] Therefore, all knowledge (including self-knowledge) depends upon external experiences. 'There is no getting hold of anything in the world except by a move in the network of practice

32 Ibid. 88–9. 'Far from concealing the soul, the body retrieves it'. (Ibid. 93–4.) Cartesianism imagines that knowledge of our own thoughts is the only indubitable knowledge. However, this process resembles a cat chasing its tail. (See Ian Ramsey, 'The Systematic elusiveness of "I"' *The Philosophical Quarterly* 5 (1955), 193–204.)

33 While Kerr sees the basis of realism as the 'givenness' of forms of life (*das leben*), he does not pick up the theological challenge that the term 'givenness' offers. (Ibid. 172–4.)

34 Ibid. 96–8.

which is the community to which we belong (our life-forms)'[35] As I have emphasised, such knowledge is not subsumed by conceptual knowledge. It must therefore present itself to human comprehension as a given. 'The given ... is the common forms of life in which one participates from the outset not one's sense-data'.[36]

If all that constitutes an individual as a sentient human being is provided externally through relation with others in the interweavings of language-world, the primacy of the individual must give way to the primacy of relation. Our being as persons is only such in relation to others.[37] Therefore our conventional assumption that individuality is equatable with personhood is open to question. An individual becomes a person only in relation to other human beings[38] and other components of language-world. A person is an individual-in-relation: a player of language-games.

4.4.3. If the Goods are not on Display

As I have argued, an ontology which takes language-games as basic may also be seen to take actuality as transient and relative and this may suggest a relativist ontology or epistemology. Jüngel has noted the human tendency to operate with the assumption that present known actuality is the sum total of reality.[39] Hardy, writing as usual within a scientific paradigm, notes that '[i]t is commonly assumed that dynamic order is derivable only from what is available through human life in the world, that is in the bounded

35 Ibid. 105.

36 Ibid. 132.

37 For further discussion on this, see Patterson, *Realist Christian Theology*, Chapter 6: 'Becoming Persons'.

38 As creatures made in the image of a Creator whose being is constituted in relation, our being must be similarly constituted. God has created us to be in relation (ibid.).

39 Jüngel, 'The World as Possibility and Actuality' and 'Metaphorical Truth' (see Part Three).

situation of an ecosystem; only such energy as can arise within this context will count as "kinetic energy" usable for work ... this is a reductionist account of the energy available for the development of relationality'.[40]

An ontology of relativism (or a relativist theory of truth) arises through a simple equation of the humanly basic with the totality of reality. As such it is positivistic and fundamentally problematic.[41] Relativism also lacks explanatory power in the face of the evidence provided by metaphorising for a source of absolute reality and truth beyond the complexes of language-games which comprise actuality. Such an absolute is not only inconceivable but also is not exhausted by any current totality of language-games. If language-games vary according to time and place (that is, if actuality is diachronic and local, is variegated and fluctuates), then metaphorised gains to actuality in the form of new moves in language-games are gains to a particular form of life: a particular context at a particular time. Metaphorising reveals that at a given time and place known actuality is not basic: gains to actuality occur through a repatterning of the known, a new relation which itself transcends known actuality. Therefore, while they are context grounded or mediated, gains to actuality are not context-created and revelation, although contextually expressed, is not subsumed within context: the absolute reality of God is both transcendent and immanent.

Hardy sees an abandonment of the positivism which confines reality to human conceptions of actuality as providing a new perspective on God's work of creating, maintaining and restoring relationality. A traditional Christian ontology (in assuming that transcendence is to be equated with separation) has ruled out an ontology of relation. However, 'the supposition that God is fundamentally isolated from the contextuality is highly questionable. Powerful as this supposition is in the Christian tradition, and richly suggestive as it is for the richness of the Divine Being, we can

40 Hardy, 'The Spirit of God in Creation and Reconciliation', 257.

41 Of course, when any relativist theory claims to be the truth about reality it claims to be absolute, thereby becoming self-referentially incoherent: absolute relativism is a contradiction in terms.

only know God through his relation to the contextuality which is ours'.[42] Therefore, language-game theology's insistence in the givenness of our forms of life, which yet requires that their ultimate foundationality be rooted in the being of God, is not as contradictory as it seems. It simply states that what is humanly basic may appear to be, but is not, the whole of reality.

It follows that to take the existence of human activities as a given is not to reduce truth to mere local meaning[43] (and thus eliminate the distinction between constructive and destructive, good and evil forms of life and language-games), but to conclude with Jüngel that such a distinction can be made only by God and is available to us only as gift.[44] Hardy has pointed out the dangerous fallacy of 'direct revelation' which must degenerate into the circular relativism of 'what is true is what is true for me'. Attempts to grasp at revelation directly in effect bypass the mutually dependent and inseparable witness of Christ and creation.[45] Yet without an exterior, objective criterion of God's reality and truth there is no way available to us to distinguish between truth and error.

In other words, a Trinitarian doctrine of God is required to save a *sola gratia* language-game theology from relativism. The given of language-world may seem to operate in a free-wheeling way but remains rooted in the Giver and as such is continually being renewed. In this process human beings participate in the redeeming as well as the creative activity of God. As Hardy observes, employing his scientific paradigm:

> [T]his ecosystem operates with and from a fuller dynamic order, and without reference to this dynamic order … The fuller dynamic order from which the ecosystem operates, by which it is energised for its unity and reconciliation, is the dynamic order of God himself which he confers on human beings in and through their world. This

42 Hardy, 'The Spirit of God in Creation and Reconciliation', 245.

43 As Phillipps does (see Part Four Chapter 2).

44 See Part Four Chapter 3.

45 Such theologies are exposed to the objection frequently levelled at Phillipps's relativist account of the relation of language-games to theology that any ontology will do so long as one utilises the appropriate set of language-games in relation to it. As Hardy shows, it takes a Trinitarian theology to dispense with such an objection.

> confers not only a richer source of energy on the world than that which is available simply by reference to the ecosystem itself, but a higher quality of relationality than is available therein; taken together, these provide a higher order of dynamic order than that available by reference to the world alone.[46]

It is through participation in the relating activity of God (in God's language-games) that humans are able to transcend their local forms of life and begin to glimpse the pattern of the whole.

4.4.4. On Building Towers of Babel

A sceptic's question which has been latent throughout this discussion is: why is there need to say more than that actuality rearranges itself and, in so doing, constantly renews itself? While it was noted in Part Four, Chapter 3 that the positing of a transcendent organiser may lead simply to a vicious regress, Hausman contends that

> unless there is something that transcends all human construction in constraining interpretation, the affirmation of new insights would need to be abandoned. If genius does sometimes give us these new creations, then it does so by transcending communities. And because these advances beyond such limits are insights, perspectives that reveal something no one and no community revealed before, then the control or the creator must transcend antecedently intelligible human construction. This is to go beyond whatever limits that may have been based on even universal structures of human intelligence. The very structures of human reality must be modified, sometimes ever so little and sometimes dramatically.[47]

Instead of wondering about how an inconceivable actuality comes to thought and speech and how concepts emerge from the incoherence of the metaphors, it may seem enough to say that it simply does. I have maintained,

46 Hardy, 'The Spirit of God in Creation and Redemption', 257.

47 Hausman, *Metaphor and Art*, 188.

however, that this doing of actuality is transcendent of human conceiving and is not therefore part of our doing. 'If there is something unique in a creation that is not in every respect under the control of the agent, then what does it mean to say that the agent is responsible for a created outcome? … [T]he primary source of responsibility must be two-fold: the agent referred to as the human creator and the external or extralinguistic – extraconceptual focus of resistance …'[48]

That which is transcendent is inconceivable unless or until it comes to speech and thought and thus in the end to concept. This greater-than-conceivable Reality may or may not be named. Hausman stops just short of requiring an explicitly divine second source:

> This responsibility of the world, however, is different from human responsibility because we would not hold mind-dependent aspects of the world accountable for their responsibilities for creative achievements. I leave aside the question of divine responsibility much less accountability. Obviously, if I were to say that a divine source is responsible for all acts and events, then the idea that something independent of human agents can be responsible would be more obvious, though no less controversial.[49]

Hardy, on the other hand, does give this source a name. In his essay 'Christ and Creation', Hardy describes the compulsive human quest for greater intelligibility as the drawing of us by the Beyond: 'the pressure of God upon us' which 'demand[s] the differentiation of God from the sum of the domains of the world'.[50] That which constitutes the reality beyond our conceiving is not uniform reality of God-world, but a differentiated system which cannot be comprehended as a whole by human components within the system unless this comprehension is given. The 'pressure' of God may be experienced as the incessant desire which fuels the search for this gift: for intelligibility or meaningfulness in 'noisy' data the paradoxes, untidinesses and logical gaps, the way the world is a 'growing complexity that lays

48 Ibid. 202.

49 Ibid. 202.

50 Hardy, 'Christ and Creation', 105–6.

waste to its own resources' and the 'entropy and negentropy of learning.'[51] The search is for the clues to a 'higher organising principle.'[52] I have argued that these clues come to speech as metaphor which is the linguistic sign of this greater comprehensiveness and higher unity.

The differentiation of reality is not a conceptual map of our making.[53] The demarcation of God from world emerges when we are given the comprehension of the world in its wholeness and are able to 'grasp the inner differentiation of the world.' Knowledge of God is a given. Therefore the distinguishing of God from language-world is not a simple dichotomomising of God and not-God: the relationship of God to world is that of Higher Organising Principle. It is God-within-world, who is at the same time God-transcending-world, who connects and combines the components of language-world into a new higher unit which is more than the totality of the components of world.[54]

Hence God (or the human need for God created by God as, among other things, the desire for intelligibility) is, according to Hardy, experienced in two ways: first, as a perception of the finiteness of incompleteness of human categories even at their most comprehensive level of synthetic theorising. (I maintain that this finiteness or incompleteness is seen in the metaphorical predication which creates and then spans a logical incoherence to discover a higher logic.) Second, God is experienced in the coming of a higher intelligibility within and between the existing categories of human knowing which, I have argued, is the new congruence (the 'higher code of pertinence'[55]) brought by metaphorising and revealed in metaphor. Greater comprehensiveness comes with new knowledge, not through further refinements to existing concepts, but through their confounding and the recombination of their component language-games into new ones which take in a greater share of reality.

51 Ibid. 108.

52 Polanyi's term. (See Polanyi, *The Tacit Dimension*, Chapter 2: Emergence.)

53 Hardy, 'Christ and Creation', 106.

54 Ibid. 106–7.

55 Ricoeur, *The Rule of Metaphor*, 150f.

It may be thought arguable that such theological conclusions are reachable without theological presuppositions: that is, as 'natural' theology.[56] If the humanly accessible actuality of language-world is contingent upon a humanly inaccessible actuality (a transcendent other), and this other is an ordering activity which shows itself in the initiation and maintenance of relationality, this other may be described as the transcendent foundation of language-world which enters that which it transcends as a new relation which disrupts, reforms and thereby extends existing relations. Given this description is plausibly consistent with definitions of the use of the term 'God', it may also seem plausible that this is not merely an implicit *analogia fidei* but (yet another) argument from evidence and reason for the existence of God. I suggest, however, that a Wittgensteinian ontology rules out this 'natural theology' option in revealing what we take as being evidence and logic to be themselves dependent on our language-games and forms of life.[57] In the end, as we have seen, even the bulwarks of fact and reason rely on an *analogia fidei*.[58] To accept the 'evidence' provided by metaphorising (or any other evidence, for that matter) for the existence of a transcendent other upon which the human language-world depends for its being, as being consistent with what theists mean by God, means ultimately, therefore, to act on faith.

56 That is, of the Enlightenment, rather than the Scholastic, variety.

57 Nor is it tenable on any other ontology for that matter. An equation of anything with God is always an equation we make without being able to justify (or 'prove') it at human level.

58 Gunton comments (in connection with Hartshorne's commitment to process) that we cannot begin to speak about the world until we have made a 'radical commitment to a particular way of understanding the world'. That is, such a commitment is not empirically derived but is an ontological 'given'. The Christian theologian must ask how consistent a particular ontological 'given' is with God's self-revelation in Jesus Christ. 'The theologian believes something to be so, and proceeds to investigate the truth of that belief. He cannot pretend, after the manner of some conceptions of natural theology, not to have the belief, for that would be the height of irrationality'. (Gunton, *Becoming and Being*, 118–20.)

4.4.5. Summary and Conclusion to Part Four

I suggested in Part Three that metaphorising (as the language-game which creates new moves in language-games through transfer and recombination) demonstrates the incompleteness of actuality (where actuality comprises the totality of such moves obtaining at a given time). Whereas language-games in general exhibit the diachronicity of actuality, the metaphorising language-game, as initiator and 'driver' of the system, reveals actuality's incompleteness. An ontology which takes language-games as basic therefore both takes relationality as primitive and views actuality as transient and relative. It therefore implies a source of reality or truth beyond the complexes of language-games which comprise actuality. Such an absolute is not only inconceivable but also is not exhausted by any current totality of language-games (thus no relativistic epistemology can be basic). Such an absolute truth/reality must be either inaccessible or accessible only as a 'given'. Paradoxically, this 'given' (as the only access to the absolute) must be given within the local and transient actuality of language-games.

With a shift to a theological paradigm (which must be seen as an *analogia fidei*, being insusceptible to logical justification), the gain to actuality through metaphorising's incorporation within actuality of that which is transcendent of actuality, may be interpreted theologically as revelation. This revelation is manifested in a disruption to, and repatterning of, conventional practices involving use of language within (a thereby extended) actuality. Ultimate Reality does not come merely to speech but comes to language-world as language-games in which thoughts and utterances are moves.

Thus metaphorising may be seen as the action of God which shows God's being to inhere in the bringing into relation of the unrelated, in the relation itself, and in the new coherence given by the relation: the metaphor or model which is the sign of the transcendent relating agency within (and transforming of) existing categories.

I conclude that for theology to be possible, a revelation is required which is of, through, and to, both linguistic and nonlinguistic reality. For revelation thus to embrace language requires, first, a doctrine of knowledge which does not restrict knowledge to purely conceptual knowledge; second, a doctrine of truth in which the totality of known true propositions does not simply correspond to actuality; and, third, an ontology and epistemology which integrate language with the physical world. I suggest that the language-game theology here advanced satisfies all these requirements.

EPILOGUE

Summary and Conclusions

Summary of the Argument

In Part One, I made a case for the foundationality of language-games and explored the implications of such an ontology.

The primacy of language-games was seen to be a logical inference. If all human experience requires language (verbal and nonverbal) for its comprehension and hence its accessibility, then language is universal medium. If language is universal medium, nonlinguistic reality is accessible only through our contact with it via language.

However, language is also a part of the physical world, in that physical-object language is what connects us to the nonlinguistic world. If the linguistic and nonlinguistic are both a part of physical reality, then language and world are integrated, not separate.

Moreover, this language-world relation takes place in time and this diachronicity involves activity. Therefore language-world connecting activities (language-games) are prior to the connections they make and cannot be justified in terms of rules inferable from them. Therefore language-games are epistemically basic.

I argued that this conclusion has the following entailments:

1. Pragmatics subsumes semantics because language-world linking activity is prior to language as such. It follows knowledge is inclusive of 'knowing-how' and not restricted to 'knowing-that', which means that language-games constitute an epistemic foundation prior to individual perceptions of world and therefore a phenomenological experience-based foundation cannot be basic.

2. Language-world linking activity is prior to any distinction between or correspondence of language and world, therefore the traditional categories of realism and idealism are superseded. This epistemic foundation as such is a relativistic one (and thus hints at its own ultimate nonbasicality).

3. A purely extralinguistic reality is either a meaningless concept, or inaccessible by definition, unless 'given' within the epistemic foundation (in which case it ceases to be extralinguistic).[1] Hence any conception of ontology is contingent on the epistemic foundation.

In Part Two, I dealt with the question of how, if extralinguistic reality is 'given', an epistemic foundation comprising language-games is able to explain and incorporate new information. I suggested that the language-game of metaphor-making was a major means of this. While Wittgenstein did address the issue of metaphor as such (and his occasional remarks in passing imply a traditional, non-incremental view), I suggested that it is consistent with his philosophy to treat metaphor as a part of ordinary language, as such subject to the same working rules.

To begin with, if language-games are basic, metaphorising (metaphor-making), as a language-game, is prior to the metaphorical statement itself. As metaphorising is a language-game, what applies to language-games in general applies to metaphorising, which means that if language-games in general are epistemically basic, so too is the metaphorising language-game.

At the same time, the language-game is no more nor less than its moves which include activities involving the use of language plus rule-like entities (propositions, facts, concepts) concerning these uses. Therefore the metaphorising language-game is the metaphorising activity, plus its product, the metaphorical statement, plus the rules which make this product a move in such a game.

I argued that, as the peculiar activity of the metaphorising language-game is to create new moves in other language-games, this entails that:

1 I explore the implications of this for a 'theistic realist' doctrine of God in *Christian Realist Theology*.

1. The metaphorising language-game is basic to, that is the source of, moves that constitute other language-games, which means that metaphorical (so-called 'indirect') reference prior to non-metaphorical (so-called 'direct') reference because the latter is often a product of the former (however, the later Wittgenstein's epistemology dispenses altogether with direct reference). As the metaphorising language-game (as the source of new references) is thereby primitive, it is not itself susceptible of verification; however, individual metaphorical statements depend for their verification on both metaphorising and 'ordinary' language-games.

2. The metaphorising language-game, as primitive, is the 'given' on which much if not all conceptual knowledge rests. Metaphorising gives rise to metaphorical statements (and other products of metaphorising) which express propositions (which should not be confused with the statements themselves). Metaphors in turn give rise to new concepts. With both metaphors and concepts, the proposition involved may remain implicit – acted upon, but not articulable within, the terms of conventional logic. This means that at any given time the totality of meaning is not subsumable by the actual (currently existing) conceptual framework.

3. Metaphorising, as a secondary language-game which involves the use of familiar terms unconventionally, and therefore parasitic on other language-games), is, however, ontologically prior to other language-games in that it creates new moves in language-games. Yet the basicality of language-games as language-world links means that it is the change in the primary language-games which effects a change in the use (and hence meaning) of terms. This change is in the nature of a transfer and combination of trainings to create a new language-world link at the growing-edge of knowledge.

4. As meaning is a function of use, and therefore pragmatics subsumes semantics, it is the change in the language-games which causes the meanings of the terms to change. Apart from the situation of new use, the primary games in question remain the same. Therefore

metaphorising effects an increment in meaning or knowledge by creating a new move in a language-game at the level of primary (unreflective) use. Thus the way in which metaphor effects a gain in knowledge is through metaphorising's novel re-patterning of conventional knowledge.

In Part Three, I argued from the conclusions arrived at so far – the basicality of language-games and the fundamental role of metaphorising in the production of new concepts – that the actuality of the complex of language-games as conceived at any given time is not basic and the actual (facts or states of affairs known to obtain *at any given time and place*) may be deduced to be less than the totality of reality.

The argument went like this:

1. If metaphorising is a language-game which creates new moves in language-games (hence brings into being new knowledge in a broad sense of the term), then metaphorising extends actuality and effects a continuing gain to language-world (or reality-truth). In metaphor unconceived and even inconceivable possibilities reveal themselves as actual in a new relation within actuality. As an assertion of what is not merely unconceived but at times *inconceivable* (logically impossible) possibility, metaphor claims to be actual while at the same time appearing to be impossible, forcing old logic and categories to give way to a new coherence and relation. The impossible, in utilising the raw material of antecedent actuality, indicates the existence of, and claims, a new, higher and wider actuality.

2. A Wittgensteinian perspective on metaphorising and possible worlds, which would require possible worlds to be small, partial and transient, is consistent with a Jüngelian view of metaphor in allowing that impossible (inconceivable properties or states of affairs) predications by metaphors may be true or actual. Yet, given the interwoven nature of language-games and their moves, the recombination effected by metaphorising cannot be atomistic. Combinatorial possible worlds models succeed in capturing the metaphorical process only when their atomism is abandoned.

The *relata* are not discrete entities. I argued that this captures the gestalt 'top-down' insight, identified in Part Two, that the whole determines the meaning of the parts: the *relata* cannot be separated from the relation.

In Part Four, I continued to argue that metaphorising, in producing new metaphors that are meaningful, provides evidence that a reality beyond human conceiving, while unverifiable, is not meaningless. While the complex of language-games is self-authenticating, metaphorising shows its incompleteness. There must be a 'higher' verification for the additions to actuality which are at odds with present actuality. I also argued that if the metaphorised new relation in effect creates or reveals a new aspect of reality, then it is not substance that is primary but relation. Moreover, if the diachronic nature of a language-game based ontology is sustained by metaphorising, then it is not so much relation itself as the becoming of relation which is basic. This finding is consistent with the Trinitarian theologies of Barth and Jüngel.

The argument went like this:

1. The 'leap of faith' to a theological paradigm entails that the gain to actuality, through metaphorising's incorporation within actuality of that which is transcendent of actuality through that which itself subsumes actuality, may be interpreted theologically as revelation. This revelation is manifested in a disruption to, and repatterning of, conventional practices involving use of language within (a thereby extended) actuality. Recent studies concerning the relationship between metaphor and theology have not adequately addressed the revelatory role of metaphor. Likewise, studies which have sought to bring a Wittgensteinian perspective to theology have been sidetracked by Wittgenstein's avowed anti-metaphysicalism and have failed to address the metaphysical implications of a language-game ontology[2] – that a theology which takes this on board must dispense with the traditional distinction between reality and truth,

2 With the notable exception of Fergus Kerr (*Theology after Wittgenstein*).

demonstrating that realism must ultimately be theistic and that absolute logic and truth are the prerogatives of God alone.

2. While the basicality of language-games might be construed as a sort of 'Wittgensteinian foundationalism' along Plantingan lines, and an affinity with Reformed epistemology is suggested by a shared emphasis on 'justification by faith', each, however, operates with quite a different view of reality, Reformed epistemology's exponents insisting in maintaining that propositions form the basis of our knowledge of the world while, of course, language-games form the foundation of a Wittgenstein world.

3. A language-game foundation, which both takes relationality as primitive and views actuality as diachronic and accessible only through the socio-linguistic filters of human forms of life, may suggest a relativist epistemology. However, an ontology, which, in addition to taking language-games as basic, sees the metaphorising language-game as primordial, takes the initiation of relation as primitive and thus demonstrates that relation is ontologically prior to substance and individuality. It therefore implies a source of reality/truth beyond the complexes of language-games which comprise human actuality. Such an absolute is not only inconceivable but also is not exhausted by any current totality of language-games (thus no relativistic epistemology can be basic). Such an absolute truth and reality must be either inaccessible or accessible only as a 'given'. Paradoxically, however this 'given' (as the only access to the absolute) must be given within the local and transient actuality of language-games. This imperative of givenness, as local, particular and diachronic, may be interpreted Christologically.

4. A 'language-game theology', in taking language to be a part of the physical world requires such a 'given' to be similarly constituted. As given, The Transcendent does not merely 'come to speech' (as per Jüngel), or 'commandeer language' (as per Barth) but comes as language-games in which the 'coming to speech' and 'commandeering of language' are moves. Thus metaphorising, according to

a 'language-game theology', is an aspect of divine agency which shows God's being to inhere in, first, the bringing into relation of the unrelated, second, the relation itself, and, third, the new coherence which is given by the relation, where metaphor is the sign of the transcendent relating agency working immanently within and transforming existing categories. This three-fold agency may be interpreted Trinitarianly.

Conclusion

The foregoing could be said to have been a linguistic-philosophical argument with a theological conclusion. The theological conclusion is orthodox enough. Why, then, trouble to arrive at it by such a complicated path? Daniel Hardy offers this justification: '[If] theological work is to have maximum impact upon today's world, it cannot simply be evocative and exhortative; it must be explanatory, and as such interact with the means by which people in other disciplines explain the world ... That is not to say the theological explanations should be identical to the explanations by other disciplines, only that they should interact with them.'[3]

The abandonment of the separation of language from world enables the resolution of the particular theological problems which are the legacy of this dualism and casts a new light on the nature of language and world which shows the rather problematic entity of metaphor to have an integral role in their relationship. Metaphor could perhaps be said to have been the stumbling block on which realist and anti-realist theologies alike have foundered. For realist theologies it has posed the problem of reference; for anti-realist theologies it has tended also to pose problems of truth or aptness (in the equating of the literal with the conventional). Here the stone

3 Hardy, 'The Spirit of God in Creation and Reconciliation', 240.

on which these theologies have stumbled could be said to have become the cornerstone.

The problem of metaphor has also been a philosophical problem in that it has proved difficult to provide an adequate explanation of metaphor within the conventional epistemological and semantical positions. The problem of metaphor thus also points to a problem in traditional epistemologies. I have suggested a solution by way of a paradigmatic and ontological shift which utilises Wittgenstein's notion of language-games. Words alone do not make a metaphor, rather it is the activity of metaphor-making (or metaphorising, as I have termed it) which gives a metaphor its meaning. Unless the semantics of metaphor are seen to be dependent on its pragmatics, symptoms will be treated rather than the cause.

According to Anthony Thiselton, 'To make constructive use of a particular philosopher's conceptual tools it is not necessary to subscribe to his view of the world'.[4] Concerns expressed by some realist theologians[5] over the use of Wittgenstein's insights in theology are, I believe, caused in large measure by various attempts (not necessarily deliberate) to reduce theology to sociology, anthropology or linguistics.[6] This interpretation stems from a failure to recognise the implicit (foundational) metaphysic of 'givenness' in Wittgenstein's work. One may either choose to work within Wittgenstein's self-imposed limits – within his 'anti-metaphysical metaphysic' so to speak – or to examine the implications of the metaphysic itself. If the latter option is taken, it is arguable (and has been argued here) that Wittgenstein's philosophy is consistent with a theology of *sola gratia*.

Once the implications of a 'givenness' metaphysic are accepted, the value to theology of Wittgenstein's thought within his stipulated limits – especially the operations of the basic language-games – may be seen to lie in its explication of the nature and process of revelation. In a language-game theology, metaphorising as the means of transfer and recombination by which we come to know new aspects of reality is seen to be revelatory. First,

4 Thiselton, *The Two Horizons*, 10.

5 T. F. Torrance, for instance (personal communications, February and April 1991).

6 By the 'Wittgenstein Fideists' and others, notably Cupitt.

the forming of new reality from new relation demonstrates the primacy of relation over substance: God's being is constituted in relation. Second, reality as humanly experienced is an inextricable interweaving of language and world. God's being must incorporate and be incorporated in both. A theology grounded in grace does not, therefore, require a traditional subject-object separation; in fact such a separation is an impediment as it poses the difficulty of explaining how God's self-gift is thinkable and expressible in speech. A 'language-game theology' not only maintains that 'pure' objectivity is impossible; it also demonstrates that it is nonsensical.

Finally, the givenness of language-games and forms of life means that all human concepts, and logical formulations as contingent upon these, are nonbasic. These too arise from, and are subject to, what is given. They cannot, of and by themselves, explain what is basic to them: the human and greater reality upon which they depend. Any such attempts at explanation are successful only insomuch as they too are given – that is, insomuch as human concepts participate in God's self-revelation. Therefore, natural theology, for all its purported reliance on rationality alone, must ultimately rely on an implicit 'analogy of faith' just as much as any other sort of theology.

The programmatic nature of the present work was noted in the introduction. It was intended that this study should provide a scaffold for further development of a 'language-game theology'. As I have indicated, this work has since been continued in my book, *Christian Realist Theology in a Postmodern Age*, in which I draw out the implications of such a theology for Christian doctrine, and its applications for ethics, worship, and Christian living.

It remains to reiterate the point with which I began my introduction. Theology, however academic, must be for the service of Christ's Church or it has no point. To be of service in this way, it cannot remain in the academy but must filter down into the daily lives and beliefs of Christians through preaching and teaching. If it is to do this, it will not be as theoretical knowledge so much as a change of perspective – an altered way of seeing how things are, and how they cohere, which, when communicated in ways that connect with people's lives, may suddenly untie some knots of perplexity and thereby remove some obstacles to belief and faith.

Bibliography

Adams, Robert, 'Theories of Actuality', in Michael J. Loux (ed.), *The Possible and the Actual: Readings in the Metaphysics of Modality*, Ithaca: Cornell University Press, 1979, 190–209.

Alston, William P., 'Plantinga's Epistemology of Religious Belief', in James E. Tomberlin and Peter van Inwagen (eds), *Profiles 5: Alvin Plantinga*, Dortrecht: D. Reidel, 1985, 289–312.

Anscombe, G. E. M., *Metaphysics and the Philosophy of Mind*, Oxford: Blackwell, 1981.

Aristotle, *De Interpretatione, The Complete Works of Aristotle*, 2 Vols, J. Barnes (ed.), Princeton: Princeton University Press, 1984.

—— *Metaphysics. The Complete Works of Aristotle*, 2 Vols: Book 1A, J. Barnes (ed.), Princeton: Princeton University Press, 1984.

Armstrong, D. M., *A Combinatorial Theory of Possibility*, Cambridge: Cambridge University Press, 1989.

Aquinas, Thomas, *Super Boethium De Trinitate*, Rose E. Brennan S.H.N. (tr.), New York: Herder and Herder, 1946.

Barth, Karl, *Church Dogmatics*, G. W. Bromiley and T. F. Torrance (eds and trs.), 2nd rev. edn, Edinburgh: T. & T. Clark, 1975 & 1977.

Berggren, Douglas, 'The Use and Abuse of Metaphor', Parts I & II, *The Review of Metaphysics* 16, 237–58, 450–72.

Black, Max, *Models and Metaphors: Studies in Language and Philosophy*, New York: Cornell University Press, 1962.

—— 'More about Metaphor', in Andrew Ortony (ed.), *Metaphor and Thought*, Cambridge UK: Cambridge University Press, 1979, 19–45.

Blackburn, S., *Spreading the Word*, Oxford: Oxford University Press, 1984.

Bogdan, Radu J. (ed.), *Profiles 8: Jaakko Hintikka*, Dortrecht: D. Reidel, 1987.

Bonhoeffer, Dietrich, *Christ The Centre*, Edward H. Robinson (tr.), New York: HarperCollins, 1960.

Boyd, Richard, 'Metaphor and Theory Change: What is "Metaphor" as Metaphor For?' in Ortony, *Metaphor and Thought*, 356–408.

Brown, S. C., *Do Religious Claims make Sense?* London: S.C.M., 1969.

Chisholm, Roderick, *Theory of Knowledge*, New Jersey: Prentice Hall, 1966.

Cohen, Jean, *Structure du Langage Poetique*, Paris: Flammarion, 1966.

Cohen, L. J. and Avishai Margalit, 'The Role of Inductive Reasoning in the Interpretation of Metaphor', in Gilbert Harman and Donald Davidson (eds), *Semantics of Natural Language*, Dortrecht: D. Reidel, 1972, 722–40.

Cresswell, M. J., 'The World is Everything That Is The Case', in Michael J. Loux (ed.), *The Possible and the Actual: Readings in the Metaphysics of Modality*, Ithaca: Cornell University Press, 1979, 129–45.

Cupitt, Don, *The Sea of Faith*, London: BBC, 1984.

Dalferth, Ingolf, *Religiose Rede von Gott*, Munchen: Christian Kaiser, 1981.

Davidson, Donald, 'On the Very Idea of a Conceptual Scheme', *Inquiries into Truth and Interpretation*, London: Oxford University Press, 1984.

—— 'What Metaphors Mean', in Sheldon Sacks (ed.), *On Metaphor*, Chicago: University of Chicago Press, 1979, 29–45.

Deely, John, *Basics of Semiotics*, Indiana: Indiana University Press, 1990.

Downey, John, *Beginning at the Beginning: Wittgenstein and Theological Conversation*, Lanham: University Press of America, 1986.

Dummett, Michael, Lectures on Gareth Evans's Varieties of Experience, Oxford, Trinity Term, 1986.

—— *Truth and Other Enigmas*, London: Duckworth, 1978.

Eliot, T. S., 'Four Quartets: Burnt Norton', *Collected Poems: 1909–1962*, London: Faber and Faber, 1963.

Evans, Gareth, 'Reply: Semantic Theory and Tacit Knowledge', in S. Holzman and C. Leich, *Wittgenstein: To Follow a Rule*, London: Routledge, 1981.

Floistad, G. (ed.), *Contemporary Philosophy: A New Survey*. Vol. 1, The Hague: Martinus Nijhoff Publishers, 1981.

Fraser, Bruce, 'The Interpretation of Novel Metaphors', in Andrew Ortony (ed.), *Metaphor and Thought*, Cambridge UK: Cambridge University Press, 1979, 172ff.

Genova, Judith, 'Philosophy and the Consideration of Other-Worldly Possibilities', in Elisabeth Leinfellner et al. (eds), *Wittgenstein and his Impact on Contemporary Philosophy (Proceedings of the Second International Wittgenstein Symposium), 1977, Kirchberg/Weschel, Austria* Vienna: Holder-Pichler-Tempsky, 1978, 398ff.

Gill, Jerry H., *On Knowing God*, Philadelphia: Westminster Press, 1981.

—— 'Wittgenstein and Metaphor', *J. Phil. and Phenom. Research* 40 (1979–1980), 272ff.

Gillett, Grant, 'An Antisceptical Fugue', *Philosophical Investigations* 13/4 (1990), 304ff.

—— 'Learning to Perceive', *Philosophical and Phenomenological Research* 48 (1987–1988), 601ff.

—— *Representation, Meaning and Thought*, London: Oxford University Press, 1992.

—— 'Tacit Semantics', *Philosophical Investigations* 2/1 (1988), 1–12.

—— 'The Generality Constraint and Conscious Thought', *Analysis* 47 (1987): 20–4.

Goodman, Nelson, *Languages of Art: an Approach to a Theory of Symbols*, 2nd edn, Indianapolis: Hackett Publishing Co., 1976.

—— *Ways of Worldmaking*, Sussex: Harvester Press, 1978.

Gunton, Colin E., *The Actuality of the Atonement: A study of Metaphor, Rationality and the Christian Tradition*, Edinburgh: T. & T. Clark, 1988.

——*Becoming and Being: The Doctrine of God in Charles Hartshorne and Karl Barth*, London: Oxford University Press, 1978.

—— *The One, The Three and the Many: Creation and the Culture of Modernity*, Cambridge UK: Cambridge University Press, 1993.

—— *Yesterday and Today: A Study of Continuities in Christology*, London: Darton, Longman and Todd, 1983.

Hardy, Daniel, 'Christ and Creation', in T. F. Torrance (ed.), *The Incarnation*, Edinburgh: Handsel, 1981.

——'The Spirit of God in Creation and Reconciliation', in H. Regan and A. J. Torrance (eds), *Christ and Context*, Edinburgh: T. & T. Clark, 1993, 237–58.

Harman, Gilbert and Donald Davidson (eds), *Semantics of Natural Language*, Dortrecht: D. Reidel, 1972.

Harre, Rom and Roger Lamb (eds), *The Encyclopaedia Dictionary of Psychology*, Cambridge, Massachusetts: MIT Press, 1983.

Hausman, Carl E., *Metaphor and Art: Interactionism and Reference in the Verbal and Nonverbal Arts*, Cambridge UK: Cambridge University Press, 1989.

Helman, David H. (ed.), *Analogical Reasoning*, Dortrecht: Kluwer, 1988.

Hepplethwaite, B. and S. R. Sutherland (eds), *The Philosophical Frontiers of Christian Theology: Essays Presented to D. M. McKinnon*, Cambridge UK: Cambridge University Press, 1982.

Hesse, Mary, 'Texts without Types and Lumps without Laws', *New Literary History* 17 (1985–6), 31ff.

—— 'Theories, Family Resemblance and Analogy', in David H. Helman (ed.), *Analogical Reasoning*, Dortrecht: Kluwer, 1988, 317–40.

Hester, Marcus, *The Meaning of Poetic Metaphor: An Analysis in the Light of Wittgenstein's Claim that Meaning is Use*, The Hague: Mouton & Co., 1967.

Hick, John, *Christianity at the Centre*, 2nd edn, London: MacMillan, 1968.

—— *Faith and Knowledge*, 2nd edn, London: MacMillan, 1967.

—— *The Centre of Christianity*, London: S.C.M., 1977.

High, Dallas M. High, *Language, Persons and Belief: Studies in Wittgenstein's Philosophical Investigations and Religious Uses of Language*, New York: Oxford University Press, 1967.

Hintikka, Jaakko, 'Degrees and Dimensions of Intentionality', in Leinfellner, Elisabeth et al. (eds), *Wittgenstein and his Impact on Contemporary Philosophy (Proceedings of the Second International Wittgenstein Symposium), 1977, Kirchberg/Weschel, Austria*, Vienna: Holder-Pichler-Tempsky, 1978, 69ff.

—— 'Jaakko Hintikka's reply to Barry Richards', in Radu J. Bogdan (ed.), *Profiles 8: Jaakko Hintikka*, Dortrecht: D. Reidel, 1987, 295f.

—— 'Reply to Romane Clark's "What is a 'Perceptually Well-Defined Individual"? Hintikka's views on Perception', in Radu J. Bogdan (ed.), *Profiles 8: Jaakko Hintikka*, Dortrecht: D. Reidel, 1987, 215–32.

—— 'Response to Robert Kraut', 'Replies and Comments', in Radu J. Bogdan (ed.), *Profiles 8: Jaakko Hintikka*, Dortrecht: D. Reidel, 1987.

—— 'Self-Profile' in Radu J. Bogdan (ed.), *Profiles 8: Jaakko Hintikka*, Dortrecht: D. Reidel, 1987, 3–38.

—— 'Semantics: a Revolt against Frege', in G. Floistad (ed.), *Contemporary Philosophy: A New Survey*. Vol. 1, The Hague: Martinus Nijhoff Publishers, 1981.

—— 'Semantics for Propositional Attitudes', in Leonard Linsky (ed.), *Reference and Modality*, London: Oxford University Press 1971, 145ff.

—— 'The Semantics of Questions and the Questions of Semantics', *Acta Philosophica Fennica* (28) No. 4.

Hintikka, Merrill B. and Jaakko, *Investigating Wittgenstein*, Oxford: Basil Blackwell, 1986.

Holzman, S. and C. Leich, *Wittgenstein: To Follow a Rule*, London: Routledge, 1981.

Hudson, W. Donald, *Wittgenstein and Religious Belief*, London: MacMillan, 1975.

Jüngel, Eberhard, 'Metaphorical Truth', *Theological Essays*, Edinburgh: T. & T. Clark, 1989, 16–71.

—— *The Doctrine of the Trinity: God's Being is in Becoming*, Horton Harris (tr.), Edinburgh: Scottish Academic Press, 1976.

—— 'The World as Actuality and Possibility', *Theological Essays*, Edinburgh: T. & T. Clark, 1989, 95–123.

Kambartel, F. and H. J. Schneider, 'Constructing a Pragmatic Foundation for Semantics', in G. Floistad (ed.), *Contemporary Philosophy: A New Survey. Vol. 1*, The Hague: Martinus Nijhoff Publishers, 1981, 155–78.

Kant, Immanuel, *Religion within the Bounds of Reason Alone*, 2nd edn, T. M. Greene and H. H. Hudson, J. R. Silber (trs.), Illinois: La Salle, 1960.

Keightley, Alan, *Wittgenstein, Grammar and God*, London: Epworth Press, 1976.

Kerr, Fergus, *Theology After Wittgenstein*, Oxford: Blackwell, 1986.

Kripke, Saul A., 'Naming and Necessity', in Gilbert Harman and Donald Davidson (eds), *Semantics of Natural Language*, Dortrecht: D. Reidel, 1972, 253–355.

Kuhn, Thomas, 'Metaphor and Science', in Andrew Ortony (ed.), *Metaphor and Thought*, Cambridge UK: Cambridge University Press, 1979, 409–19.

Lakoff, George and Mark Johnson, *Metaphors We Live By*, Chicago: University of Chicago Press, 1980.

Langer, Suzanne K., *Feeling and Form: A Theory of Art*, New York: Charles Scribner's Sons, 1973.

Lash, Nicholas, 'How Large is a "Language Game"?' *Theology* 87 (1984) 19–28.

Leinfellner, Elisabeth et al. (eds), *Wittgenstein and his Impact on Contemporary Philosophy (Proceedings of the Second International Wittgenstein Symposium), 1977, Kirchberg/Weschel, Austria*, Vienna: Holder-Pichler-Tempsky, 1978.

Levin, Samuel R., 'Standard Approaches to Metaphor and a Proposal for Literary Metaphor', in Andrew Ortony (ed.), *Metaphor and Thought*, Cambridge UK: Cambridge University Press, 1979, 124–35.

Lindbeck, George, *The Nature of Doctrine*, Philadelphia: Westminster, 1983.

Linsky, Leonard (ed.), *Reference and Modality*, London: Oxford University Press 1971.

Loux, Michael J., 'Introduction', in Michael J. Loux (ed.), *The Possible and the Actual: Readings in the Metaphysics of Modality*, Ithaca: Cornell University Press, 1979.

—— (ed.), *The Possible and the Actual: Readings in the Metaphysics of Modality*, Ithaca: Cornell University Press, 1979.

Luther, Martin, 'Confession Concerning Christ's Supper', *Luther's Works*. American ed., 55 vols. Jaroslav Pelikan and Helmut T. Lehman (eds), Philadelphia: Muehlenberg and Fortress, and St. Louis: Concordia, 1955–86, vol. 37, 172ff.

Lycan, William, 'The Trouble with Possible Worlds', in Michael J. Loux (ed.), *The Possible and the Actual: Readings in the Metaphysics of Modality*, Ithaca: Cornell University Press, 1979, 274–316.

Mac Cormac, Earl, *A Cognitive Theory of Metaphor*, Cambridge, Massachusetts: MIT Press, 1985.

McFague, Sallie, *Metaphorical Theology: Models of God in Religious Language*, London: S.C.M. Press, 1983.

Marshall, Bruce D., 'Absorbing the World: Christianity and the Universe of Truths', in B. D. Marshall (ed.), *Theology and Dialogue: Essays in Conversation with George Lindbeck*, Indiana: University of Notre Dame Press, 1990, 69ff.

—— (ed.), *Theology and Dialogue: Essays in Conversation with George Lindbeck*, Indiana: University of Notre Dame Press, 1990, 69ff.

Martin, Janet C., 'Uses of Metaphor in Religious Language with Special Reference to Wittgenstein's Views of Language and to Metaphor in the Biblical Writings', unpublished dissertation submitted as partial requirement for the degree of Master of Arts, The Department of Biblical Studies, University of Sheffield, 2 September 1975.

Mason, H. E., 'On the Multiplicity of Language-Games', in Leinfellner, Elisabeth et al. (eds) *Wittgenstein and his Impact on Contemporary Philosophy (Proceedings of the Second International Wittgenstein Symposium), 1977, Kirchberg/Weschel, Austria*, Vienna: Holder-Pichler-Tempsky, 1978, 332ff.

Miller, George A., 'Images and Models, Similes and Metaphors', in Andrew Ortony (ed.), *Metaphor and Thought*, Cambridge UK: Cambridge University Press, 1979, 240ff.

Morawetz, Thomas, *Wittgenstein and Knowledge*, Amherst: University of Massachusetts Press, 1978.

Morgan, Jerry L., 'Observations on the Pragmatics of Metaphor', in Andrew Ortony (ed.), *Metaphor and Thought*, Cambridge UK: Cambridge University Press, 1979, 136ff.

Neilson, Kai, 'Wittgensteinian Fideism', *Philosophy* 42 (1967), 191–209.

Ortony, Andrew (ed.), *Metaphor and Thought*, Cambridge UK: Cambridge University Press, 1979.

Osgood, Charles E., *Method and Theory in Experimental Psychology*, New York: Oxford University Press, 1953.

Patterson, Sue, 'Gratuitous Truth: Metaphor and Revelation' *Colloquium* 23/3 (1991), 29–43.

——'Janet Martin Soskice, Metaphor and a Theology of Grace', *Scottish Journal of Theology*, 46 (1993), 1–26.

——*Realist Christian Theology in a Postmodern Age*, Cambridge UK: Cambridge University Press, 1999.

——'*Word*, Words and World', *Colloquium* 23/2 (1991) 71–84.

Petrie, Hugh G., 'Metaphor and Learning', in Andrew Ortony (ed.), *Metaphor and Thought*, Cambridge UK: Cambridge University Press, 1979, 438–61.

Phillipps, D. Z., *Belief, Change and Forms of Life*, London: MacMillan, 1986.

——*Faith After Foundationalism*, London: Routledge, 1988.

——*Faith and Philosophical Enquiry*, London: Routledge, 1970.

——*Religion Without Explanation*, Oxford: Blackwell, 1976.

Plantinga, Alvin, 'Is Belief in God Properly Basic?' *Nous* 15, 41–51.

——'Reason and Belief in God', in Alvin Plantinga and Nicholas Wolterstorff (eds), *Faith and Rationality*, Indiana: University of Notre Dame Press, 1983.

——'Self-Profile', in James E. Tomberlin and Peter van Inwagen (eds), *Profiles 5: Alvin Plantinga*, Dortrecht: D. Reidel, 1985, 31–2.

——*The Nature of Necessity*, New York: Oxford University Press, 1974.

——and Nicholas Wolterstorff (eds), *Faith and Rationality*, Indiana: University of Notre Dame Press, 1983.

Polanyi, Michael, *Personal Knowledge*, London: Routledge, 1958.

——*The Tacit Dimension*, London: Routledge, 1966.

Premack, D., 'Toward Empirical Behaviour Laws. I: Positive Reinforcement', *Psychological Review* 66 (1959), 219–33.

Pylyshyn, Zenon W., 'Metaphorical Imprecision and the "Top-Down" Research Strategy', in Andrew Ortony (ed.), *Metaphor and Thought*, Cambridge UK: Cambridge University Press, 1979, 420ff.

Ramsey, Ian, 'The Systematic elusiveness of "I"' *The Philosophical Quarterly* 5 (1955), 193–204.

Regan, H. and A. J. Torrance (eds), *Christ and Context*, Edinburgh: T. & T. Clark, 1993.

Ricoeur, Paul, 'The Metaphorical Process as Cognition, Imagination and Feeling', in Sheldon Sacks (ed.), *On Metaphor*, Chicago: University of Chicago Press, 1979, 153–9.

—— *The Rule of Metaphor*, Robert Czerny et al. (trs.), London: Routledge, 1978.

Robbins, Wesley J., 'Pragmatism and the Deconstruction of Theology', *Religious Studies* 24 (1988), 377ff.

Rosche, E. and C. B. Mervis, 'Family Resemblances Studies in the Internal Structure of Categories', *Cognitive Psychology* (7) (1975), 573ff.

Ross, Jacob Joshua, 'Wittgenstein on the Learning of a Language', in Leinfellner, Elisabeth et al. (eds), *Wittgenstein and his Impact on Contemporary Philosophy (Proceedings of the Second International Wittgenstein Symposium), 1977, Kirchberg/ Weschel, Austria*, Vienna: Holder-Pichler-Tempsky, 1978, 398ff.

Rumelhart, David E., 'Some Problems with the Notion of Literal Meanings', in Andrew Ortony (ed.), *Metaphor and Thought*, Cambridge UK: Cambridge University Press, 1979, 78–91.

Ryle, Gilbert, 'Heidegger's "Sein und Zeit"', *Critical Essays: Collected Papers* Vol. 1, London: Hutchison, 1971, 200ff.

Saarinen, Esa, 'Continuity and Similarity in Cross-Identification', in E. Saarinen, R. Hilpinen, I. Niiniluoto and M. Provence Hintikka (eds), *Essays in Honour of Jaakko Hintikka*, Dortrecht: D. Reidel, 1979, 89–215.

——R. Hilpinen, I. Niiniluoto and M. Provence Hintikka (eds), *Essays in Honour of Jaakko Hintikka*, Dortrecht: D. Reidel, 1979.

——'Quantifying in and on Trans-World Identity', in Radu Bogdan (ed.), *Profiles 8: Jaakko Hintikka*, 91ff.

Sacks, Sheldon (ed.), *On Metaphor*, Chicago: University of Chicago Press, 1979.

Sadock, Jerrold, 'Figurative Speech and Linguistics', in Andrew Ortony (ed.), *Metaphor and Thought*, Cambridge UK: Cambridge University Press, 1979, 46–63.

Searle, John R., 'Metaphor', in Andrew Ortony (ed.), *Metaphor and Thought*, Cambridge UK: Cambridge University Press, 1979, 92ff.

Seneca, Clara, 'Family Resemblance and Partial Interpretation', in Leinfellner, Elisabeth et al. (eds), *Wittgenstein and his Impact on Contemporary Philosophy (Proceedings of the Second International Wittgenstein Symposium), 1977, Kirchberg/Weschel, Austria*, Vienna: Holder-Pichler-Tempsky, 1978, 277ff: 277.

Sherry, Patrick, *Religion, Truth and Language Games*, London: MacMillan, 1977.

Soskice, Janet Martin, *Metaphor and Religious Language*, London: Oxford University Press, 1985.

Stalnaker, Robert C., 'Possible Worlds', in Michael J. Loux (ed.), *The Possible and the Actual: Readings in the Metaphysics of Modality*, Ithaca: Cornell University Press, 1979, 225–34.

—— 'Pragmatics', in Gilbert Harman and Donald Davidson (eds), *Semantics of Natural Language*, Dortrecht: D. Reidel, 1972.

Thiselton, Anthony C., *The Two Horizons: New Testament Hermeneutics and Philosophical Description with Special Reference to Heidegger, Bultmann, Gadamer and Wittgenstein*, Grand Rapids, Michigan: Eerdmans, 1980.

Thorndike, E. L. and R. S. Woodworth, 'The Influence of Improvement in One Mental Function upon the Efficiency of Other Functions (I); II The Estimation of Magnitudes; III Functions Involving Attention, Observation and Discrimination', *Psychological Review* 8 (1901), 247–61, 384–95, 553–64.

Tomberlin, James E. and Peter van Inwagen (eds), *Profiles 5: Alvin Plantinga*, Dortrecht: D. Reidel, 1985.

Torrance, Alan J., *Persons in Communion: Trinitarian Participation and Human Description*, Edinburgh: T. & T. Clark, 1996.

Torrance, T. F. (ed.), *The Incarnation*, Edinburgh: Handsel, 1981.

—— *Theological Science*, London: Oxford University Press, 1989.

Toulmin, Stephen, 'Ludwig Wittgenstein', *Encounter* 32 (1969), 58–71.

Travis, Charles, *The Uses of Sense: Wittgenstein's Philosophy of Language*, London: Oxford University Press, 1989.

Turbayne, Colin, *The Myth of Metaphor*, Revised Ed., Columbia: University of South Carolina Press, 1970.

White, Roger, 'Notes on Analogical Predication and Speaking about God', in B. Hepplethwaite & S. R. Sutherland (eds), *The Philosophical Frontiers of Christian Theology: Essays Presented to D. M. McKinnon*, Cambridge UK: Cambridge University Press, 1982, 197–226.

Williams, Michael, *Groundless Belief*, Oxford: Blackwell, 1977.

Winch, Peter, *Ethics and Action*, London: Routledge, 1972.

—— *The Idea of a Social Science*, London: Routledge, 1958.

Wittgenstein, Ludwig, *Blue and Brown Books*, Oxford: Blackwell, 1958.

—— *Culture and Value*, G. H. von Wright with Heikki Nyman (eds), Peter Winch (tr.), Oxford: Blackwell, 1980, 82ff.

——*On Certainty*, G. E. M. Anscombe and G. H. von Wright (eds), Oxford: Blackwell, 1969.

—— *Philosophical Grammar*, Rush Rhees (ed.), Anthony Kenny (tr.), Oxford: Blackwell, 1974.

——*Philosophical Investigations*, Oxford: Blackwell, 2nd edn, 1958.

——*Philosophical Remarks*, Rush Rhees (ed.), Raymond Hargreaves and Roger White (trs.), Oxford: Blackwell, 1975.

——*Remarks on Colour*, G. E. M. Anscombe (ed. and tr.), Oxford: Blackwell, 1977.

——*Remarks on the Philosophy of Psychology*, Vol. II, G. H. von Wright and Heikki Nyman (eds), E. G. Luckhardt and M. A. E. Aue (trs.), Oxford: Blackwell, 1980.

—— *Tractatus Logico-Philosophicus*, London: Routledge, 1922.

—— *Vermischte Bemerkungen*, Frankfurt am Main: Suhrkamp Verlag, 1977.

Wittgenstein's Lectures on the Foundations of Mathematics, Cambridge, 1939, from the notes of R. G. Bosanquet, Norman Malcolm, Rush Rhees and Yorick Smythies, Cora Diamond (ed.), Ithaca, New York: Cornell University Press, 1976.

Index

Religions and Discourse

Edited by James M. M. Francis

Religions and Discourse explores religious language in the major world faiths from various viewpoints, including semiotics, pragmatics and cognitive linguistics, and reflects on how it is situated within wider intellectual and cultural contexts. In particular a key issue is the role of figurative speech. Many fascinating metaphors originate in religion e.g. revelation as a 'garment', apostasy as 'adultery', loving kindness as the 'circumcision of the heart'. Every religion rests its specific orientations upon symbols such as these, to name but a few. The series strives after the interdisciplinary approach that brings together such diverse disciplines as religious studies, theology, sociology, philosophy, linguistics and literature, guided by an international editorial board of scholars representative of the aforementioned disciplines. Though scholarly in its scope, the series also seeks to facilitate discussions pertaining to central religious issues in contemporary contexts.
The series will publish monographs and collected essays of a high scholarly standard.

Volume 1	Ralph Bisschops and James Francis (eds): *Metaphor, Canon and Community.* 307 pages. 1999. ISBN 3-906762-40-8 / US-ISBN 0-8204-4234-8
Volume 2	Lieven Boeve and Kurt Feyaerts (eds): *Metaphor and God Talk.* 291 pages. 1999. ISBN 3-906762-51-3 / US-ISBN 0-8204-4235-6
Volume 3	Jean-Pierre van Noppen: *Transforming Words.* 248 pages. 1999. ISBN 3-906762-52-1 / US-ISBN 0-8204-4236-4
Volume 4	Robert Innes: *Discourses of the Self.* 236 pages. 1999. ISBN 3-906762-53-X / US-ISBN 0-8204-4237-2
Volume 5	Noel Heather: *Religious Language and Critical Discourse Analysis.* 319 pages. 2000. ISBN 3-906762-54-8 / US-ISBN 0-8204-4238-0

Volume 6 Stuart Sim and David Walker: *Bunyan and Authority.* 239 pages. 2000. ISBN 3-906764-44-3 / US-ISBN 0-8204-4634-3

Volume 7 Simon Harrison: *Conceptions of Unity in Recent Ecumenical Discussion.* 282 pages. 2000. ISBN 3-906758-51-6 / US-ISBN 0-8204-5073-1

Volume 8 Gill Goulding: *On the Edge of Mystery.* 256 pages. 2000. ISBN 3-906758-80-X / US-ISBN 0-8204-5087-1

Volume 9 Kune Biezeveld and Anne-Claire Mulder (eds.): *Towards a Different Transcendence.* 358 pages. 2001. ISBN 3-906765-66-0 / US-ISBN 0-8204-5303-X

Volume 10 George Newlands: *John and Donald Baillie: Transatlantic Theology.* 451 pages. 2002. ISBN 3-906768-41-4 / US-ISBN 0-8204-5853-8

Volume 11 Kenneth Fleming: *Asian Christian Theologians in Dialogue with Buddhism.* 388 pages. 2002. ISBN 3-906768-42-2 / US-ISBN 0-8204-5854-6

Volume 12 N. H. Keeble (ed.): *John Bunyan: Reading Dissenting Writing.* 277 pages. 2002. ISBN 3-906768-52-X / US-ISBN 0-8204-5864-3

Volume 13 Robert L. Platzner (ed.): *Gender, Tradition and Renewal.* 165 pages. 2005. ISBN 3-906769-64-X / US-ISBN 0-8204-5901-1

Volume 14 Michael Ipgrave: *Trinity and Inter Faith Dialogue: Plenitude and Plurality.* 397 pages. 2003. ISBN 3-906769-77-1 / US-ISBN 0-8204-5914-3

Volume 15 Kurt Feyaerts (ed.): *The Bible through Metaphor and Translation: A Cognitive Semantic Perspective.* 298 pages. 2003. ISBN 3-906769-82-8 / US-ISBN 0-8204-5919-4

Volume 16 Andrew Britton and Peter Sedgwick: *Economic Theory and Christian Belief.* 310 pages. 2003. ISBN 3-03910-015-7 / US-ISBN 0-8204-6284-5

Volume 17 James M. M. Francis: *Adults as Children: Images of Childhood in the Ancient World and the New Testament.* 346 pages. 2006. ISBN 3-03910-020-3 / US-ISBN 0-8204-6289-6

Volume 18 David Jasper and George Newlands (eds): *Believing in the Text: Essays from the Centre for the Study of Literature, Theology and the Arts, University of Glasgow* 248 pages. 2004. ISBN 3-03910-076-9 / US-ISBN 0-8204-6892-4

Volume 19 Leonardo De Chirico: *Evangelical Theological Perspectives on post-Vatican II Roman Catholicism.* 337 pages. 2003. ISBN 3-03910-145-5 / US-ISBN 0-8204-6955-6

Volume 20 Heather Ingman: *Women's Spirituality in the Twentieth Century: An Exploration through Fiction.* 232 pages. 2004. ISBN 3-03910-149-8 / US-ISBN 0-8204-6959-9

Volume 21 Ian R. Boyd: *Dogmatics among the Ruins: German Expressionism and the Enlightenment as Contexts for Karl Barth's Theological Development.* 349 pages. 2004. ISBN 3-03910-147-1 / US-ISBN 0-8204-6957-2

Volume 22 Anne Dunan-Page: *Grace Overwhelming: John Bunyan, The Pilgrim's Progress and the Extremes of the Baptist Mind.* 355 pages. 2006. ISBN 3-03910-055-6 / US-ISBN 0-8204-6296-9

Volume 23 Malcolm Brown: *After the Market: Economics, Moral Agreement and the Churches' Mission.* 321 pages. 2004. ISBN 3-03910-154-4 / US-ISBN 0-8204-6964-5

Volume 24 Vivienne Blackburn: *Dietrich Bonhoeffer and Simone Weil: A Study in Christian Responsiveness.* 272 pages. 2004. ISBN 3-03910-253-2 / US-ISBN 0-8204-7182-8

Volume 25 Thomas G. Grenham: *The Unknown God: Religious and Theological Interculturation.* 320 pages. 2005. ISBN 3-03910-261-3 / US-ISBN 0-8204-7190-9

Volume 26 George Newlands: *Traces of Liberality: Collected Essays.* 313 pages. 2006. ISBN 3-03910-296-6/ US-ISBN 0-8204-7222-0

Volume 27 Forthcoming.

Volume 28 James Barnett (ed.): *A Theology for Europe: The Churches and the European Institutions.* 294 pages. 2005. ISBN 3-03910-505-1 / US-ISBN 0-8204-7511-4

Volume 29 Thomas Hoebel: *Laity and Participation: A Theology of Being the Church.* 401 pages. 2006.
ISBN 3-03910-503-5 / US-ISBN 0-8204-7509-2

Volume 30 Frances Shaw: *Discernment of Revelation in the Gospel of Matthew.* 370 pages. 2007.
ISBN 3-03910-564-7 / US-ISBN 0-8204-7591-2

Volume 31 Eolene M.Boyd-MacMillan: *Transformation: James Loder, Mystical Spirituality, and James Hillman.* 313 pages. 2006.
ISBN 3-03910-720-8

Volume 32 Sean Doyle: *Synthesizing the Vedanta: The Theology of Pierre Johanns S.J.* 353 pages. 2006.
ISBN 3-03910-708-9

Volume 33 W. R. Owens and Stuart Sim (eds): *Reception, Appropriation, Recollection: Bunyan's* Pilgrim's Progress. 253 pages. 2007.
ISBN 3-03910-720-8 / US-ISBN 0-8204-7983-7

Volume 34 Sister Veronica Donnelly O.P.: *Saving Beauty: Form as the Key to Balthasar's Christology.* 269 pages. 2007.
ISBN 978-3-03910-723-0

Volume 35 Younhee Kim: *The Quest for Plausible Christian Discourse in a World of Pluralities: The Evolution of David Tracy's Understanding of 'Public Theology'* 411 pages. 2008.
ISBN 978-3-03910-733-9

Volume 36 Forthcoming.

Volume 37 Brendan Lovett: *For the Joy Set Before Us: Methodology of Adequate Theological Reflection on Mission.* 235 pages. 2007.
ISBN 978-3-03911-056-8

Volume 38 Allen Permar Smith: *From Pulpit to Fiction: Sermonic Texts and Fictive Transformations.* 212 pages. 2007.
ISBN 978-3-03911-328-6

Volume 39 Mark W. Elliott: *The Reality of Biblical Theology.* 386 pages. 2007.
ISBN 978-3-03911-356-9

Volume 40 Noel O'Sullivan: *Christ and Creation: Christology as the Key to Interpreting the Theology of Creation in the Works of Henri de Lubac.*
490 pages. 2009.
ISBN 978-3-03911-379-8

Volume 41 Bernhard Nausner: *Human Experience and the Triune God: A Theological Exploration of the Relevance of Human Experience for Trinitarian Theology.*
324 pages. 2008.
ISBN 978-3-03911-390-3

Volume 42 Kathleen McGarvey: *Muslim and Christian Women in Dialogue: The Case of Northern Nigeria.* 450 pages. 2009.
ISBN 978-3-03911-417-7

Volume 43 Sue Yore: *The Mystic Way in Postmodernity: Transcending Theological Boundaries in the Writings of Iris Murdoch, Denise Levertov and Annie Dillard.* 334 pages. 2009.
ISBN 978-3-03911-536-5

Volume 44 Forthcoming.

Volume 45 Ankur Barua: *The Divine Body in History: A comparative study of the symbolism of time and embodiment in St Augustine and Rāmānuja.*
267 pages. 2009.
ISBN 978-3-03911-917-2

Volume 46 Mark Corner: *Death be not Proud: The Problem of the Afterlife.*
293 pages. 2011.
ISBN 978-3-03911-998-1

Volume 47 Scott Robertson: *Henry Fielding: Literary and Theological Misplacement.*
303 pages. 2010.
ISBN 978-3-0343-0155-8

Volume 48 Glenn A. Chestnutt: *Challenging the Stereotype: The Theology of Karl Barth as a Resource for Inter-religious Encounter in a European Context.*
280 pages. 2010.
ISBN 978-3-0343-0184-8

Volume 49 Francesca Bugliani Knox: *The Eye of the Eagle: John Donne and the Legacy of Ignatius Loyola.* 356 pages. 2011.
ISBN 978-3-0343-0225-8

Volume 50 Sue Patterson: Word, *Words and World: How a Wittgensteinian Perspective on Metaphor-Making Reveals the Theo-logic of Reality.* 261 pages. 2013. ISBN 978-3-0343-0230-2

Volume 51 Tobias O. Okoro: *Dancing to the Post-Modern Tune: The Future of the Sacrament of Reconciliation among the Igbo People.* 526 pages. 2010. ISBN 978-3-0343-0240-1

Volume 52 René Gothóni: *Words Matter: Hermeneutics in the Study of Religions.* 234 pages. 2011. ISBN 978-3-0343-0268-5

Volume 53 Patricia Madigan: *Women and Fundamentalism in Islam and Catholicism: Negotiating Modernity in a Globalized World.* 346 pages. 2011. ISBN 978-3-0343-0276-0

Volume 54 Johnson Kĩriakũ Kĩnyua: *Introducing Ordinary African Readers' Hermeneutics: A Case Study of the Agĩkũyũ Encounter with the Bible.* 385 pages. 2011. ISBN 978-3-0343-0289-0

Volume 55 Frans Wijsen: *Religious Discourse, Social Cohesion and Conflict: Studying Muslim–Christian Relations.* 231 pages. 2013. ISBN 978-3-0343-0944-8